BANK MARKETING HANDBOOK

Other books from Bankers Publishing Company

Banker's Handbook for Strategic Planning
Douglas V. Austin and Mark S. Mandula

Compensation Management for Banks
Donald L. Caruth

Improving Bank Profits
Paul F. Jannott

Personal Financial Planning in Banks
Jeffrey L. Seglin and Jeffrey R. Lauterbach

Pricing Deposit Services
L. Biff Motley

BANK MARKETING HANDBOOK

How to Compete in the Financial Services Industry

ROBERT J. McMAHON

BANKERS PUBLISHING COMPANY
BOSTON

Library of Congress Cataloging-in-Publication Data

McMahon, Robert J., 1923–
  Bank marketing handbook.

  Includes index.
  1. Bank marketing. I. Title.
HG1616.M3M385   1986   332.1′068′8   86-20555
ISBN 0-87267-102-X

Executive Editor: Jack R. Bruggeman

Production Coordinator: Sandy J. Crooms

Cover and interior design: Outside Designs

To John S. Reed of Citicorp
whose personal efforts
have increased the acceptance
of bank marketing

ROBERT J. McMAHON, A.B., A.M., Ph.D.

Dr. McMahon is a Professor of World Business at the American Graduate School of Management (Thunderbird). He was formerly Senior Vice President and member of the Managing Committee of Lloyds Bank California, where he was responsible for the marketing as well as corporate planning of this North American member of the worldwide Lloyds Bank Group.

McMahon has extensive experience in both consumer and industrial marketing as well as corporate organization and management through affiliation with or consultant assignments for such national and international firms as Eastman Kodak, TRW, Westinghouse, Motorola, Raytheon, Esmark, Dentsu, Carrier, UTA French Airlines, Alcoa, and Mellon Bank. He is currently on the Executive Committee and a member of the Board of Directors of Citibank (Arizona). He is also a board member at Springfield Remanufacturing Corporation and Linch and Waxman, and he serves as well on the President's Advisory Committee of the University of Phoenix. He is a former Trustee of Mount St. Mary's College.

He received his Ph.D. from the University of Southern California and has published numerous articles in the business press as well as technical journals on subjects as varied as organization conflict, line management, interpersonal communication, bank marketing, industrial advertising, and sales management for consumer products. Dr. McMahon has lectured at the University of Southern California Graduate School of Business, UCLA, Loyola-Marymount, and Mount St. Mary's College.

McMahon served on the personal staff of General Douglas MacArthur in World War II and is a colonel in the U.S. Army Reserve. He also served as aide de camp to General Walter Bedel Smith, former ambassador to the USSR and head of the CIA. McMahon is a Fellow of the Institute of Electrical and Electronic Engineers and is a member of the honor societies Phi Kappa Phi and Alpha Epsilon Rho. He is also a graduate of the Industrial College of the Armed Forces as well as the U.S. Army Command and General Staff College.

McMahon's publications include *Marketing in the Real World, Marketing Planning, and Marketing Planning for Banks.*

PREFACE

Those who market products and services outside the banking industry have some difficulty understanding why it has taken our industry so long to embrace the marketing concept. The fact that our industry was the first to make widespread use of computer technology has made it difficult for others to understand our lack of marketing sophistication and appreciation. As an industry we are now discovering the strengths and potential contributions of sound bank marketing programs. We are also paying the high costs of ill-conceived and unprofessional efforts. We must catch up quickly because of the presence of nonbank institutions on our turf.

This handbook is a reference tool for marketing practitioners. It will provide guidance for the financial services marketing manager to apply productive methods and techniques to the marketing efforts of a bank. The content of the various chapters has been shaped by over two decades of experience in the marketing of products and services of commercial banks. Along the way the author was fortunate enough to have mentors, critics, associates, and competitors to give valuable substance to this experience.

There are some suggestions which, if followed, may increase the value of this handbook. First, each chapter has been written to stand on its own. It is not necessary to start with the first chapter and read sequentially from front to back; this is not intended to be a textbook with scholarly principles explicated in precise order. The chapters are titled according to the various components of the bank marketing function. The reader can use the appropriate chapter to match the current marketing management dilemma.

There are numerous charts, worksheets, and checklists that can be extracted from the handbook and adapted for use by the reader's particular bank or financial institution. Most of them can be easily programmed for personal computers or for the mainframe of the institution. Standard spreadsheet type software such as Lotus 1-2-3 can be used for the process.

Because there is so much to be gleaned from successful marketers of other consumer and industrial products, some of the material has been based on nonbanking marketing. This material has been combined with bank marketing material to prepare a state-of-the-art handbook that can be used for reference or refreshment.

Few writing efforts are solely the result of isolation in a writing chamber. This handbook and the methods and techniques it advocates are the result of an association with many good people and several outstanding banks and consumer product companies. To acknowledge all, inside and out of the banking industry, would require a full chapter of appreciation. Some, however, were so important that their contribution cannot go unreported.

The late Hugh Redhead of Mellon, one of the early visionaries in bank marketing, revealed his ideas to me in a most contagious way. Others, such as Dick Rosenberg of Wells Fargo and Jim Hillestad of Chemical, added a practical dimension. Long and close associations with people in my own bank, Lloyds, helped put these original bank marketing principles to the test. On the academic side, Staff Grady of Lloyds let me return to campus for seasoning in theory, and Bill Voris of the American Graduate School (Thunderbird) provided the academic support that helped commit this knowledge to paper.

During the recent beginnings of deregulation, I was exposed to a young, vibrant group of professional bankers who added the quality of reality to my knowledge and experience. This group includes David Zacharias of First Commercial, Howard McCrady of Valley National, and fellow board member David Brooks of Citibank.

Among the bank marketing managers who use this handbook, I do not expect immediate and universal agreement with the contents or philosophy espoused. This handbook represents an outcome of the trial and error of experience involving a great variety of bank products and services. It is presented for the improvement of the bank marketing management process and is intended to be nothing more nor less.

CONTENTS

QUICK INDEX
TO TABLES AND FIGURES

BANK MARKETING HANDBOOK

I

INTRODUCTION

1

THE STATE OF BANK MARKETING

> . . . the government is implementing its national economic policy through consumer-oriented controls on banking. It is, however, a fact of life that we must accept—although it certainly makes business more difficult.
>
> John S. Reed
> Chairman, Citicorp

The arena for marketing financial services is growing in size and scope with new players entering the game. The relatively stable banking environment is being altered with innovation, opportunism, and government intervention. The era of deregulation is broadening consumer options to the extent that commercial banking must now become an aggressively competing member of the financial services industry.

According to the Federal Deposit Insurance Corporation, there are more than 14,000 commercial banks in the United States, and many metropolitan intersections have either a gasoline station or a commercial or thrift bank on every corner. The retailers of gasoline products have already discovered the ills of overcapacity and are closing their lower-volume locations and adding a more diverse product line to those remaining. Unfortunately, commercial banks are reluctant to come to grips with overcapacity, although some few, like the Bank of America with the recent closure of 12 to 15 percent of its branches or Bankers Trust with its mass retail branch divestiture to concentrate on the wholesale market, are facing the realities of the bank marketing evolution.

Many commercial bankers are clinging to the industry that was, instead of accepting the new role of banking as a leading member of the financial services industry. The former position of the banking industry as a distinct line of business remains in the minds of many bankers. They continue to operate with the heritage of a tightly controlled marketing environment. This is particularly prevalent among the smaller banks. Since, according to the FDIC the majority of the U.S. commercial banks are small—almost 9,567 of the total, each possessing less than $49.9 million in assets—it is apparent that the changes are taking place in money centers rather than on the grass roots level where the majority conducts business.

The reluctance of banks to change is understandable although not acceptable in the new competitive environment of the financial services industry. The controlled marketing environment of the past made the banking business extremely attractive for conservative investors. The price of raw material, deposits, was legislated to be free of cost other than the expenses of acquisition and administration. Profit margins were almost guaranteed as the result of certain cost ceilings and product mark-up formulas that attempted to make all commercial banks equal. It required poor credit judgment and inept operations management to affect profitability severely.

Probably the most damaging by-product of the controlled marketing environment was the industry norm that there was no compelling reason for mounting a strong, aggressive marketing effort. This situation existed in spite of the fact that management usually dealt with the key components of bank marketing on a daily basis. In the new financial services competitive environment, however, key marketing components such as regulation, consumers, product, competition, and delivery systems can no longer be ignored. Thus, the current state of bank marketing ebbs and flows with the idiosyncrasies of these components as manipulated by chameleon competitors.

DEREGULATION. The bank regulators, federal and state, are moving to the left under intense pressure from the marketplace and the players. Territorial control, as required by the McFadden Act of 1927, is weakening. The distribution millstone of over a half century is being lifted through an assault from all financial services quarters. In 1985 the U.S. Supreme Court upheld laws that permit states to join together to form regional banking compacts. This decision affirmed the legality of mergers and acquisitions across state lines and recognized the right of states to establish their own geographic boundaries for banking.

Such a ruling by the U.S. Supreme Court supported the constitutionality of a two-state compact previously approved by the Federal Reserve Board, which permitted Connecticut and Massachusetts banks to acquire banks from each of their states. The *American Banker* considers regional pacts to be favorable for interstate banking on a limited basis while preventing unfriendly takeovers by the large banks located in the New York and California money centers.

In another 1985 development affecting deregulation, the Banking Committee of the House of Representatives approved legislation that would close the loophole for nonbank banks. This loophole has enabled commercial companies such as stock brokerages, life and casualty insurers, mass retailers, and others to create nonbank banks by eliminating the commercial lending function in favor of demand deposit gathering. Under a new definition, the term *bank* will mean any institution that is insured by the Federal Deposit Insurance Corporation or any institution that both accepts transaction accounts and makes commercial loans. Those nonbank banks established in 1984 and earlier will continue to operate under the "grandfather clause." Because of a subsequent U.S. Supreme Court ruling, the nonbank loophole will continue, subject to future legislative action by the Congress. The Court held that the Federal Reserve Board acted beyond the scope of its authority in expanding the definition of "bank" under the Bank Holding Company Act.

In addition to federal deregulatory action, several states have exercised states rights and passed new laws affecting interstate banking. Delaware, for example, passed its Financial Center Development Act of 1981 to permit limited-purpose interstate banking. This law allows out-of-state banks to operate in Delaware with a charter that places severe restrictions on their retail banking activities. In 1986 Arizona and Utah also enacted new laws to permit in-state banks to be acquired by out-of-state banks. South Dakota has made laws favorable to the marketing of credit card and insurance products by state-chartered banks. Those statutes also permit local banks to be acquired by merger or acquisition.

Although unrestricted interstate banking is not permitted officially, the use of the Edge Act, loan production offices, consumer finance, commercial finance, and trust subsidiaries serve as advance outposts for expansion across state lines. Even at this stage of deregulation, Citicorp claims that it provides some form of financial service to one out of every seven U.S. households. This is accomplished by over 2,000 corporate lending officers in some thirty U.S. cities as well as through almost nine hundred consumer banking and finance offices in forty-four states. The realities of the marketplace such as this make interstate banking inevitable. The major element to be resolved is the constitutional level for the form interstate banking will take.

CUSTOMERS. As disruptive as deregulation may be to the status quo of bank marketing, customer behavior may undergo an equally disquieting change. Whether banks are well established, newly opened, or greatly enhanced by merger or acquisition, the next five to ten years will separate losers from winners. Industry estimates on the number of surviving banks have varied widely, but not a single prognosticator has predicted an increase in the number of banks. Since population increases mean customer growth to marketers, there appears to be a marketing paradox in the making.

One hard fact of marketing may explain the paradox of fewer banks in the era of more customers and greater marketing potential. A survey by the *American Banker* in 1984 reported that 36 percent of the respondents had less confidence in their bankers. A Gallup survey revealed that the percentage of respondents who expressed faith in bankers has fallen from 60 to 51 percent since 1980. One analysis of this less than favorable trend is that customers may be transcending some of the old barriers to switching financial institutions. The old deterrents of loyalty, fear, habit, inertia, or the mere hassle involved with bank change are no longer keeping customers in the fold. The days of captive banking seem to be over, and customers are becoming less intimidated by traditional bankers on their architecturally hostile platforms.

To counteract this trend of independence that is being reinforced by the various avenues of choice, customers are demonstrating a preference for relationship banking. With working families subject to the demands of business and leisure, they seek the convenience of one-stop shopping for financial as well as other services. As more people bank, the individual transactions are increasing dramatically. To cater to convenience, automated teller machines (ATMs), videotex, telemarketing, and other innovations in bank delivery systems have been utilized by those institutions who are on the leading edge of bank marketing. Citibank has reported that their Citicard Banking Centers are handling transactions at the rate of 55 million a year, which accounts for almost two transactions a second, twenty-four hours a day. Citibank estimates that more than half of all their banking transactions are now conducted off the premises of traditional brick and mortar structures.

It is obvious that a variety of consumer marketing techniques are being used to deliver the financial services that respond to the needs of the customer. In an effort to target the most desirable customers, *segmentation*, or *niching*, is being used by bank marketers. Traditionally, commercial banks have targeted the affluent segment of the market. Demographics have been scrutinized for high-income, high-net-worth individuals. Even on the corporate side, Dun and Bradstreet lists have been combed for AAA titans of commerce and the identity of decision makers. Through the years there have been some successful deviants such as A. P. Giannini and his depression-spawned marketing effort to the less affluent, but the norm of today is to seek the high end of the market. The 80/20 theory that a small number of consumers is responsible for the largest percentage of sales continues to permeate the bank marketplace and the aspirations of its marketers.

Any marketing research professional worth his or her salt can identify with statistical ease a market segment that banks continue to take for granted. To describe the extent of this neglected niche, there are some compelling statistics from the U.S. Department of Commerce that indicate that 80 percent of the U.S. households earn less than $39,000 annually. There appears to be a clamor to do business with the "yuppies" of the day and their fellow affluents, although only 4 percent of the population earn

$50,000 to $100,000 annually, and only 3 percent earn more than that amount.

Newly arrived financial services competitors have been quick to recognize the potential of mass rather than class. Sears and J. C. Penney are offering financial services to a large customer base that they have courted and served well for generations and one that duplicates those that commercial banks have served without particular distinction in the past. To make marketing matters worse, these newcomers are applying the retail merchandising expertise that most bank marketers lack. These giant retailers are making the traditional banking customer more aware of product and service alternatives so that the aura of financial omnipotence no longer resides exclusively on the platform of a commercial bank.

In corporate banking increasing competition for customers has reduced profit margins so that most commercial customer marketing is now concentrated in the middle market of companies with annual sales between $5 million and $100 million. The large corporations are using commercial paper and other money market instruments for their normal financial needs. Thus, the money center and large regional banks have lowered their sights from the Fortune 500 to the middle market. The marketing problem has not been solved through this target maneuver, however. The more innovative banks are discovering the virtues of the smallest companies. The return on assets employed in a customer relationship has been declining with an increase in company size. The principal reason seems to be the changing mix of business that the bank handles. Smaller-size customers usually leave excess balances that are interest-free on deposit, or they may open money market accounts with limited transaction activity and no reserve requirements. In addition to being less concerned with pricing, these small-balance customers pay higher prices for fee-based services, and they pay more loan interest. Although this additional income to banks is offset to some degree by the extra costs of servicing small business accounts, the profit margins are greater for the total relationship.

COMPETITION. The most significant customer need has been the ability to make frequent, efficient transactions with a minimum of inconvenience. The services that are identified most positively with individual banking customers are checking accounts and convenient credit. Commercial customers often seek sympathetic loan consideration as well as transaction accommodation. Competition is becoming intense for both of these major targets. At present, retail merchants serve the convenience credit needs of about 24 million more customers than banks and generate 28 percent of the credit card charge volume. The current marketing arena for financial services is concentrated on the competition for credit card utilization.

For the moment, the big players in credit cards are Visa and Mastercard with over 150 million cardholders. However, formidable competitors have entered the bank card marketplace. Sears has introduced its Discover card through its Delaware bank, Greenwood Trust, which will ultimately provide a broad range of retail credit, banking, brokerage, and insurance services. In spite of its ownership of Sears Savings Bank in California as well as Greenwood Trust, Sears has also proposed that congress authorize an interstate system of consumer-focused banks for the marketing of personal banking services. If their proposal is successful, these banks will be established on the premises of the Sears retail stores in conjunction with their real estate, brokerage, and insurance operations. It is also only a matter of time before the Sears card will be part of a national ATM network. Its archcompetitor, J. C. Penney, now issues credit cards on a limited basis through the J. C. Penney National Bank, also headquartered as a unit bank in the small community of Harrington, Delaware. American Express continues to provide major competition in the up-scale market for travel and entertainment cards with over 15 million cardholders. Two oil companies, Amoco and Shell, have a large customer base of 8 million each and are considering general-purpose credit cards for use with financial services such as insurance. The adaptability of these cards for use in ATM networks is obvious.

Competitors to banks that are often overlooked are the more than eighteen thousand credit unions whose assets now total over $100 billion. Nearly 53 million customers have deposit accounts in these facilities. They have share draft privileges, which are tantamount to an interest-bearing checking account. They also offer personal loans that often require less stringent qualifications and have faster, more convenient approval procedures. The product lines of credit unions are broadening with such additions as credit card affiliations, individual retirement accounts (IRAs), discount brokerage, ATM network membership, and computer-authorized loans. A strong competitive edge is obtained by operating costs and tax benefits of nonprofit cooperatives, which are owned and operated by credit union members who share an occupational, religious, or geographical affiliation. Most credit unions are associated with government agencies or profit-oriented corporations who make facilities and administrative support available at little or no cost. Their great marketing strength is in their savings accounts and consumer finance, which offer rates that commercial banks are reluctant or unable to match.

Competition is also active on other product fronts. For example, the marketing effort of most commercial banks for two particularly appropriate products has been less effective than that of some financial service competitors. The products involved are IRAs and cash management accounts. According to the *American Banker*, Merrill Lynch has over 1 million cash management customers and over 10 thousand brokers seeking additional business. By 1985, over $200 billion was invested in IRAs with only $58 billion of it deposited in commercial banks. At present, the future of IRAs is subject to a determination by the Congress and may be affected by changes either favorable or unfavorable to commercial banks. In consumer finance receivables, traditionally an area of expertise for commercial banks, Sears has more than Chemical Bank, one of the ten largest banks in the U. S. Another of the top ten, Morgan Guaranty, is reviewing the state of commercial banking and is considering relinquishing its bank charter in favor of becoming an investment bank.

PRODUCT. It is difficult to separate product from competition since product specialization has become the primary basis for competitive advantage. In an effort to become more competitive, banks have introduced a flood of products seeking differentiation into the marketplace. Negotiable order of withdrawals (NOWs), superNOWs, money market accounts, and so on, are adding to the noise level in the arena, to the confusion of buyers as well as sellers: customers are as confused as tellers. In the haste to facilitate market entry, several sound marketing principles were either violated or ignored. The marketing mistakes are being compounded in an effort to protect customer turf from other financial institutions. Banks are offering discount brokerage services at little or no profit and are even moving subsidiaries to South Dakota for insurance product origination.

As product lines have increased there has been a change in the historical pricing patterns. States have reevaluated their usury laws, and the federal government has preempted state usury ceilings on mortgages and mobile home loans. The free market has not been so kind on the liability side of the ledger. All banks are experiencing diminishing margins as NOW, superNOW, and money market accounts are offered almost universally. Innovative banks have discovered that in a cost-sensitive environment, self-service products must prevail. Thus, improved technology has become essential to reduce the cost of servicing transaction accounts while offering relatively attractive rates for deposits.

The need for income has resulted in changes in product mix and fee structure. Bank fees have risen dramatically since 1984 and are expected to continue to rise. Charges for passbook accounts have increased by over one-third. Small savers are becoming less welcome, so that most banks now have minimum balances for these accounts to earn interest; or, if interest is paid, the charges for less than the minimum balance exceed the interest credited. The issue of account minimums and charges for checking accounts has become political, with legislators' pressuring for "lifeline" accounts for the market segment that has low balances perennially.

The commercial loan product mix has concentrated primarily on mitigating risk by tightening credit standards, reducing loan-to-value ratios for collateral, and making more widespread application of variable interest rates. Products remain quite similar but the marketing philosophy has changed during the recent loan problems in the energy, agriculture, and international sectors. Loan marketers are now being criticized less for making a bad loan than they are for failing to recognize during their course of calling on clients that the loan is getting into difficulty. Bank marketers are concerned not only with adding earning assets but with secondary markets for unloading assets and problem loan workouts as well.

DELIVERY SYSTEM. Deregulation has already encouraged the assault of geographic barriers, and the demise of the McFadden Act seems imminent. The nonbank loophole, the U.S. Supreme Court decision affecting regional bank mergers, and the liberalized statutes by numerous states have added a national dimension to bank distribution. Coincident with interstate marketing, advances in banking technology through the development of new systems have revolutionized the delivery of financial services to consumers. This changing technological environment has brought new opportunities in bank marketing that were only contemplated at the strategic planning level a few years ago. The financial services offered through new delivery systems cover a full range of transactions. These computer-based systems have proved to be reliable and cost-effective as they utilize readily accessible terminals by means of a communication network.

Dependable service is available at geographically dispersed, convenient locations, twenty-four hours a day, and ATMs are not labor-intensive. Labor savings are significant when the incremental transaction cost of a teller is considered in comparison with ATM transaction costs—fifty cents versus twelve cents, a 75 percent saving. By removing some of the constraints of banking hours, staffing requirements and by closing some of the costly full-service branch locations, banks now have the ability to offer customers a range of differentiated products and cost-effective levels of convenient service not previously possible.

Citibank has reported an exceptional reliability record of service available more than 99 percent of the time with none of its Consumer Banking Centers out of service more than twelve minutes in any twenty-four-hour period. The service capability has resulted in marketing and sales support to develop multiaccount relationships and to extend out-branch service into

nonbranch retail outlets, corporate offices and factories, shopping mall cor-
ridors, parking lots, and the home. The latter has permitted delivery of
some financial services at the end of a telephone jack or on the screen of a
television set.

The growth in ATM networks has made a tremendous impact on
product delivery. After a modest beginning in 1970 when some of the major
banks established proprietory systems, the ATM network concept has expanded into shared use on an interstate basis. The transactions provided are
interaccount deposit and transfer as well as cash dispensing. The rush of
banks to provide such customer convenience has resulted in the rapid installation of over sixty thousand ATMs in the U. S. Unfortunately, many
banks have made capital commitments for ATMs, which may have a return
that is slow or inadequate. According to the United States League of Savings, a typical household uses an ATM only once every three months. This
is either an indictment of the marketing effort or the result of an inflated
expectation of the convenience factor by bank managements. Retailers such
as Circle K and Publix Super Markets have recognized the traffic-building
potential of an on-premises ATM. The next development in the evolution
of product delivery off bank premises is expected to be the direct debit
point-of-sale (POS) system, in which customers initiate a transaction that
is the equivalent of cash. This is the more practical version of the cashless
society often predicted by business romantics. At this point there are capital
investment considerations for the POS system that have not been resolved
between retailers and banks. Oil retailers such as Exxon, Mobil, and Arco,
in cooperation with local banks, have pioneered the POS concept on an
expanded test mode.

When evaluating the new bank delivery systems, most futurists consider home banking to possess the greatest potential. They expect it to become an essential component of the home information industry. It is part
of a home information center that includes home shopping, budgeting, and
security, in addition to the entertainment devices such as television and
stereo sets. In 1983, Booz-Allen and Hamilton predicted that 20 to 30 million households would utilize home information systems by the mid-1990s.
Whether teletex or videotex, transmitted by computer modem or coaxial
cables, home banking service is technically feasible today; the PRONTO
system of Chemical Bank is a case in point. In spite of some penetration in
home banking, its transaction potential appears to be limited, and the banking service available is restricted to account information, account debit for
bill payment, and funds transfer between accounts.

This review of the key components in commercial banking gives an
insight into the state of bank marketing. It is a function whose importance
to banking can no longer be questioned. The competitive arena, the sales
requirements for increasing assets and liabilities, the high noise level of

communication in the marketplace, and the reconciliation of customer need with product offerings are dimensions of the scope of the study needed by thoughtful banking professionals. To provide for such study, both pragmatic and theoretical considerations must be reviewed. The banking industry is in a magnificent state of flux, offering unequaled opportunity for putting the principles of bank marketing to work for bank survival in the battle for financial services superiority.

2

THE BANK MARKETING FUNCTION

Most bankers are in agreement about the existence of the marketing function. Its relative importance in the business of banking, however, continues to be debated within the industry. In large money center banks, marketing is accepted as not only an essential function, but one requiring a staff of professional marketers, highly trained in the principles of finance. This is a radical change from the initial period of bank marketing's emergence, when it was considered to be primarily a public relations function, staffed by gregarious individuals who had less than an enviable record in client credit approval.

BANK MARKETING. The generic definition of *marketing* has been presented in various ways. Distinguished academicians like Peter Drucker consider marketing to be the organized performance of all selling functions, and Philip Kotler believes it to be a social process of creating a product that is exchanged for value. Theodore Levitt writes that marketing is the function of buying customers, rather than considering it to be the process of producing goods and services for resale.

When applied to banking, *marketing* has been loosely defined by some bankers as a general term describing a collection of specific activities such as business development, installment loan merchandising, credit card solicitation, institutional advertising, retail service premium promotions, public relations, and product or customer research. Rather than serve as a catch-all term for those functions resulting in some form of customer communication or contact to promote and sell products and services, marketing should be considered a disciplined management function involving the commitment of valuable corporate resources that must deliver an acceptable return on investment. The bottom line is that the marketing function must include those activities in aggregate that are performed to make banking possible and desirable by facilitating the exchange of money for financial related services between interested parties.

Marketing Concept. A successful bank marketing effort requires more than an understanding of what the function entails. It is essential that the banking organization embrace the concept of marketing so that proper planning and effective implementation of the marketing effort can be initiated. The key element of the concept is to understand that marketing must be customer-driven and that it has its origins with the identification of customer need. Once this need is identified and analyzed, the marketing effort is to be directed toward the development of products and services to satisfy these needs.

In the process of establishing the marketing concept, there are other banking functions whose relationships with the marketing function are often antagonistic. Such key banking functions as credit analysis, asset and liability management, regulator relations, liquidity control, and auditing are no less essential and can provide not only support but synergy for a successful marketing effort. Marketing is a requirement for deposit gathering, loan generation, or service utilization. In such a context, it can be considered an equally essential function in the banking process.

Under such circumstances, the marketing concept can be easily defined for an individual bank. To seat the concept, the following five criteria should be applied:

1. Senior bank management must accept the premise of the essentiality of the marketing function and its parity with the credit function.
2. Products and services must be provided to satisfy customer needs.
3. The bank must conduct its business with an acute awareness of the changing marketing environment.
4. Marketing activities must not only help deliver an adequate return on assets but result in a reasonable profit relative to the volume of loans and deposits and the type of service that is provided.
5. Although senior management must require adherence to the current banking laws and regulations, it must be sympathetic to and supportive of innovative marketing efforts in activities whose legal parameters have not yet been defined.

It would seem to be self-evident that providing customers with the products and services they need is one of the most important roles of any bank. Unfortunately, the desks on the platform and the counters at teller stations are crowded with the necessary policy manuals, pro formas, and operations procedures concerning the handling of specific transactions or service requests that are nonroutine. This often results in "rule book marketing" and regimentation to the self-interest of the bank instead of the customer. Outstanding bank marketing requires innovation at all customer contact levels. This can be fostered by educating employees about the marketing concept as well as the purposes and application of bank marketing. It also requires that the responsibility for marketing be cascaded from the office of the chief executive officer (CEO) to the teller line. The players at every level make or break the marketing effort of the bank.

Once the concept has been endorsed by senior management, it should become a part of the bank's corporate culture. Thus, account or loan officers will accept the selling dimension of their calling activity; credit analysts will develop a philosophy of structuring loans for the benefit of both bank and customer; loan approval authority will consider facilitation as well as risk; customer contact personnel at the retail level will cross-sell effectively without causing the operations function to deteriorate. In short, the bank will become marketing-driven with customer need established firmly in the driver's seat.

Bank Marketing Components. With the bankwide acceptance of the marketing concept, it is appropriate to consider the various components of bank marketing. In the broadest sense, there are more people in the marketplace than customers and potential customers. Customers should never be generalized; they require specificity. For example, there are those in the marketplace who make the decision as to where and with whom to bank, those who actually use the product or service, those who serve as referents, those who regulate through audits as well as legislation, those who affect public opinion, and those who serve the retail competitors on one hand and commercial partners in syndication on the other. Therefore, it is difficult to generalize when identifying bank customers. Because of this, the components of bank marketing are also very specialized to permit adaptation or modification for the numerous bank marketing targets involved.

In undergraduate college courses, marketing students are exposed to the four Ps—product, price, place, and promotion. This is an overly simplistic approach for the identification and memorization of the key components of marketing. Once identified, they are blended together in various types and amounts to become the marketing mix. These basic principles hold just as much for banking as they do for packaged goods such as toothpaste, appliances such as VCRs, and capital goods such as Boeing 747s. In banking, however, the mix is peculiar to such environmental conditions as government regulation, competition of nonbanks, and the unusual nature of the principal raw material—money.

In banking, *product* is represented by a selling proposition that includes not only products that are both tangible and intangible, but a critical addition of customer service and safety. It is a mixture of innovative ideas that can be duplicated by competition overnight, semi-fixed restrictions of existing computer support systems, and an environment where product differentiation is often only a matter of geographic location. The degree of expertise through training is one area in which banks usually differ.

Price is a particularly multi-dimensional component. Because of its complicated nature, many banks are not absolutely certain of the true costs of each product. Rather than be based on cost of goods sold and competitive pressures, which is usually the case in other industries, bank pricing is a complex determination based on a collection of variables that include cost of funds, reserve requirements, regulatory parameters, minimum amounts, maturities, risk, and social responsibilities. Ever present, also, are the competitors in the marketplace, government, and private enterprise.

Promotion is another generic term to cover many diverse activities such as personal sales, advertising, sales promotion, merchandising, public relations, and other customer communication functions. Again, banking has many peculiarities that differentiate the promotion component from other retail and commercial product marketing. There are some similarities, however. Tellers and supermarket check-out clerks have limitations against cross-selling in common; both are too busy on operational matters. The technical expertise required by calling officers in the credit area is just as severe as the requirements that IBM account representatives have in electronic data processing systems. There are some important differences in bank promotion. For example, in bank sales promotion and merchandising, laws in some instances restrict the cost of premiums, the hours of retail operation, the size of loans to be offered to a single borrower, the nature of the loan collateral, and the time constraints of the relationship with both loan and deposit offerings, all of which affect the banks' ability to promote products and services. Bank advertising is also affected; it must contain strict revelations on rate and disclaimers on customers served, including special trade marks which must appear in certain printed advertisements. Another key promotion family member is public relations. Not only is this an extremely sensitive area in bank marketing, but contrary to the system in other industries, public relations activities are usually devoted to image or situation repair rather than preventive maintenance. Product information for publicity's sake is very difficult to communicate unless advertising is used.

Place is the generic term in the four Ps acronym that is used to describe distribution. In banking, distribution can be described more accurately as a product and service delivery system. Traditional channels of distribution for manufactured products bear little similarity to those required for money products. However, money-based products utilize a wide variety of distribution methods. Banking product delivery uses branches, which serve as dealerships, ATMs that are a form of vending machine, loan production offices (LPOs) that duplicate the services of a field sales office, and correspondents whose function is similar to that of a manufacturer's agent. And, in growing numbers, banks are becoming franchised, joining ATM networks, and utilizing telephone sales solicitation with professional telemarketing efforts.

To assess properly the nature of the various marketing components in a particular bank, it is helpful to prepare a simple audit as the initial stage in the consideration of an effective bank marketing effort (Table 2-1). The audit will not only help identify the specific components being used currently, but establish the frequency with which they are being used as well as the individual within the bank responsible for their use. The audit can also indicate whether the component's place of origination is inside the bank or an outside source such as a regulator, advertising agency, printer, service bureau, correspondent, or other supplier.

ROLE OF BANK MANAGEMENT. It is essential that the bank marketing function be understood and appreciated by bank management. As the services offered by the financial services industry, of which banking institutions must now acknowledge membership, become more sophisticated and varied, the marketing effort of banks must keep pace. With the introduction of professional marketers in bank organizations, management problems are encountered, some of them were encountered by other industries many years earlier as they traveled the same route of marketing evolution. Along their paths of progress, these industries discovered that one of the most basic management problems in the marketing function concerned the need for change and the reluctance of industry traditionalists to accept new concepts for conducting business.

This is not surprising and should not be considered an indictment of traditionalists whose loyalty and continuity are essential within the ranks of a successful organization because some blending of marketing hawks and doves after their inevitable confrontation has always been the essence of progress. Conflict between these two well-meaning camps usually results in a change for the better. That the banking industry, particularly at this time of deregulation and heightened competition, is having similar problems inducing traditionalists to accept the bank marketer is to be expected.

One area in particular where traditionalists and marketers meet head-on is retail banking. Some traditionalists do not understand or accept the need for continuous reminders at the point of contact where loans and deposits are actually transacted. They resist point-of-purchase advertising in the form of signs and displays and fight most attempts by bank marketers to alter the merchandising climate of marble, mahogany fences, and thick pile. They seem to use fine artifacts in bronze and oil instead of more self-serving lobby displays and floor-traffic-inducing promotions.

Table 2-1. Bank Marketing Component Audit

Marketing component	Usage frequency			Responsibility			Source	
	Always	Some	None	CEO office	HQ staff	Line	Internal	External
Product								
Research and Development								
Systems Development								
Programming								
Test Marketing								
Product Training								
Pricing								
Loan Interest Rate								
Loan Maturities								
Loan Collateral								
Deposit Interest Rate								
Deposit Maturities								
Service Fees								
Participations								
Marketing communication								
Business Development								
Sales Aids								
Sales Training								
Broadcast Media Advertising								
Print Media Advertising								
Outdoor Media Advertising								
Direct Mail Advertising								
Literature								
Signs and Displays								
Trade Shows								
Premiums and Incentives								
Advertising Specialties								
Marketing Research								
Product Publicity								
Delivery system								
Retail Branch System								
Remote Drive-up Facilities								
ATMs								
POS Terminals								
Loan Production Offices								
International Offices								
Correspondents								
Telemarketing								
Franchisee								

One way to reduce such resistance is to make the reluctant banking traditionalist more comfortable with the principles of bank marketing by communicating the contribution that components such as advertising and sales promotion can make to the success of the bank. Unfortunately, bank marketing is not a high priority for some banks and their senior managements, although most banks have established marketing departments in their organization structure. What is occurring is that these departments are often structured to function outside the mainstream of the business development effort of the bank; the mainstream flows through the line organization without the professional marketing expertise that has been so productive in other industries. Some traditionalists go so far as to avoid association with the standard marketing activities unless senior management implies a strong endorsement of the marketing function and directs the planning and application of sound marketing principles throughout the organization.

The good news is that the traditional marketing manager of the past, who was considered a public relations technician primarily, is being replaced with well-trained professionals. In the initial stages of this evolution of professionalism many banks were forced to go outside the banking industry to recruit such qualified individuals. The bad news in the early days of this movement was that these professionals knew little about finance and the basics of money and banking. In spite of this, these innovative marketers from the outside were able to make valuable contributions to the development of bank marketing techniques. Today, the industry is growing its marketing expertise from within, and this new breed of professional bank marketer has not been reluctant to assume promotional risks, complimentary to a risk-oriented industry, to increase market share, to develop new products and services, and to adapt successful techniques from other industries to banking. This effort has been enhanced by their understanding of banking and their newly found acceptance by their peers within the bank.

It is important for bank management at all levels to understand and appreciate that approaches to bank marketing are selective, legislative, duplicated from other industries, and ideally, innovative in the face of competition. Bank marketers must provide productive programs while banking is being controlled and influenced by a host of environmental variables that range from the type of banking product or service to be promoted to internal variables of management style, philosophy of risk, and resource availability, to the regulated and legislated external variables of local and national government. To complicate matters even more, there exist the inevitable pressures of competition and the seldom predictable state of the economy. As participants in the loan and deposit arena, similar to others engaged in marketing highly competitive products, bank management must be prepared for change and counteract with sound, innovative plans for marketing action. The alternative is to react defensively or to follow the course of banking tradition, which cannot prevail in the face of deregulation and the emergence of a competitive financial services industry.

Whether the appropriate action involves a calling officer's generating loans and deposits, a telemarketing specialist's soliciting IRA accounts, a trust officer's developing a pension and profit sharing plan, an operations and computer specialist's working with liability experts meeting a client's cash management needs, or an advertising officer's producing a television commercial, senior management must demand that these marketing actions be synergistic as part of a predetermined use of marketing components. If the marketing components are applied in a spontaneous, intuitive, uncoordinated manner or without a preplanned cause and effect sequence, the marketing effort will become reactive and defensive. It is management's responsibility to control and implement the use of marketing components accordingly.

II

BANK MARKETING SITUATION

3

BANK MARKETING ENVIRONMENT

Prior to any formal marketing action, it is necessary to appraise the marketing situation and to determine the current and future states of the bank marketing environment. The role of such an appraisal is to identify, monitor, and analyze those current and potential trends and situations that will create marketing problems or opportunities affecting the marketing effort. In the course of such an analysis, numerous variables whose interaction will establish the nature of the marketing situation will be identified.

There are marketing variables within each bank whose control lies outside the hands of the marketing manager. Depending upon his or her acceptance by the organization or upon the specific authority granted by senior management, the marketing manager has varying degrees of influence over these variables. In most instances, he or she exercises little control over those internal variables that deal with long-standing corporate policies and procedures that are based on bank operating traditions. On the other hand, the increased acceptance of the bank marketing function has improved the internal environment so that marketing managers have a greater opportunity for membership in the council of corporate decision.

The macrocomponents of the environment are the same for all business entities whether they be banks, manufacturers, or public agencies. These can be identified in the broadest sense as the community, its culture, its physical features, and the productivity of man's efforts within the community. However, we are faced with the need for more specificity when considering the environment for an analysis of the marketing situation. Therefore, the environmental variables most influential in the marketing situation can be classified as those operating outside the bank in the *external environment* or within the organization in the *internal environment*. Each interacts to make the bank marketing situation quite dynamic amid a continually changing business climate.

EXTERNAL ENVIRONMENT. The microelements of the external environment consist of a broad range of uncontrollable factors with varying interactive influences. They include such diverse components as pending legislation, the prime rate, the nature of competition, local business practices, and operation technology. Foremost in the external environment, however, is the effect of the national and regional or local economy on the marketing situation. Obviously, the marketing manager must review the economic outlook and analyze those trends in the business climate that may influence marketing. These include such basic indicators as gross national product (GNP) and various forecasts of production as well as such items as capital spending surveys, inventory levels, reports on corporate profits, and personal income projections.

In the consumer or retail banking sector, one key indicator is the rise or fall in real disposable income (DPI). Other factors include the rate of unemployment, retail sales in both durable and nondurable goods, and residential housing starts. Inflation affects both the commercial and the consumer sectors, and its rate has a profound effect on the bank marketing situation. Because of the increasing influence of international political and economic considerations, such items as the balance of payments and foreign exchange rates involving the U.S. dollar can affect a local marketing effort as much as the national marketing of bank products and services.

In spite of the current trend of deregulation, there will always remain a modicum of state and federal regulation and other government actions outside the control of individual banks. For example, the Federal Reserve Board deals with matters affecting monetary policy, and the congress and the executive branch are engaged in fiscal machinations. These activities not only affect the supply of the banks' raw material, money, but, in concert with other regulatory bodies such as the Comptroller of the Currency, establish regulations limiting or expanding the activities of the banking industry as a whole.

Some of the most reliable indicators of economic climate have been categorized on the basis of time—before, during, and after the existence of the economic situation in question. These indicators have been identified as leading, coincident, or lagging by economists. In order to provide for a systematic analysis of economic indicator data, it is helpful for the marketing manager to gather the basic information from several authoritative sources and to review each indicator and its possible effect on the marketing of key bank products and services. The worksheet (Table 3-1) can serve as a helpful tool for such an analysis.

Closely allied to the economic and political considerations in the external environment are the accepted business customs and practices of the banking industry, not only as an industry, but among individual banks or according to regional idiosyncrasies. These accepted methods of conducting business involve such marketing-related activities as the nature and extent of bank credit (loans on unimproved land versus single-family dwellings),

Table 3-1. Economic Indicator Analysis

Indicators	Retail deposits			Wholesale deposits			Consumer loans			Commercial loans			Trust and investment		
	+	0	−	+	0	−	+	0	−	+	0	−	+	0	−
Leading															
Manufacturers' New Orders															
Residential Housing Starts															
Building Construction															
Plant and Equipment Orders															
New Business Incorporations															
Number of Business Failures															
Corporate Profits															
Labor Cost Index (Price per Unit)															
Stock Price Index															
Change in Inventory Book Value															
Industrial Material Price Index															
Manufacturing Layoff Rate															
Unemployment Insurance Claims															
Coincident															
Unemployment Rate															
Nonagricultural Employment															
Help Wanted Advertising Index															
Industrial Production Index															
Gross National Product															
Bank Debits (Outside NYC)															
Personal Income															
Retail Stores' Sales															
Wholesale Price Index															
Inflation Rate															
Prime Interest Rate															
Lagging															
Wage and Salary Cost Index															
Labor Cost Index (Per Unit)															
Manufacturers' Inventory															
Finished Goods Inventory															
Consumer Installment Debt															

+ = Positive effect.
0 = Not affected.
− = Negative effect.

the degree and type of risk accepted (for example, Minnesota banks do not make citrus crop loans), the use and capability of computer support (daily versus monthly compounding), and even business hours (after-hour and Saturday retail banking). Business customs and practices not only vary according to tradition and bank management philosophy, but by type of customers and industries served, many of whom have their own individual or industry practices or behavior that must be understood by bank marketers.

Of particular significance to the nature of the marketing situation is the uncontrollable variable of competitive action and reaction. Understanding the precise extent of the influence of competition on the bank marketing situation necessitates that the various players in the marketplace be identified by name and type. This identification process includes not only the commercial banks, but thrifts, credit unions, and all other financial services institutions vying for a share of the market. Once each is identified by name, an analysis of how each competitor is positioned must also be concluded. Other competitive information that must be considered includes institutional strengths and weaknesses; specific share of market data; loan and deposit volume, including type emphasized, interest, and fee structures; and any significant trends in growth or reduction.

Closely related to the competitive environment are consumer attitudes, the degree of institutional acceptance by customers and prospects, the calibre and expertise of bank personnel, and the availability and excellence of service. The extent of the effects of the variable for competition is often determined by the degree to which competitors in each marketplace vie actively for human or financial resources, political or economic leverage, a niche or particular market segment, types of product and service offered, customer loyalty, or other elements and conditions favorable to the marketing situation. Because of the extreme importance of competition as an environmental variable, Chapter 4 will be devoted to competition later to provide guidance on its identification and analysis.

The growing importance of bank technology is more easily recognized in the present era of deregulation. This environmental variable not only includes the technological support required to handle the mountains of data in bank operations to sustain and support the marketing effort, but the data base and the facilities necessary to satisfy the information and service requirements of the banks' customers. Banks and their managers at all staff levels must be aware of the technological trends and events happening outside as well as inside the banking industry. Such technologies have the potential to impact the ability of banks to serve their customers. Not only are the new technological developments well known by financial services competitors, but many have been developed, tested, and put on-line to gain a competitive advantage.

It is essential that marketing managers recognize that most technologies have life cycles in the same manner as products. The critical action in an environment of changing technology is not only to become aware of possible changes but to manage the transition from one technology to another when the currently used technology is in the decline or obsolete phase. The evolution of the growth of ATM transactions instead of bank lobbies is a case in point. The introduction of the automated teller machine technology has made some retail banking transactions available on a twenty-four-hour basis; with further technology, the ATM networks have permitted out-of-market transactions as well. Waiting in the wings are point-of-sale terminals as part of the electronic funds transfer systems that will make additional banking services available on the premises of retail merchants. Of some concern is the effect of the POS terminal installation on float, another marketing consideration as well as a revenue factor in the technological analysis.

The use of technology in customer information files (CIFs) will provide valuable demographic data for review and exploitation by the marketing manager. The information available is not only useful for prospecting for cross-selling opportunities, but for providing an information source for real-time inquiry by customers concerning their accounts in the bank. This information storage and retrieval capability will become the cornerstone for the perceived ultimate in off-site financial services, banking in the home. This new delivery system is being promoted by such marketing pioneers as Chemical Bank in New York. Thus, the technological factors cross many banking areas that affect marketing.

There are also cultural and sociological considerations in the external environment that must be reviewed. There are the basic consumer behavioral factors involving tradition, value systems, knowledge, belief, art, morality, laws, and other social, psychological, and intellectual idiosyncrasies. These mores of society are responsible for usury laws, the opulence of bank architecture, the privacy requirement of the money transaction process, and the use of nonverbal symbols for bank safety such as teller cages and platform fences.

Sociologically, bank marketing managers must be constantly aware of the rising expectations of customers and prospects as members of society. Any shift in the public's perception of the safety of a bank can be catastrophic. The insensitivity of bank personnel to financial problems as inconsequential as the levying of a small fee for service or to any act of discrimination according to customer account size can also result in customer defections. Citibank was faced with a minor revolution when customers below a certain account balance were directed to use ATMs instead of the personal teller service. Demographic and psychographic factors that affect customer behavior in banking are also of such importance that Chapter 6 will be devoted to a better understanding of this element in bank marketing.

Finally, the financial needs of society are also important considerations in any cultural analysis of the bank marketing situation. For example, banks are subject to adverse criticism from both customers and the regulatory agencies if service to low-income consumers, loans to women or minorities, low-interest-rate mortgages, and business loans in distressed areas are not made readily available. Even bank advertising must communicate the availability of these services. The risk and the cost of fulfilling these social responsibilities must be subsidized by the more conventional and profitable services in the marketing portfolio.

Because of the remaining restrictions against interstate banking by commercial banks, the lack of definitive parameters for the operating of nonbank banks, and the legally acceptable local representation of national financial services institutions, geographical factors are also of some importance in a marketing environment analysis. However, the biased regulatory constraints are only one consideration involving geographical location. For example, geographical factors can influence the specialized types of loans (loans by banks in the centers of the petroleum or the entertainment industries such as Texas and California), the nature of deposits (customers of banks in the smaller communities have a stronger savings discipline), the condition of the local economy (dependence on agribusiness in farming communities), and even the physical location of branches (urban versus suburban). Weather can also become an important marketing variable. Variations in the length, time, and condition of specific marketing programs, particularly agribusiness, can be influenced by such extremes in weather as heavy snows, floods, droughts, or any unplanned by-products such as brown-outs and early business closings.

Thus, the number and type of variables in the external environment that can affect the marketing effort are varied, extensive, and uncontrollable. The precise nature of their interaction is also difficult to predict. In spite of this difficulty, marketing managers must develop a method for identification and analysis of the external environment as a basis for determining which problems can be neutralized, minimized, or overcome as well as which opportunities can be exploited through a well-conceived and executed marketing program.

INTERNAL ENVIRONMENT. In contrast to the external variables outside the control of the bank, internal environmental factors are those originating within the bank. These variables are usually the result of the corporate policies and procedures established by senior management. It is true that many of these have their origins in compliance with regulatory requirements; however, there is a certain range of approaches to compliance from which management can select specific policies and procedures in keeping with the philosophy they have adopted for conducting business. Although some marketing managers participate in establishing corporate policies and procedures as members of senior management, they are able to exert only a limited degree of influence over the many internal variables in the bank. Therefore, the internal environmental variables, although considered to be controllable by senior management, are actually outside the control of the marketing manager in the implementation of the marketing effort.

From a marketing point of view, one of the most significant and inflexible internal variables is the corporate philosophy of banking. This philosophy can be stated in a formal document such as a corporate charter, a pro forma for a formal bank corporate charter is illustrated in Figure 3-1. In the absence of a formal charter, the corporate philosophy is usually stated with a series of memoranda. It may even be unwritten and communicated by word of mouth or through the overt behavior of senior executives by means of demonstration with the traditional, repeated actions of senior management. Whatever the method of communication, the general philosophy of conducting business is usually understood by marketing managers through the interpretation of bank practices, policies, and procedures that are established by the leaders of the corporation.

One important characteristic of an unwritten or informal bank management philosophy is that it is often a reflection of the personal value system of the organization's chief executive officer or a consensus of the board of directors on the way business should be conducted. Thus, the corporate philosophy of any bank is subject to change or revision by successive administrations through the actions of directors. Such administrations may be given a specific direction for change or one for the perpetuation of the current philosophy of business.

Obviously, a corporate philosophy can impact the selection of a corporate marketing strategy. It is sufficient to state at this time that the strategy is best expressed in the form of corporate objectives. These objectives are established by senior management on the basis of analyses and recommendations submitted by managers at subordinate levels. The set of corporate objectives indicates what the bank intends to accomplish in response to the problems and opportunities identified in both the external and internal environments. The strategy to which marketing managers must adhere includes not only setting general objectives consistent with the corporate philosophy but working within major policy guidelines that govern ways that bank resources are to be committed in the pursuit of the objectives.

One key objective that bank marketing managers must accept as primary and having a priority over other objectives is the one devoted to

Figure 3-1. Bank Corporate Charter Pro Forma

At _____ Bank, we will assume the corporate responsibilities necessary to assure not only a proper return on assets to justify our capital investment, but to provide outstanding financial service in a key banking market. Toward this end, _____ Bank will require innovative action resulting from the application of mature judgment, bold concepts, and decisive implementation. The specific corporate charter for the _____ Bank includes the following:

1. To increase pretax earnings of _____ Bank to a level that is equal to or better than that of comparable banking institutions in a manner that is consistent with sound banking practices and to consider only the results obtained as the acceptable measure of performance.

2. To increase dramatically the level of recognition and acceptance of _____ Bank by the financial community of _____ and to establish _____ Bank as a highly acceptable source for corporate banking service in this important market.

3. To establish _____ Bank in the U.S. market and to provide wholesale and retail banking services that are competitive to all financial institutions to the degree permitted by government regulation.

4. To provide complete coverage of the _____ market by expanding distribution through _____ Bank's delivery system and to exert aggressive sales coverage of both commercial and retail banking customers.

5. To foster a strong organizational pride in _____ Bank and to develop a corporate reputation within as well as outside the organization that develops, attracts, and retains competent professionals who are goal-oriented, performance-conscious, highly trained, and strongly motivated.

6. To motivate the employees of _____ Bank to perform at levels consistent with their individual abilities by providing them with the training, materials, facilities, and opportunities to achieve individual potentials in the course of fulfilling this charter.

7. To help discharge the social responsibilities of financial institutions as a member of the local and national communities and to improve the course of human endeavor by the innovative use of our individual and collective talents and services in the process.

profit. Bank earnings are the most common measure of business accomplishment. Regardless of the corporate charter or an organization's basic banking philosophy, a commercial bank must establish some basic objectives related to revenue and earnings. These objectives can be stated as a specific return on assets, an increase in revenue, improved earnings per share, or an improvement in some of the key ratios applied to loans and deposits. Whatever the criteria selected for corporate achievement, bank earnings objectives are usually established by senior management with the approval of the board of directors. As such, they are considered to be outside the direct control of the marketing manager.

A logical extension of banking philosophy of conducting business and the corporate marketing strategy to be pursued is reflected in the style of management exercised within the bank. The specific style can usually be identified by using the classic theory X and theory Y management methods developed by Douglas McGregor. Although developed for organizations in general, it is particularly applicable to banking. Theory X assumes that personnel are lazy and dislike work; that they are incapable of accepting responsibility and must be managed firmly. Theory Y assumes that employees have a psychological need to work and want achievement and responsibility. Whether the precise style of management in a bank is participative, authoritative, or some of each, the prevailing style is an important variable for consideration in the marketing function. The style setters in banking are the senior officers and key department heads. They normally evoke emulation by their subordinates that becomes a general style of management that cascades through the organization. Obviously, the supervisory environment has a profound effect on the implementation of the marketing programs.

Another internal environmental variable is concerned with the structure of the banking organization. This is a method for implementing the basic management function of the bank as a prelude to coordinating and controlling the efforts of the bank as a whole. It serves to equalize the work load by assigning the responsibility and authority required within the various bank units and individuals. The organization structure is vulnerable to repeated revision because bank management often turns to reorganization in an attempt to find an immediate solution to banking problems. This exercise has a disruptive effect on the marketing program implementation and must be considered by the marketing manager during plans for reorganization.

In addition to the organization structure, the various corporate functions should be reviewed periodically by the marketing manager in light of inadequate responsibilities, possible overlaps, and standard personality conflicts. Occasionally, the specific functions assigned to individuals and the authority perceived are misunderstood or ambiguously defined for historical, political, or nepotistic considerations. Since such situations are seldom under the control of the marketing manager, these must also be accepted as factors presenting possible problems or opportunities affecting the marketing effort.

The last of the key internal environmental variables concerns the resources available for commitment by the bank. Those in this category include human, physical, and financial resources. Bank resources such as industrious, well-trained people; state-of-the art operations equipment and facilities; sources of funds; and access to operating capital must be analyzed in the light of their effect on the marketing effort. It should be noted that the resources of the bank are severely influenced by such external environmental variables as the state of the economy and the climate of government regulation. These and the other internal and external variables engage in continuous interaction in the environment.

SOURCES OF ENVIRONMENTAL INFORMATION. The marketing manager will require many sources in order to gather the data necessary for an analysis of the marketing situation. Outstanding sources for data on the external environmental variables are the state and federal governments and their various agencies. The Federal Reserve Board and its district banks are a particularly fruitful source. They provide data in depth in relation to the banking industry nationally as well as within prescribed regions and individual markets. This information is quite thorough as far as competitive data are concerned. They also provide interpretation of data as well as forecasts by well-qualified experts. Marketing managers should avail themselves of such information to determine the nature of the external environment. There are several specific reports for use by the marketing manager.

The Functional Cost Analysis is issued annually by the Federal Reserve Board. It provides data and interprets information received from several hundred U.S. banks, which are grouped by size of deposits—less than $40 million, $50 to $200 million, more than $200 million. The publication reports gross earnings, major expense categories, and net earnings on income-producing functions.

The Federal Reserve District Banks provide annual reports on operating ratios. These reports contain data on banks under each Reserve Bank's jurisdiction. The information is reported by state and in some cases by specific metro-markets. The type of data in the reports is used primarily for comparative purposes between banks. In addition to this useful information for competitive analysis, *Bank Operating Statistics* is issued annually by the Federal Deposit Insurance Corporation. It contains the following five tables on designated economic areas within each state:

1. Assets and liabilities; capital accounts
2. Selected balance sheet ratios
3. Income and expenses by area
4. Income and expenses as a percentage of total operating revenue
5. Selected operating ratios

The Office of the Comptroller of the Currency publishes the *National Bank Surveillance System Report* on a quarterly basis. This report compares individual bank performance to a specific peer group. The source of this information is the call reports from individual banks, and the report contains significant ratios from the data submitted. The Federal Home Loan

Banks provide specialized information on the savings and loan institutions by reporting monthly on the flow of deposits. Additional reports by the Federal Reserve Banks include similar data for commercial banks with their quarterly Time and Savings Deposit Survey. They also provide weekly data on commercial loans by industry and a monthly report on bank debits.

There are several reliable sources for economic data other than information directly related to banks. The Federal Reserve Banks publish excellent regional economic studies, and the Department of Commerce provides surveys of current business. *Sales and Marketing Management,* a trade magazine, publishes an Annual Survey of Buying Power, which segments data by state, county, and metropolitan area. Various state agencies report on industry employment, state economic data, automobile registrations, and revenue receipts. F. W. Dodge, a private firm, provides data in depth on the construction industry. One final outstanding source of demographic data is the information collected by the U.S. Census Bureau. The data are correlated by census tract as well as by Standard Industrial Classification.

The interaction process in the environment is the key to the marketing situation. The result of this interaction is a dynamic cause and effect progression. Therefore, the importance of the internal and external environment should not be minimized by a marketing manager. In the process of developing a successful marketing effort, each program must be assessed for the effects of the environment before bank resources are committed. It is crucial that marketing managers understand that the direction given for the marketing effort to achieve success within such a dynamic environment be monitored constantly for revision. As the environment changes, so must the marketing effort.

4

COMPETITION IN
FINANCIAL SERVICES

Although financial services have always been indispensible to individuals, business, and government, the nature of such services has favored specialization because of such restraints as capital requirements, laws and regulations, and technical complexity. This specialization has embraced such broad service segments as insurance, investment, and credit. The one factor all financial services had in common was the need for management of risk.

As management became more concerned with such considerations as the relationships between risk and reward, there began an evolutionary movement to expand the services offered by not only specializing within the three broad segments of insurance, investment, or credit, but invading provinces within those segments other than the one that had been traditionally primary. This movement in the United States has been encouraged by less government restriction, consumer acceptance, and the favorable climate in the capital market.

The result is a competitive arena that has a spectrum of players that runs from international institutions with assets greater than many of the countries they do business in to specialized boutiquelike firms who serve small market niches. Well-known corporate names such as General Motors, Sears, American Express, Citibank, Prudential, and Merrill Lynch compete, not only with each other, but with the Northrup Credit Union, Wells Fargo, Dime Savings Bank, Bank of Scottsdale, and thousands of other institutions, large and small. Companies whose primary business has been marginally in the financial services area have expanded their services directly into the financial area. For example, it is fair to say that the importance of credit to retail merchants such as Sears and J. C. Penney makes this form of financial service critical to their marketing success. However, expansion into consumer deposit gathering, stock and bond brokerage, insurance, or real estate brokerage is only marginally related to the principal business of mass retailing.

The effect on the long accepted concept of commercial banking as a distinct line of business has been traumatic, to say the least; banking is now part of the financial services industry whether it wants to be or not. The size of the financial services market has been estimated as one providing an annual revenue of $300 billion, and it is divided inequitably among over fifty-thousand financial institutions. The good news is that the market is large enough to accommodate those whose marketing effort can provide an effective presence.

The commercial banking segment of financial services has been subject to product modification and changes in methods of operation through the deregulation process. This has fostered many changes that appear to be revolutionary rather than evolutionary. For example, demand deposit accounts that have been non–interest-bearing are now earning interest, and the failures of some banks and thrift institutions have permitted the circumvention of the McFadden Act by allowing acquisitions by out–of-state institutions and operation across state boundaries. There have been other causal factors than deregulation, however, including an unexpected instability in interest rates that not only assaulted traditional rate behavior but developed an unusual climate of volatility. There have also been major technological improvements in the collection, transmission, processing, and storage of financial information as well as enhanced development of electronic-driven financial services.

This revolutionary business climate in the marketplace has affected the competitive posture of individual banks and has placed greater emphasis on the need for positioning the bank advantageously. The importance of positioning in bank marketing is such that it will be covered in detail later in this chapter. For individual banks, management must anticipate the possibility for an erosion of market share and slower rates of growth as new players enter the arena. Slow growth and loss of share may affect profitability adversely so that there may be a need for management to consider changes in corporate strategy from such minor variations as geographic representation to the major alternative of acquisition or franchising. The product and service offerings will be a key competitive tool with the possible reduction in the relative importance of asset-based activities; fee-based services are expected to become the principal front for competitive survival.

Competition in financial services can be categorized into major groups. These include the direct competition provided by other commercial banks as well as specialized financial institutions such as savings banks or savings and loan associations. However, the category of growing importance and concern to commercial banks consists of nonbank competitors. These are represented by experienced and well-capitalized retailers of consumer products and services that are dependent upon customers and based on some type of credit, an investment of assets, or some form of coverage against risk. Understanding and appreciating the nature of the competitive situations demand that the key types of institutions in each category be identified and analyzed.

DIRECT COMPETITORS. The greatest source of competition in the financial services marketplace is found among other commercial banks, domestic and foreign-owned. However, specific ownership is not necessarily a critical factor. Direct competition is best measured or evaluated on the basis of products and services offered and markets served. It is true that assets, bank reputation, and philosophy of doing business affect the competitive posture of a commercial bank, but assets must be considered as resources that provide a return through serving markets with appropriate products and services. Ownership, size, and philosophy are important but only as a means to a marketing end.

All commercial banks are not competitive with each other. This statement does not refer to the fact that some direct competitors at the retail level are also joint participants in a commercial credit; rather, the lack of direct competition by one bank with another is often due to geographical considerations. If commercial banks are categorized by their geographical presence, much is evident concerning the market served.

The key segment for large bank competition can be identified as those labeled *money center banks*. This category includes those banks based in the U. S. money centers of New York, Chicago, Los Angeles, and San Francisco. Citibank, Chase Manhattan, Manufacturers Hanover, Bank of America, First Chicago, Chemical, Continental of Illinois, and Security Pacific are a few of the key competitors. Some banks in Boston and Mellon in Pittsburgh are also considered money center competitors. One particularly significant group in the money centers are the foreign-owned banks from the United Kingdom, Japan, Canada, and Hong Kong. In fact, Japanese banks now have over an 8 percent share of the U.S. market. Foreign-owned banks have not only gained market entry *de novo* but established a strong presence through the purchase of regional banking systems such as Marine Midland (Hong Kong and Shanghai Bank), First Western (Lloyds Bank), Southern California First (Bank of Tokyo), Harris Trust (Bank of Montreal), and Crocker (National Westminster). The latter was subsequently resold to Wells Fargo while Lloyds Bank sold its California operation to Sanwa of Japan.

The money center banks compete not only among themselves in the various money centers, but through Edge Act or other loan production offices in key metropolitan centers throughout the United States as well as in selected cities overseas. They are particularly active in the commercial sector, dealing with large corporate credits. Many of these competitors have extensive delivery systems in their primary markets, thus heightening the competitive environment in the retail banking sector as well.

There is a growing arena of competition in the various geographical regions in the United States. There are many strong banks in the regional bank category. These include Wachovia and North Carolina National in the

Southeast, Valley National in the Rocky Mountain region, Wells Fargo and Rainier in the far West, Bank of New York in the East, The Bank of New England, Bank One in Mid America, and Republic in the Southwest. The regional bank competition is a factor nationally for certain specific financial services. However, the predominant marketing effort is usually confined to their headquarters area and to the contiguous states and metropolitan centers. The primary competition is with other regional banks, of which there are usually only a few, and with the local banks that are well established in each community within the region. The principal competitive advantages of a regional bank over other banks, national and local, are its depth of expertise in the people, businesses, and industries indigenous to the region as well as its usually extensive local delivery system.

The local bank category is obviously the one with the most members, and many of them are organizations well entrenched in their local communities. They offer a wide variety of products, services, and locations. There are vast differences between the positioning of these banks as determined by their selling propositions. Any competitive analysis usually considers only those banks that can be categorized realistically as direct competitors. For example, Citibank may be represented in the California market and competing for large commercial credits through a loan production office; however, they may not be a factor in small commercial lending or retail banking, with the exception of such specialized retail segments as consumer finance, credit cards or home mortgages, which Citibank offers on a national basis. These aspects of the competitive situation must be reviewed in any analysis. The fact that all commercial banks may not be direct competitors is a prime consideration in the identification process.

SPECIALIZED FINANCIAL INSTITUTIONS. Although the category of specialized financial institutions has been identified on the basis of its specialization, there are only two principal entities in this group—one includes savings and loan associations and savings banks, which are considered to be in the category of *thrift institutions* and the other consists of *credit unions*. These specialized institutions have begun to offer more competition to commercial banks by delivering a wider range of financial products and services than marketed by them in the past. For example, major thrift institutions now provide some forms of commercial loans as well as consumer credit in addition to their more traditional products, home mortgages and interest-bearing deposit accounts. Credit unions have also begun to offer home mortgages as well as a share draft adaptation of bank checks to serve as transaction accounts while providing traditional low-cost installment loans for personal use.

Legislation in 1980 not only permitted savings and loans to offer transaction accounts but provided for consumer lending, retail credit cards, second mortgages, and trust services. The Garn–St. Germain Act two years later granted them the authority to offer demand deposits in conjunction with commercial loans to corporations. From a competitive standpoint, the savings and loans have moved slowly into the marketing of these products and services and are not major players at this point. Although they have the regulatory authority to compete by using additional products, they are generally only competitive with commercial banks in home mortgages and in the generation of deposit accounts.

Credit unions are the second principal type of institution in the specialized financial group, and they occupy a unique position. In addition, they are particularly well suited to succeed in a deregulated environment. The eighteen-thousand credit unions have a membership of over 50 million, or one out of five people, and are unique in that they are nonprofit financial cooperatives that are owned and operated by members who share an occupational, religious, or regional affiliation. Their nonprofit status as well as some organization subsidization of occupancy and clerical costs usually make them very competitive with better rates and terms for consumer loans and higher interest on deposits.

Another unique characteristic of credit unions is that they belong to a single informal financial system. They differ from other financial institutions in that they cooperate through membership in trade associations rather than compete head-on with each other. These associations, or state credit union leagues, develop consumer products and services cooperatively, provide correspondent banking services, write credit life and disability insurance, structure pension plans, and participate in maintaining a national telecommunication system. Accounts at most credit unions are federally insured to $100,000. Their product line includes many consumer services such as unsecured personal loans, auto loans, ATM network access, debit and credit cards, IRAs, discount brokerage, share drafts (checks), travelers checks, and money orders. As the fee structure in banks and thrifts continues to rise, nonprofit credit unions will provide greater competition with free transaction accounts that are not usually subject to deposit minimums. Membership fees, if any, are nominal, and the locations of credit union offices are very convenient to their members, often within the plant or office of the members' employer.

NONBANK COMPETITION. The nonbank group of market participants has the potential to provide formidable competition to banks. The marketing innovations developed and implemented by these nonbankers are responsible for more new consumer products than the deregulation process. For example, financial services such as money market accounts, commercial paper, and cash management accounts are meeting the needs of both individuals and companies. In some cases these new products caused an outflow of deposits from the banks that was only subdued by some emergency changes in banking regulations. The players in this nonbank group can be identified within one of four major categories—mass retailers, large industrials, diversified financials, and insurance companies. And there is some overlap within these categories.

Mass retailers are in business to satisfy many of the same consumer needs as banks. They are leaders in the small personal loan business since retail credit is the capstone of retail merchandising. There are some startling statistics about retail stores. For instance, they issue over 60 percent of the credit cards in the United States and satisfy the credit requirements of approximately 24 million more customers than banks or oil companies, previously the major providers of consumer credit. Retail stores also generate 28 percent of the credit card charge volume. There are two large, national retailers, Sears and J. C. Penney, who provide competition for banks. Their long-term marketing strategies appear to be directed toward increasing their involvement in financial services.

In the past few years, Sears has added to its retail eminence in the mass merchandising, insurance, and thrift institution lines of business by the acquisition of a major stock and bond brokerage (Dean Witter Reynolds) and a real estate brokerage (Coldwell Banker). With its more than 850 retail outlets, Sears is also the nation's largest retail lender with 60 million credit cardholders. As the owner of the twenty-fifth largest thrift institution (Sears Savings Bank) and one of the largest insurance companies (Allstate), this mass retailer is positioned to provide one-stop financial services by structuring its retail stores to become financial supermarkets. In addition to these operations, Sears is lobbying vigorously for legislation permitting the establishment of a new type of banking institution, the *consumer bank*.

The core of the Sears proposal is to allow direct competition with commercial banks and thrift institutions through a specific type of bank that is limited in its franchise to conduct business. The proposed consumer bank would accept deposits and make only consumer, small-business, and family farm loans. Restrictions on the mix and the extent of the loan portfolio would assure that the lending emphasis would be directed in the local community served by each bank. As an indication of the competitiveness commercial banks can expect from Sears, the charter proposed for the consumer banks states that there is a need for additional financial service that the present banking system is not providing. Sears cites, as an example, the need for non–interest-bearing checking accounts without monthly fees or a minimum balance requirement. These "lifeline accounts" have a strong political appeal, and legislators have indicated support for such a product.

Sears has also proposed that these new consumer banks be well capitalized and operate under rigid rules that prevent the upstreaming of funds to the parent organization.

The magnitude of Sears' presence in the retail credit arena can be best appreciated by their volume of installment credit. In 1982 it was nearly $10 billion, and by 1983 it had increased to $14 billion. The impact of the more than three hundred in-store financial centers it has opened has also been particularly significant in generating customers new to certain financial services. Sixty percent of the brokerage accounts and 15 percent of the savings bank accounts opened at these in-store centers have been first-time accounts. With the introduction of the Discover Card, Sears has not only provided an access card for its credit services but promoted its use as a general-purpose credit card accepted by other retail establishments as well as for travel and entertainment. Sears had already signed up fifty-thousand retailers nationwide and is recruiting new participants at the rate of over one-thousand a day. To make it highly competitive to bank credit cards, users of the Discover Card also have access to a national ATM network, and the card can be applied for such Sears financial services as money market funding and IRA contributions.

J. C. Penney is also a nonbank competitor, although the small J. C. Penney National Bank in Harrington, Delaware, qualifies it as a direct competitor of minimal consequence at this time. It is apparently providing a base for banking services to be offered through the Penney stores. The major competitive thrust of J. C. Penney is its $5 billion annual volume in consumer credit. It is also increasing its presence in the credit card market by providing retail credit cards for its in-store merchandising effort as well as issuing bank credit cards through its bank subsidiary in Delaware. Regardless of which credit card is used by Penney's cardholders, these pieces of plastic are an important and competitive financial asset. They become the entry device for introducing Penney's customers in its two thousand stores to a growing number of financial services that complement its national retail base of services. Of eventual interest to those commercial banks considering offering insurance services, J. C. Penney has already established itself as one of the largest direct response insurance marketers in the United States. In 1983, through both in-store and direct response sales, Penney had in excess of $200 million in annual premiums from more than 1 million policyholders.

The large industrial companies are another important segment in the nonbank competitor category. These large conglomerates have established subsidiaries that offer a wide assortment of financial services. General Motors Acceptance Corporation (GMAC), Ford Motor Credit Company, Chrysler Financial Corporation, and IBM Credit Corporation are all financial subsidiaries of their parent companies. General Electric (GE) Credit,

Westinghouse Credit, and Borg-Warner Acceptance Corporation were subsidiaries at one time but are now independent finance companies with widely accepted corporate identity. American Can acquired Borg Enterprises and now offers mortgages in selected K-Mart stores.

The subsidiary companies have a credit function that is related directly to the sale of their parent company's products. However, these subsidiaries have expanded into other financial services areas. For example, GMAC not only provides consumer installment credit as evidenced by their $40 billion portfolio, but the commercial finance of equipment and inventory as well. They have over a 25 percent share of the auto loan market. Bank of America, the largest auto lender among commercial banks, has less than a 2 percent share of the national market (bear in mind, however, that it operates primarily in the California market). GMAC is also the second largest mortgage lender after having acquired two large mortgage firms as it expanded its financial services capability. GMAC does not accept deposits at this time. If it did, its $75 billion in assets would make it the fifth-largest U.S. bank. A credit card for automotive services is being test marketed and GMAC is also considering lending to small and medium-size businesses based on their experience in lending to automotive dealers.

Borg-Warner not only finances dealers' inventories of its former owner, but it provides equipment leasing services to unrelated dealers and other manufacturers. Westinghouse and GE credit entities are also active in equipment leasing. By 1983, industrial firms such as these accounted for approximately 8 percent of the commercial loans outstanding. Because of their vested interest in the sale and leasing of high-value manufactured products, they will remain very competitive in the loan and lease product area, consumer and commercial. There is some indication that their expansion will continue; Ford acquired a thrift institution in 1985 to increase its involvement in financial services and is now considering opening S&L branches in fifty-six hundred automobile dealerships.

The diversified financials consist of such companies as American Express, Avco, Merrill Lynch, E. F. Hutton, Dreyfus, Household and Beneficial. These firms provide specialized financial services such as travel and entertainment cards, consumer loans, stock and bond brokerage, and insurance. Among the most competitive aspects are the density of their distribution network and the nature of their delivery systems. For example, Merrill Lynch has a branch network of over four hundred offices in key areas of business and affluence staffed with over ten thousand brokers engaged in customer contact. Merrill Lynch was the first to offer cash management accounts on a mass retail sales basis, and they are currently one of the country's largest home equity loan originators with over $1 billion in second mortgage outstandings.

Until 1971, American Express was primarily a travel services company whose presence in the bank marketing area was represented by its travel and entertainment card and travelers checks. Both products were marketed through commercial banks acting as retail dealers in their distribution system. In 1981, American Express changed its corporate strategy to become a major source of financial services instead of primarily a leader in the travel industry. As a result, they acquired Shearson, the securities firm; Investors Diversified Services (IDS), a distributor of middle market investment products; as well as the investment banking firm of Lehman Brothers. They have also become very active in the mortgage market through their subsidiary, Shearson Lehman Mortgage Corporation. American Express is preparing to provide consumer funded services. They are opening a nationally chartered bank in Delaware and a state bank in Minnesota. They also plan to offer personal credit lines and mortgage loans to American Express card holders as well as to customers of their IDS subsidiary. It is significant that they maintain a larger discretionary asset pool than any U. S. bank.

During the period of 1981–83, the leading diversified financial companies were very active in commercial lending. For example, Merrill Lynch increased their outstandings by 152 percent. These large firms were particularly active with deposit-generating products to fund their commercial lending effort. By 1984, Merrill Lynch, through their money market funds, had generated over $39 billion in assets. Ironically, much of this was invested in jumbo certificates of deposit issued by commercial banks. Congress finally provided competitive relief for the banks with the Garn St. Germain Act, which gave banks and thrifts the right to offer a directly competitive product. Once the banks and thrifts had a product of comparable benefit to consumers, some of the deposits that departed the banking system returned but not until an intensive marketing effort that featured attractive rates and government insurance coverage of the deposits was initiated.

The large insurance companies make up the last category of nonbank competitors. These include such ubiquitous giants as Transamerica and Prudential-Bache. These two companies could also qualify for inclusion in the diversified financials category with subsidiaries in consumer finance and the stock and bond brokerage business. At one time, Transamerica had a multi-state banking system in the western United States. Many of its former banks are now part of First Interstate Bank. Other major players in this category include Aetna, Equitable Life, American General, and Travelers. These firms compete with banks primarily through the investment portfolios that make them particularly competitive in long-term commercial lending. Other specific products offered by this group that are competitive to bank products include mutual funds, brokerage, cash management, IRA accounts, mortgage banking, and equipment leasing.

Life insurance companies have always been highly competitive in the lending area, commercial and consumer. They offer personal loans at interest rates that are well below market because the cash value of policies is pledged as collateral. By 1983, life insurance companies had almost $70 billion in consumer loans. In commercial mortgage lending, insurance companies are also very active, and they participate in loans to business either directly or through private placement. Indirect lending is accomplished through their ownership of corporate bonds and equity securities, both of which are alternatives to bank financing. In 1983 Prudential-Bache was one of the largest commercial lenders, with over $38 billion in business loans.

SOURCES OF COMPETITIVE INFORMATION. Because competition is both direct and indirect, information can be gathered from many sources. The most economical is that information obtained from secondary rather than primary research methods. In general terms, competitive information is available from the public at large, from customers, from within the industry, from government agencies, or from trade publications and business book publishers. To cite all sources would be an impossible task; however, there are many excellent secondary sources that bank marketing managers should be familiar with when attempting to gather the data necessary for a comprehensive analysis of the competitive situation. A list of suggested reading as well as specific services for pertinent information has been included in the back of the book. In addition, the following government agencies have excellent resources that can be used to obtain specific information.

Helpful Government Agencies

Comptroller of the Currency
Federal Deposit Insurance Corporation (FDIC)
Federal Home Loan Bank Board
Federal Reserve Board
Federal Savings and Loan Insurance Corporation (FSLIC)
Securities Exchange Commission (SEC)
State Banking Departments/Commissions
State Economic Development Offices
State Insurance Departments/Commissions
U.S. Census Bureau

Note: There are also several computer data bases such as Dialog that are available by subscription and with modem access.

COMPETITIVE ANALYSIS PROCESS. The lack of an intimate knowledge of competition, direct and indirect, in the marketplace can result in an ineffective marketing effort that is usually followed by a decline in market share and, ultimately, reduced profits. Some banks attempt to react to competitive pressures from all participants in the marketplace by trying to be all things to all people. In the attempt, they initiate inconsistent marketing programs that not only turn out to be unproductive but add to the noise level of the promotion effort in the marketplace and tend to confuse the customer. To select the most opportunistic strategy for marketing success, the bank marketing manager must understand how his or her competitive market is structured and how the bank might be positioned for a successful competitive assault.

Competition can be classified broadly as described previously into three groups—direct competition, specialized financial institutions, and nonbank competition. The analysis worksheet in Table 4-1 can be used by bank marketing managers to identify and conduct a comparative evaluation of local competition. Initially this is completed on the basis of the products and services provided. Once the worksheet has been filled out, a thoughtful analysis can be made in preparation for positioning the individual bank concerned.

The following financial services competitive analysis worksheet is only intended to serve as a tool for collecting and storing data; it can be reproduced in a computer by using software that has a spreadsheet capability. The initial stage of the analysis is to determine whether to define the market in a micro or macro dimension: to decide whether it should be considered in total or in specific segments. Once the geographic limits have been established, the market boundaries should be drawn to identify primary and secondary areas for marketing emphasis. The areas can be as encompassing as the continental United States or as specific as a two-mile radius from a particular retail branch. Statistical data from the U.S. Census Bureau will provide the necessary demographics of the market and in as finite detail as census tracts. Knowing the age, occupation, and income mix of the market as well as psychographic data on life-styles from other sources will provide guidance for the bank positioning process and the products and services to be marketed. Once the specific market areas are selected, meaningful groupings of existing and potential customers should be developed. Some quantitative measure of potential penetration into each group should also be determined. This may require using marketing research techniques and will be discussed in Chapter 6.

These data are the basis for understanding the intensity of competition as a prelude for positioning. Competitors can also be evaluated by size, growth rate, or profitability, which gives some indication of the resource strength for commitment to the marketing effort. Another approach in the competitive analysis is to determine the objectives of the parent company or subsidiaries in the marketplace, that is, increased share of the national or local market, corporate profitability, or strategies of expansion, harvest, or withdrawal. In some cases much can be projected on the basis of previous competitive strategies. The organization and corporate cultures can also provide more insights as to whether competition is cost-oriented, highly structured, decentralized, risk-prone, well experienced, or prestige-conscious. These should all be reviewed in order to identify the strengths and weaknesses of all of the market participants. Once this analysis is completed, the marketing manager can make appropriate recommendations for positioning the bank.

BANK POSITIONING. The aspect of the marketing strategy selection process known as *positioning* is relatively new in banking. This element was added to the marketing strategy development as an extension of the differentiation quest. Marketing managers discovered that knowing what the customer wants does not assure success if many competitors are already satisfying these wants successfully. This meant that marketing eminence required marketers not only to satisfy the wants and needs of customers but to discover weaknesses in the positions of competitors and to exploit these failures or omissions by filling the unserved niche. Traditionally, banks have been positioned generically, perpetuating the widely accepted consumer perception that all banks or all thrifts were essentially the same. Once the concept of financial services rather than banking was understood, many banks realized that they could no longer be "full-service" to the degree that they were making a commitment to be all things to all people. Thus, bank positioning has become a key element in the determination of the marketing strategy.

Bank positioning is still in its developing stage, particularly as more and more entrants flock to the growth opportunities in the financial services industry. Because of the critical nature of bank positioning, marketing managers have relied on some basic principles that could be adapted from other more experienced industries. Business organizations are positioned on the basis of the nature and extent that their corporate resources can be committed in the marketplace. These resources have been identified as either financial, human, or material, and they are committed through the marketing process of providing products and services to customers. Because of this process of resource commitment, the positioning of a company can be based on the type of the organization and its resources, the nature of the product or service as represented by its selling proposition, or the specific type of customer to be served. To assist the bank marketing manager in the positioning process, the bank positioning check list in Table 4-2 has been pro-

Table 4-1. Financial Services Competitive Analysis

Institutions	Personal deposits		Commercial deposits		Consumer loans		Commercial loans		Trust services		Investment services		Insurance services		Electronic services		Branch offices	
	Types	Rates	Types	Rates	Types	Rates	Types	Rates	Types	Fees	Types	Fees	Types	Cost	Types	Fees	Types	No.
Commercial banks																		
1. ___																		
2. ___																		
3. ___																		
4. ___																		
5. ___																		
Savings banks/S&Ls																		
1. ___																		
2. ___																		
3. ___																		
4. ___																		
5. ___																		
Credit unions																		
1. ___																		
2. ___																		

47

Finance companies			
1.			
2.			
3.			
Stock brokers			
1.			
2.			
3.			
Insurance companies			
1.			
2.			
Mass retailers			
1.			
2.			

Table 4-2. Bank Positioning Check List

Components of positioning	Own bank	Competition						
		Bank A	Bank B	Bank C	Bank D	Bank E	Thrift A	Thrift B
Organization								
Ownership								
Absentee								
Local								
Wholesale bank								
National								
Regional								
Local								
Retail bank								
National								
Regional								
Local								
Banking leader								
Technology								
Marketing								
Personnel								
Banking follower								
Technology								
Marketing								
Personnel								
Banking laggard								
Technology								
Marketing								
Personnel								
Delivery system								
Urban								
Suburban								
Community								
Rural								
Franchisee								
ATM/network								
Home banking								
Drive-up banking								
Extended hours								
Target market								
Business								
Large								
Medium								
Small								
Individuals								
Blue-collar								
White-collar								
Professional								
Retiree								
Gov't. worker								
Military								
Industry specialty								
1. _____								
2. _____								
3. _____								
4. _____								
Government								
City								
County								
State								
Federal								

Table 4-2 (continued)

Components of positioning	Own bank	Competition						
		Bank A	Bank B	Bank C	Bank D	Bank E	Thrift A	Thrift B
Selling proposition								
Multi-product line								
Personal deposits								
Commercial deposits								
Consumer loans								
Commercial loans								
Limited product line								
Personal deposits								
Commercial deposits								
Consumer loans								
Commercial loans								
Specialized product line								
Credit/debit card								
Trust								
Investment								
Insurance								
International								
Other								
1. _____								
2. _____								
3. _____								
4. _____								
Pricing								
High value								
Market rate								
Discount								
Promotion								
Dominant advertising								
Average advertising								
Conservative claims								
Premium-dependent								
Price-driven								
Prestige-oriented								
Niche emphasis								
1. _____								
2. _____								
3. _____								
4. _____								

vided. It will be helpful in making a comparison of the positions of the various key competitors in a specific marketplace.

Once the check list is completed, the bank marketing manager can determine the most advantageous position for the bank. The purpose of the bank positioning check list is to review the positioning in the market prior to establishing a recognizable and sustainable differentiation from competition. Opportunities for differentiation are usually to be found in the selling proposition or in one of the niches in the target market. Any organization can be restructured to foster a change in positioning, but such restructuring is usually a costly and lengthy process. Any changes in organization should only be those necessary to complement and support repositioning in the selling proposition or target market.

III

BANK MARKETING STRATEGY

5

BANK STRATEGY REVIEW
AND SELECTION

In bank marketing the principal ingredient for success is the selection and implementation of a viable strategy for competing with other financial institutions. Strategy has many definitions and interpretations. Although most members of management consider *strategy* to be a synonym for *action programs,* it is actually a conceptualization of how an organization proposes to conduct business in the marketplace; it is a detailed statement of what the bank intends to do rather than an explanation of how it intends to do it. Bank management builds its strategy by establishing a foundation of corporate objectives that fulfill the purpose or charter of the organization while exploiting opportunities present in the marketplace. Additional clarification of the strategy is provided by management by the selection of a broad set of constraints, policies, and operating philosophies that encourage or restrict the scope of business action. The strategy of the bank is implemented through the setting of attainable objectives and goals and the targeting of potential customers to help achieve the corporate objectives.

It is apparent that the selection of a suitable bank strategy requires an identification of options, an analysis of each, and a set of strategic decisions by management. As banks continue through the maze of deregulation the determination of a viable strategy is primate. It must be more than an inspirational statement of objectives and goals; the strategy must offer guidance to assist subordinate department and branch managers in making the routine, everyday decisions necessary to achieve the corporate objectives. These key people must understand and accept the bank strategy and their roles in the successful implementation of action programs that bring it to life.

Over the long term, senior management on the macro level and marketing management on the micro level are concerned with the operating perspectives of the markets to be served. For example, bank management may decide on a scope of operation that serves the market broadly or one that concentrates on smaller segments; the scope of the market is a key element in the structuring of a strategy. Another key variable is the strategic time frame of immediacy or long term as well as the market entry timing factor of being an early or late entrant. The operating theater to be selected can focus on neighborhood representation or be directed toward global presence. There is also the consideration of the operating posture by becoming a major player or a marginal participant.

The market for financial services is not homogeneous; it is made up of segments that in turn consist of specialized niches. They vary substantially from each other, and one of the most critical of the strategy decisions is to determine the target markets and the marketing priorities within them. The methods of target identification and designation are numerous, but most are based on demographic, psychographic, or socioeconomic variables and whether the decision is to serve a distinct niche, several segments, or an entire mass market. Obviously, strategy determination is complex as well as crucial in bank marketing. Its complexity is caused by the numerous components that must be recognized and considered in the process of establishing a proper bank strategy.

COMPONENTS OF STRATEGY. Prior to the consideration of such micro components as marketing targets, objectives, and goals, the bank marketing manager must receive direction from senior management relative to the strategic priorities of the corporation regarding growth and profitability. It has to be determined whether to invest for future growth, to manage for increased earnings, to sustain the bank at current levels, or to contract or shrink the bank to a lower asset base. This determination affects the type of strategy selected for the bank because there are so many alternative courses of marketing action with each.

A.   To invest for growth:

  1. Penetrate additional market segments
  2. Increase share of market
  3. Lower prices and expand volume
  4. Increase number of products and services
  5. Make acquisitions

B.   To manage for increased earnings:

  1. Target high-return market segments
  2. Emphasize higher-profit products
  3. Add high-value, fee-based services
  4. Increase prices
  5. Apply economies of scale

C. To sustain present levels:

  1. Defend current position
  2. Maintain share of market
  3. Stabilize market pricing
  4. Invest as the market dictates
  5. Add new products and services selectively

D. To contract from present levels:

  1. Reduce assets selectively
  2. Abandon less productive advertising and promotion
  3. Harvest low-contribution products and services
  4. Reduce administrative overhead
  5. Forego increases in market share

The time frame of the bank strategy is another decision to be made by senior management; marketing managers need to know whether the strategy to be selected is long-term (three to five years) or short-term (one to three years). For example, candidates for acquisition would implement a short-term strategy, and acquirers or noncandidates would probably select a long-term strategy. Exceptions to this might be based on short-term marketing opportunities that require a more immediate exploitation. In a period of uncertainty such as the current deregulation environment, strategies of many banks might be more realistic and productive if they were based on the short term instead of the long term.

The individual bank's philosophy of doing business usually determines the operating posture of the bank. By tradition banks have operated on a highly cooperative basis, recognizing that the difficulties of one bank are transferred to the industry as a whole. This is in contrast to many industries in which one competitor's demise is another company's triumph; the semiconductor industry is a case in point. Nevertheless, it is possible to assume a posture of seeking dominance or strong visibility aggressively. There is also the alternative of remaining defensive but with respectable market presence. The cooperative posture is often one of a market follower who tends to react with the pack, is neither first nor last. In general, most markets have aggressive or defensive advocates, but the majority of the players remain in the cooperative posture as followers rather than leaders. Whether this heavy cooperative mix can survive the new competitive environment of the financial services industry remains to be seen.

The operating mode can provide critical guidance for the marketing manager by indicating whether the manner of the market thrust is driven by cost considerations, a differentiated product line, or the nature of the market itself. If the operating mode is price-sensitive, it can be said to be cost-driven. A *cost-driven strategy* is characterized by standard, no-frills products and spartanlike service and operations support. Products and services are generic with little differentiation. Staff costs are kept at reduced levels and automation is emphasized, sacrificing the personal service atmosphere. The cost-driven mode requires appropriate target customers that are price-sensitive and place less emphasis on highly personalized service.

The *product-driven operating mode* is one that seeks differentiation. The marketing emphasis is on product quality and reliable service. This mode is achieved with higher costs, and the result is above-market pricing and greater perceived value by customers. The product mode usually delivers a better return on investment, but because of higher pricing, it is considered by customers to be somewhat exclusive or upscale. This perception and customer appeal often results in a reduced share of market and a smaller but more affluent target segment or niche. A product-driven mode places product considerations over market emphasis or cost containment. Thus, this mode requires an innovative product development effort or a rapid response capability for successful product imitation if differentiation is difficult. Product innovation is based less on cost than on creativity. However, there is less risk of failure by duplicating or modifying proven product or service ideas.

Product differentiation can also be achieved by attractive packaging, by an unusual delivery system, or by a unique application. One highly successful example of differentiation was Wells Fargo's Gold Account, which packaged deposit and credit products together with an implied special customer treatment. The Bank of California has a unique delivery system that emphasizes private banking by providing off-bank-premises service for busy upscale customers. Although offered by many banks, there is a unique application involving bank credit cards during the busy holiday season: card users are given a skip payment option for December or January. These are examples of product differentiation that are possible in an industry of product similarity.

Operating in a mode that is *market driven* is the most common among commercial banks. Branch offices are opened in geographic locations consistent with the other components of strategy such as the operating posture, target markets, and operating theater. Specific segments or niches are served with products that are most appropriate to the market. In many situations the strategy may be mass-oriented instead of class-directed; however, the nature of the market is primate with cost and product secondary considerations. There are many examples of banks in this operating mode. Citibank has a philosophy of customer service that classifies this large bank as market-driven. Morgan Guaranty is also market-driven but has targeted a specific niche that does not necessarily compete with Citibank's market. Both of these excellent banks develop products and services for their specific markets, and cost is not the primary consideration.

Since the marketing strategy is concerned with what is to be done rather than the specific product or program to be used to implement the strategy, certain target priorities of a general nature are necessary to define what is to be done before determining how to accomplish it. These targets are overly simplified in that they only consider customers and whether the bank strategy is to retain present customers, increase the customer base, or eliminate certain types for economic or risk-related reasons. Another priority may be expanding the services provided to each customer by establishing the banking relationship on the long-term, multiproduct basis or as a short-term, single-product emphasis.

The operating theater identifies the geographical scope of the strategy and requires variations in product and service as well as personnel and the delivery system. The bank that operates in a rural community has a set of action plans far different from those of its counterparts in metropolitan or statewide areas. The objectives and goals appropriate to a regional bank are not entirely applicable to a national or international banking strategy. In a money center bank such as Manufacturers Hanover the strategy for its New York City retail operation is very dissimilar from its strategy involving international credits in Latin America. Thus, many banks must consider a multistrategy posture by selecting strategies within strategies.

Banks tend to be identified or closely associated with the type of customers served and the group of products offered. In the components of strategy these are represented by the operating emphasis or the various products offered by the bank and the market segments that the bank has elected to serve. Because of their importance, the variety of products available will be covered in detail in Chapter 7. It is also essential that the universe of customers be identified before the target market selection process is begun. These two components are particularly significant, and they provide banks with an especially broad product and customer menu from which to select a bank marketing strategy.

STRATEGY SELECTION. The identification of the marketing strategy components permits the marketing manager to review the various factors that affect the strategy options available. However, it is necessary to understand the current strategy of the bank to determine whether revisions or radical changes are appropriate. This requires an analysis of the current strategy and can be initiated by making some of the following determinations:

1. Establish the key operating guidelines of management, such as return on assets, return on equity, earnings per share, share of market, total assets, loan volume, and deposit mix.
2. Identify the specific lines of business of the bank, including its concepts of social responsibility and obligations to shareholders, customers, employees, and government agencies.
3. Consider the current business environment and possible conditions favorable or adverse to the present bank strategy as revealed by apparent weaknesses or untapped strengths that might make the current strategy less appropriate.
4. Review the current strategy for its consistency with the expertise and resources of the bank to provide sufficient competitive advantage and operating opportunity.

There is a particular process or methodology for selecting the marketing strategy for a bank. Although the process illustrated in Figure 5-1 proposes a specific order, some of these process actions may be accomplished concurrently or in a slightly different order. The key to the process is to complete each stage prior to the adoption of a final strategy. As the flowchart indicates, before attempting to recommend a specific marketing strategy, there are some management decisions affecting the strategy that are concerned with the investment to be made in marketing. The basic business strategies determined by senior management provide the basis for achieving a marketing advantage; however, more specialized information is necessary from management for marketing investment decisions. For instance, management decisions regarding the corporate priorities for operating the bank are necessary. In its broadest sense, senior management must determine whether the marketing strategy is to be growth-oriented or seeking nongrowth. *Growth-oriented strategies* can be accomplished by a gain in share of market and increased product usage. Action programs such as aggressive branch promotion or intensive calling programs, heavy mass communication, or discount pricing usually result in growth. However, the immediate gains from such programs are difficult to sustain. It is usually more productive to develop resources that eliminate some of the bank's weaknesses relative to competition and that also result in a distinctive product or service advantage.

This strategy can best be implemented successfully by developing new products for existing markets or new markets for existing products. To facilitate the former, the current product line can be expanded by adding a debit card capability to the present bank credit card or adding features of

Figure 5-1. Marketing Strategy Selection Process

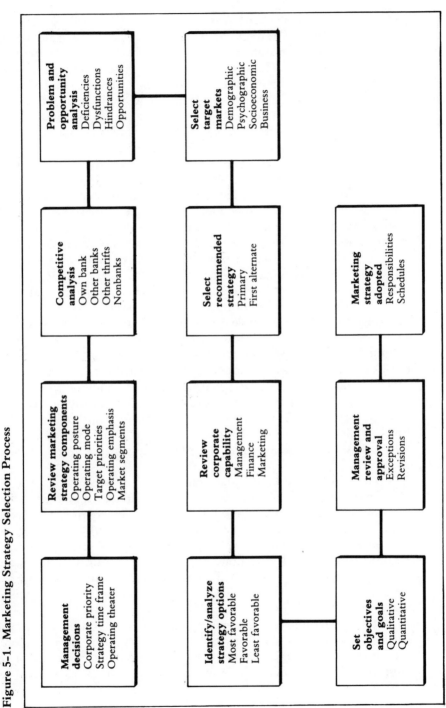

convenience such as membership in a national ATM network. New product development also increases growth in an existing market with a cross-selling effort to present customers. If new market expansion is selected as a course of action, the bank has to expand geographically or target new segments or niches in the present marketplace. This targeting can be accomplished by identifying nonusers of specific bank products or services, by developing new delivery systems, or by revising the pricing schedule.

A *non–growth-oriented strategy* is one that both banks and thrifts have been reluctant to follow voluntarily. This reluctance has worked against some institutions and might have prevented some failures or forced mergers and acquisitions had this alternative been selected in time. A nongrowth strategy should not be considered as applicable solely to a bank in total. It can and should probably be used more frequently on specific product lines, customer niches, branch locations, or operating subsidiaries. The most radical application is divestment or liquidation. A common example of this is the sale of credit card operations by some banks to improve their capital position or eliminate further consumer loan losses. The situation in which this nongrowth strategy is most appropriate is one in which the product is losing money after a sufficient opportunity for profitability; the discount brokerage service is an example for many banks. In another situation consumer use is declining or a competitor is so dominant in the marketplace that further competition may not be sound economically; branch closures or customer niche exits are solutions to this situation, although many banks have been unable to take such action for reasons of tradition, community reputation, or restrictions by the regulators. The key to any management strategy of nongrowth is to initiate an appropriate course of action that enhances the effectiveness of bank resources. If followed, this strategy results in a "shrink the bank" effort by reducing the asset side of the balance sheet.

The most practical use of the nongrowth strategy is to hold or maintain market position. This is usually an interim strategy during periods of economic or industry uncertainty. Whether pursuing a controlled reduction or maintaining current levels, this strategy requires an adequate marketing investment. Neither strategy can be applied successfully without appropriate financial strength. If divestiture is forced by severe financial problems, this strategy should not be selected because it has little chance of being implemented in an orderly and effective manner without adequate financial resources.

When determining recommendations for a marketing investment strategy, there are also some basic considerations and consequences regarding growth versus nongrowth. Growth geographically may be different because of the expansion of well-known banks when interstate banking becomes a reality. To achieve growth, most banks have to become specialty institutions with well-defined product lines and target market segments. Many large local banks may be unable to isolate product or market niches to support their current overhead and infrastructure. This may result in the adoption of a nongrowth strategy until their products and targets have been redefined. It is axiomatic that every market has its share of new entrants and that the current strategies pursued by banks and thrifts will be altered considerably.

PROBLEM AND OPPORTUNITY ANALYSIS. The bank marketing strategy selected is strongly affected, not by products and targets exclusively, but by the problems and opportunities that exist in the marketplace. It is these problems and opportunities that clearly define the marketing situation confronting the bank. A *problem* has been defined as a condition that requires attention and correction, whereas an *opportunity* is a situation that invites attention and exploitation. If the current situation is described accurately in the analysis of the marketing environment, the identification of problem areas and growth and profit opportunities is very evident. Major problems should be considered regardless of the immediate prospects for solutions. In most cases, problems and opportunities feed upon each other: where one is found, the other is lurking nearby. Problems can be found in fairly predictable locations; however, they can be more easily identified by three indicators of danger.

The first of these is the *deficiency danger.* This will indicate undesirable changes from the normal or that the action results being realized are less than forecast. Typical deficiencies of concern to a marketing manager include the following:

1. Declining market share of deposits
2. Reduced customer base
3. Lack of market penetration in loans
4. Drop in demand deposits
5. Net loss of checking accounts
6. Lower installment loan volume
7. Lower commercial loan volume
8. Reduced profitability
9. Lower consumer awareness of the bank and its services
10. Increase in nonperforming assets

The second indicators concern *dysfunction*. This suggests that there is some interruption in the smooth operation of the marketing function. Typical indicators of dysfunction include the following:

1. Inadequate sales representation by calling officers
2. Attrition of calling officers
3. Increased complaints about bank service
4. Unproductive advertising and promotion
5. Regulator restraints on advertising and promotion
6. Ineffective literature and sales aids
7. Inadequate or incorrect market information
8. Delayed loan processing
9. Conflicting or restrictive bank procedures

The third classification concerns *hindrance* that indicates obstacles that delay or reduce the possibility for achieving the marketing objectives and goals. Typical hindrance circumstances include the following:

1. Low margin pricing structure
2. Nonbank competition
3. Mismatch or limited funds for use
4. Obsolete or inefficient delivery system
5. Market dominance by regional or national competitors
6. Nonexclusive selling proposition
7. Customer apathy or dissatisfaction
8. Poor bank or service reputation
9. Confusion of bank with thrift institution
10. Lack of corporate recognition in key market
11. Inconsistent operations support
12. Low market presence or visibility
13. Limitations on products and services
14. Distance from key local markets

Once these indicators are evident, a more detailed analysis should be made to separate the actual problems from their symptomatic elements. For example, the indicator of a declining market share might only be symptomatic of the actual marketing problem; the real problem could be the impact of a major advertising effort by a competitor and compounded by the inadequacy of the effort to counter its effect. The actual problem might also be poor service, rate or service charge differential, an inconvenient or inadequate delivery system, lack of competitive product features, or a combination of several of these factors. In some cases, the problem may be industrywide instead of confined to a single bank. If so, its solution, after separating the real problem from its symptoms, may require a strong, dominant marketing position by the bank to minimize or reduce the advantage of nonbank competitors.

The problem identity effort also requires that problems be designated as solvable, unsolvable, or neutralized. If they can be solved realistically and economically, considering the time and resources to be committed, the problems can become opportunities and, perhaps, restated as marketing objectives or goals. If they are not solvable, they become part of the external or internal environment that must be considered in the evolution of the bank marketing strategy and the ultimate courses of action selected.

Although problems have often been described as opportunities, they can be more accurately defined as pathfinders for opportunities. The identification and analysis of problems leads to opportunities through those areas to which bank marketing managers turn for solutions. Thus, opportunities can sometimes be found among the following:

1. New or revised industry technologies
2. Specific bank strengths in financial expertise
3. Secondary product features or consumer benefits
4. Changing customer life-styles
5. Changing customer service needs
6. Improved delivery system facilities
7. Comparative financial strength
8. Geographic presence in key local markets
9. Effective, well-trained calling officers
10. Dense branch distribution patterns
11. Competitive interest rates and fee charges
12. Strong correspondent bank relationships
13. Favorable bank image and reputation
14. Role as industry leader in the community

Once the identification and analysis of marketing problems and opportunities have been completed, the strategy selection process provides for a review of the various options for strategy selection. Although it is essential that an innovative strategy be selected, there are some practical considerations that may limit the options available. These are referred to as the capabilities of the bank that affect its ability to follow a given strategy; usually they are described as the bank's strengths and weaknesses. The list of some measures that may affect the bank's capability includes the following as related to key operating functions within the bank:

1. Does senior management attract and maintain highly qualified personnel and have a process for the training and development of future managers?
2. Has senior management demonstrated sound judgment through an acceptable decision-making process?
3. Has management established a standard operating procedure that results in adequate strategic planning and functions within an efficient organization structure for proper control and coordination?
4. Does financial management have access to long-term capital at a favorable cost, and can short-term capital be raised at a reasonable cost?
5. Is the bank in a position to maximize the value of shareholders and still provide a competitive return on investment?
6. Will financial management be willing to assume operating risks when justified by business conditions and marketing opportunities by committing adequate funds?
7. Can the bank finance diversification through merger or acquisition?
8. Can the marketing effort establish an appropriate customer base?
9. Does marketing management have access to current marketing information?
10. Are bank products and services available through an efficient and convenient delivery system?
11. Can marketing management provide effective promotion and market communication?
12. Are marketing programs implemented through a well-organized, motivated, and supportive sales and service organization?
13. Does the marketing effort have an attractive selling proposition that has a competitive advantage?
14. Can marketing resources provide for continuing product development and improvement?

In advance of or coincident with an analysis of problems and opportunities as well as an evaluation of the functional strengths and weaknesses of the bank is a review of the components of the marketing strategy. This can be accomplished with the completion of a detailed competitive analysis. This analysis will assist the bank marketing manager in not only identifying the strategy options available or uncovered, but in determining which options are the most favorable. This comparative review of the various strategy components can be completed by using the Marketing Strategy Selection Worksheet (Table 5-1), which lists many of the components in detail.

When the comparative analysis has been completed the strategy options can be evaluated and a primary strategy recommended. Because mar-

Table 5-1. Marketing Strategy Selection Worksheet

Components of strategy	Competition						Own bank	
	Bank A	Bank B	Bank C	Bank D	Thrift A	Thrift B	Present	Future
Corporate priority Growth Earnings Contraction Sustain								

Strategy time frame
Short term
    (1–3 yr)
Long term
    (3–5 yr)								

Operating posture Agressive Cooperative Defensive								
Operating mode Cost-driven Product-driven Market-driven								

Target priorities
Customer
    retention
Customer increase
Customer
    reduction
Relationship
    expansion								

Operating theater Community Metropolitan Statewide Regional National International								

Operating emphasis
Personal deposits
Commercial
    deposits
Consumer finance
Commercial
    finance
Corporate lending
Correspondent
    banking
Trust/custodial
Investment
Electronic services
Insurance
International
Special services								

Table 5-1 (continued)

Components of strategy	Competition						Own bank	
	Bank A	Bank B	Bank C	Bank D	Thrift A	Thrift B	Present	Future
Market segments								
Demographic								
Student								
Blue-collar								
White-collar								
Retireds								
Professionals								
Civil service								
Military								
Psychographic								
Leaders								
Followers								
Traditionalists								
Egocentrics								
Achievers								
Intellectuals								
Risk-takers								
Innovators								
Family-centered								
Prestige-conscious								
Socioeconomic								
Lower-class								
Middle-class								
Upper-class								
Singles								
Young marrieds								
Middle marrieds								
Old marrieds								
Volume users								
Light users								
Price-sensitive								
Service-driven								
Business								
Large manufacturers								
Medium manufacturers								
Small manufacturers								
Service companies								
Distributors								
Professionals								
Private institutions								
Govt. institutions								

keting situations change so rapidly, it is always prudent to select a first alternative strategy for contingency purposes. It should be one of the previously designated favorable options and will probably include many of the components of the primary strategy recommended. On the basis of the recommendation, it is then appropriate to select the specific targets that offer the most potential in support of the strategy selected.

TARGET MARKET SELECTION. Bank marketing targets are usually identified in terms of ultimate consumers or users of the product or service, although the regulators, employees, civic leaders, and personnel of other financial institutions can be considered as special targets for marketing attention. In basic or primary target determination, markets are usually defined in terms of a specific group of prospects or customers with demographic, psychographic, or socioeconomic characteristics who will receive a benefit in common through the satisfying of a financial service need. These needs are usually dominated by a primary service requirement that differentiates the group from others in the marketplace. For example, one group of retirees on a fixed income in a retirement community may be price-sensitive and seek higher interest rates or lower service fees and be willing to bank in areas outside their immediate vicinity. However, within the same residential location, another group may require better service and closer proximity because of less mobility. In some respects this is a Catch-22 situation since providing more service is costly and may affect the rate of interest that is available. Demographically, the groups would appear in the same statistical set, but from a psychographic or socioeconomic standpoint, they have some strong differences. To complicate targeting further, the situation described may also result in part of each group maintaining at least two banking relationships in separate institutions that are committed to opposing marketing strategies and, yet, serve portions of each group.

Bank customers can also be identified on the basis of their banking behavior as well as the product or service benefit received. Banking behavior is more than tracking the actions of the one whose name appears on the account. There are various individuals who influence the banking decision. Thus, these influentials as well as the account holders or users can be designated as targets. When viewed in total, marketing targets for banks usually fall into one or more of the following categories:

1. **Initiator.** One who first suggests the bank or its products, e.g., the wife who suggests a bank loan for home improvement, a vacation, or a child's education.
2. **Informer.** One who provides more specific information, e.g., a

friend with a word–of–mouth recommendation or bank personnel who provide product knowledge.

3. **Decision maker.** One who determines all or part of the banking decision on whether, what, how, when, and where to bank, e.g., the wife for a convenient household account, the husband for the IRA account, the company treasurer for the business account.

4. **Patron.** One who actually serves as the customer of record, e.g., signators of a loan agreement or the checking account or credit cardholder.

5. **Account user.** One who conducts the banking transaction, e.g., those who visit branch offices, ATM and credit card users, cash depositors.

Each target group can also be identified on the basis of the function performed in society. This classification is very general and is categorized by mass communication specialists as *publics*. This method of target designation is most useful when seeking information of a macro nature and is used to identify a more universal grouping rather than a specific segment or niche. These functional categories of a micro nature include the following:

1. Customers and prospects
   Individual consumers
   Business and professional
   Government agencies
   Nonprofit organizations and institutions
   Other financial institutions
2. Own organization
   Present employees
   Prospective employees
   Retired employees
   Former employees
   Spouses and families
   Directors and advisors
3. Financial community
   Debtholders
   Competitors
   Vendors
   Trade and professional organizations
   Shareholders
   Investing public
   Financial analysts
   Financial counselors
   Consulting firms

        Accounting firms
        Legal firms
4. Influence centers
        Mass information media
        Government regulatory agencies
        Public officials
        Community leaders
        Civic and service organizations
        Academics
        Consumer advocacy groups
        Public-at-large

In spite of the numerous ways available to categorize and target customers, the most definitive are those that use methods developed by behavioral scientists, aided by statisticians and economists. The markets for individual consumers can be well defined by demographic, psychographic, or socioeconomic classification. *Demographics* is essentially a quantitative approach that relies on income levels, amount of education, gender, and occupational groupings. These have a somewhat predictable cause and effect relationship that provides a commonality for assessing banking potential. For example, banking characteristics can be established on a macro basis for those in certain demographic groups. Students have little discretionary income for deposit, retirees have fixed income levels and have less need for loans, military people move frequently and either bank on an absentee basis or have shorter-term banking relationships, and professionals are often large users of capital funds.

Psychographics is a second target segment and tends to be more qualitative. It defines banking customers according to their interests and activities. Opinions are also an essential consideration since they affect personal interests and the activities pursued. Interests include such concerns as home and the family, work, recreation, community involvement, and such personal items as food and fashion preferences. Activities include hobbies, social events, entertainment, club and organization membership, shopping patterns, sports participation, television viewing habits, and work as an activity as well as an interest. Behavioralists consider an interest to be a degree of excitement, whereas an activity is a manifest action. They can both be applied to banking by translating participation and interest into such categories of individual life-styles as leaders, followers, egocentrics, intellectuals, risk takers, and those who are family-centered or prestige-conscious.

From a *socioeconomic perspective*, targets can be classified by social class behavior. This is a particularly dynamic categorization because it reacts to the changing social environment and develops diverse and quick changing life-styles. On a qualitative basis, class strata that have an immediate application in banking can be constructed. For example, the lower-class stratum is more difficult to qualify for credit although its loan requirements are many. This group reacts more favorably to the specific amount of the monthly payment than to the rate of interest or term. The upper-class category or the more upscale customer is more likely to consider the actual rate or some visual demonstration of prestige through such instruments as bank cards with a discriminating color, extensive credit line, and semiexclusive privileges. The social classification by behavioralists is as finite as a division of upper, middle, and lower into the further subsets of upper upper, lower upper, upper middle, lower middle, and so on. For the purpose of bank customer behavior and its relation to market segmentation, it is sufficient to confine it to upper, middle, and lower. However, the circumstances of marriage, age, usage, and sensitivity to price and service are also economic considerations that are particularly germane to banking.

On the commercial side, customer behavior is analyzed with statistical data and economic considerations. It is difficult to categorize a business banking customer on the basis of company behavioral strata. Although the size of a company gives some indication of capital needs, asset-based financing requirements, and other peculiarities of specific banking products and services, it is more appropriate to analyze on the basis of government and industry data. Size of company is an immediate consideration only because the size of the bank limits its resources to serve companies of a certain size.

The basis for most statistical data and economic analysis is the government-assigned Standard Industrial Classification (SIC) (Table 5-2). Most government data and industry performance reports are published with reference to SIC: Both Robert Morris and Dun and Bradstreet use it for reference in their reports. Marketing managers should be aware of the precise categories that are identified with the SIC since this will provide valuable statistical and economic data for use in establishing viable commercial targets. The complete listing for Standard Industrial Classification covering U.S. businesses is provided for the convenience of the marketing manager to use in the process of target segment selection.

MARKETING OBJECTIVES AND GOALS. With the selection of the recommended strategy and the designation of target markets, the setting of objectives and goals is necessary to establish the specific intent of the bank for marketing action. Either one can be qualitative, quantitative, or a combination of both. Objectives and goals are established on the basis of an actual result to be achieved within a specified time period. They can be related to bank growth or profit, loan or deposit volume, earnings, improvement of the bank's image and reputation, or satisfying the social responsibilities of the company. Objectives are the essence of the marketing effort.

Growth objectives can be stated in terms of share of market as compared to the shares of competition, growth in specific product and service volume, increased branch distribution, or expansion of the range of products offered. Profit objectives can be related to the return on equity, return on assets, or a specified improvement over previous profit performance. The altering of a bank's image and the improvement of its reputation are recurring objectives, particularly during those periods when a specific image problem exists.

Unfortunately, the terms *objectives* and *goals* are often used interchangeably although, in fact, they are used to denote two different entities. An objective is an aspiration to be working toward for future accomplishment. It may even be timeless in certain instances in the sense that a qualitative objective is often continuous: even when achieved, the objective remains. There are four dimensions that can be used to differentiate between objectives and goals—time frame, specificity, focus, and measurement. The time frame of an objective may be timeless and enduring; a goal is temporal, time-phased, and intended to be revised or replaced by new goals over the short term.

To ensure specificity, objectives are stated in broad, general terms and often deal with matters of corporate image, management style, or an expression of self-perception. Goals are more specific and are stated in terms of a particular result to be accomplished within a specified period of time. Because of their enduring qualities, objectives may never be achieved in total; goals are set to be attained within a relatively short period of time. Objectives are also expressed with reference to some external variable, whereas goals are often internal in that they involve the commitment of bank resources in an immediate period. Objectives are frequently established for the purpose of achieving leadership or recognition in a certain sector within the industry or by a particular segment of the market. Goals require the organization to apply the bank's resources in a prescribed way to achieve the desired results.

Objectives can take the form of the immeasurable in some instances; however, both objectives and goals are best stated in terms that are quantifiable; the character of the measurement is different for each. Quantified objectives are stated in relative terms such as compounding the rate of growth in deposits and loans sufficiently to make the bank the leader in its market. This objective might be attained in a year or two, but the mission of remaining on top is the relevant element that makes the objective timeless and provides an ongoing objective for the bank. A quantified goal, on the other hand, is simply stated and expressed in absolute terms. For additional

Table 5-2. Standard Industrial Classification (SIC) (Numerical Order)

SIC DESCRIPTION

AGRICULTURE. FORESTRY & FISHING

01   Agricultural Production—Crops
0111 Wheat
0112 Rice
0115 Corn
0116 Soybeans
0119 Cash Grains, nec
0131 Cotton
0132 Tobacco
0133 Sugar Crops
0134 Potatoes, Irish
0139 Field Crops Except Cash Grains, nec
0161 Vegetables & Melons
0171 Berry Crops
0172 Grapes
0173 Tree Nuts
0174 Citrus Fruits
0175 Deciduous Tree Fruits
0179 Fruits & Tree Nuts, nec
0181 Nursery Products, Ornamental
0182 Foods Crops Grown Undercover
0189 Horticulture Specialties, nec
0191 Farm Crops, General

02   Agricultural Production— Livestock
0211 Beef Cattle Feedlots
0212 Beef Cattle Except Feedlots
0213 Hogs
0214 Sheep & Goats
0219 General Livestock
0241 Dairy Farms
0251 Fowls, Broiler & Fryer
0252 Chicken Eggs
0253 Turkeys & Turkey Eggs
0254 Poultry Hatcheries
0259 Poultry & Eggs, nec
0271 Fur-bearing Animals & Rabbits
0272 Horses & Other Equine
0279 Animal Specialties, nec
0291 Farms, Primarily Livestock

07   Agricultural Services
0711 Soil Preparation Services
0721 Crop Planting & Protection
0722 Crop Harvesting
0723 Crop Preparation Services for Market
0724 Cotton Ginning
0729 Crop Services General
0741 Veterinarian Services, Farm Stock
0742 Veterinarian Services, Specialities
0751 Livestock Services

0752 Animal Specialty Services
0761 Farm Labor Contractor
0762 Farm Management Services
0781 Landscape Counseling
0782 Lawn & Garden Services
0783 Shrub & Tree Services

08   Forestry
0811 Timber Tracts
0821 Forest Nurseries & Tree Seed
0843 Extraction Pine Gum
0849 Forest Products Gathering of, nec
0651 Forestry Services

09   Fishing, Hunting & Trapping
0912 Finfish
0913 Shellfish
0919 Marine Products, Misc
0921 Fish Hatcheries & Preserves
0971 Hunting & Trapping Game Propagation

MINING

10   Metal Mining
1011 Iron Ores
1021 Copper Ores
1031 Lead, Zinc Ores
1041 Gold Ores
1044 Silver Ores
1051 Bauxite, Aluminum Ores
1061 Ferroalloy Ores
1081 Metal Mining Services
1092 Mercury Ores
1094 Uranium-Radium Ores
1099 Metal Ores, nec

11   Anthracite Mining
1111 Anthracite
1112 Anthracite Mining Services

12   Bituminous Coal & Lignite Mining
1211 Bituminous Coal & Lignite
1213 Bituminous, Lignite, Mining Services

13   Oil & Gas Extraction
1311 Crude Oil & Natural Gas
1321 Natural Gas Liquids
1381 Drilling Oil & Gas Wells
1382 Oil, Gas Exploration Services
1389 Oil, Gas Field Services, nec

14   Nonmetallic Minerals, Except Fuels
1411 Dimension Stone
1422 Limestone, Crushed & Broken
1423 Granite, Crushed & Broken

Table 5-2 (continued)

1429 Stone, Crushed & Broken, nec
1442 Construction Sand & Gravel
1446 Industrial Sand
1452 Bentonite
1453 Fire Clay
1454 Fuller's Earth
1455 Kaolin, Ball Clay
1459 Clay & Related Minerals, nec
1472 Barite
1473 Fluorspar
1474 Potash Soda & Borate Minerals
1475 Phosphate Rock
1476 Rock Salt
1477 Sulfur
1479 Chemical And Fertilizer Mining, nec
1481 Nonmetallic Minerals (Except Fuels)
      services
1492 Gypsum
1496 Talc, Soapstone And Pyrophyllite
1499 Nonmetallic Minerals, nec

CONSTRUCTION

15   General Building Contractors
1511 Contractors General Building
1521 Single Family Housing Construction
1522 Residential Construction
1531 Operative Builders
1541 Industrial Buildings & Warehouses
1542 Nonresidential Construction

16   Heavy Construction Contractors
1611 Highway & Street Construction
1622 Bridge Tunnel & Elevated Highway
1623 Water Sewer & Utility
1629 Heavy Construction, nec

17   Special Trade Contractors
1711 Plumbing, Heating (Except
      Electrical) & Air Conditioning
1721 Painting, Paper Hanging &
      Decorations
1731 Electrical Work
1741 Masonry, Other Stonework
1742 Plastering Drywall, Insulation
1743 Terrazzo, Tile, Marble & Mosaic
      Work
1751 Carpentering
1752 Floor Laying, Floor Work, nec
1761 Roofing Sheet Metal Work
1771 Concrete Work
1781 Water Well Drilling
1791 Structural Steel Erection
1793 Glass, Glazing Work
1794 Excavating & Foundation Work
1795 Wrecking, Demolition Work

1796 Installion, Building Equipment, nec
1799 Special Trade Contractors, nec

MANUFACTURING

20   Feed & Kindred Products
2011 Meat Packing Plants
2013 Sausages & Other Prepared Meat
2016 Poultry Dressing Plant
2017 Poultry & Egg Processing
2021 Butter
2022 Cheese, Natural & Processed
2023 Milk, Condensed & Evaporated
2024 Ice Cream & Frozen Dessert
2026 Milk, Fluid
2032 Canned Specialties
2033 Canned Fruits, Vegetables & Related
      Products
2034 Dried & Dehydrated Fruits,
      Vegetables & Related
2035 Pickled Fruits & Vegetables, Sauces &
      Salad Dressings
2037 Frozen Fruits & Vegetables
2038 Frozen Specialties
2041 Flour & Grain Mill Products
2043 Cereal Preparations
2044 Rice Milling
2045 Flour, Blended & Prepared
2046 Wet Corn Milling
2047 Pet Food, Dog, Cat & Other
2048 Prepared Feeds, nec
2051 Bread, Cake & Related Products
2052 Cookies & Crackers
2061 Sugar, Raw Cane
2062 Sugar, Refining Cane
2063 Sugar, Beet
2065 Confectionary Products
2066 Chocolate & Cocoa Products
2067 Chewing Gum
2074 Cottonseed Oil Mills
2075 Soybean Oil Mills
2076 Vegetable Oil Mills
2077 Animal & Marine Fats & Oils
2079 Lard & Cooking Oils, nec
2082 Malt Liquors
2083 Malt
2084 Wine, Brandy & Brandy Spirits
2085 Distilled & Blended Liquor Except
      Brandy
2086 Soft Drinks, Bottled & Canned
2087 Flavoring Extracts & Flavoring
      Syrups, nec
2091 Canned & Cured Seafoods
2092 Fish, Fresh or Frozen
2095 Coffee, Roasted

Table 5-2 (continued)

2097 Ice
2098 Macaroni & Spaghetti
2099 Food Preparations, nec

21   Tobacco Manufacturers
2111 Cigarettes
2121 Cigars
2131 Tobacco, Chewing & Smoking
2141 Tobacco Stemming & Redrying

22   Textile Mill Products
2211 Weaving Mills, Cotton
2221 Weaving Mills, Synthetics
2231 Weaving & Finishing Mills, Wool
2241 Fabric Mills
2251 Women's Hosiery
2252 Hosiery, nec
2253 Knit Outerwear Mills
2254 Knit Underwear Mills
2257 Circle Knit Fabric Mills
2258 Warp Knit Fabric Mills
2259 Knitting Mills, nec
2261 Finishing Plants, Cotton
2262 Finishing Plants, Synthetics
2269 Finishing Plants, Misc
2271 Carpets, Rugs—Woven
2272 Carpets, Rugs—Tufted
2279 Carpets, Rugs, nec
2281 Yarn Mills, Except Wool
2282 Mills, Throwing & Winding
2283 Mills, Wool Yarn
2284 Mills, Thread
2291 Felt Goods, Misc
2292 Lace Goods
2293 Upholstery Fillings & Padding
2294 Textile Waste, Processed
2295 Fabrics, Coated Not Rubberized
2296 Tire Cord, Fabric
2297 Fabrics, Nonwoven
2298 Cordage & Twine
2299 Textile Goods, nec

23   Apparel & Other Textile Products
2311 Men's & Boys' Suits
2321 Men's & Boys' Nightwear
2322 Men's & Boys' Underwear
2323 Men's & Boys' neckwear
2327 Men's & Boys' Trousers
2328 Men's & Boys' Work Clothing
2329 Men's & Boys' Clothing, nec
2331 Women's & Misses' Blouses
2335 Women's & Misses' Dresses
2337 Women's & Misses' Suits
2339 Women's & Misses' Outerwear, nec
2341 Women's & Children's Underwear

2342 Corsets & Garments
2351 Millinery
2352 Hats & Caps
2361 Children's Dresses
2363 Children's Coats
2369 Children's Outerwear, nec
2371 Fur Coats
2381 Gloves, Dress & Work
2384 Robes & Dress Gowns
2385 Waterproof Garments
2386 Leather-lined Cloths
2387 Apparel Belts
2389 Apparel & Accessories, nec
2391 Curtains, Draperies
2392 Housefurnishings
2393 Textile Bags
2394 Canvas Products
2395 Pleating & Stitching
2396 Apparel Findings
2397 Schiffli Machine Embroideries
2399 Fabricated Textile Products, nec

24   Lumber & Wood Products
2411 Logging Camps & Contractors
2421 Sawmills & Planing Mills, General
2426 Hardwood Dimension Flooring
2429 Special Product Sawmills, nec
2431 Millwork
2434 Wood Kitchen Cabinets
2435 Hardwood Veneer & Plywood
2436 Softwood Veneer Plywood
2439 Structural Wood, nec
2441 Boxes, Wood
2448 Wood Pallets & Skids
2449 Wood Containers, nec
2451 Mobile Homes
2452 Wood Buildings, Prefabricated
2491 Wood Preserving
2492 Particleboard
2499 Wood Products, nec

25   Furniture & Fixtures
2511 Wood Household Furniture
2512 Furniture, Household, Upholstered
2514 Metal Household Furniture
2515 Mattresses & Bedsprings
2517 Wooden TV & Radio Cabinets
2519 Household Furniture, nec
2521 Wood office Furniture
2522 Metal office Furniture
2531 Furniture For Public Buildings
2541 Wood Partitions & Fixtures
2542 Metal Partitions & Fixtures
2591 Venetian Blinds, Shades
2599 Furniture & Fixtures, nec

Table 5-2 (continued)

26   Paper & Allied Products
2611 Pulp Mills
2621 Paper Mills Except Building Paper
     Mills
2631 Paperboard Mills
2641 Paper Coating & Glazing
2642 Envelopes
2643 Bags, Except Textile Bags
2645 Die Cut Paper, Board
2646 Pulp Goods, Pressure Molded
2647 Sanitary Paper Products
2648 Stationery Products
2649 Converted Paper Products
2651 Boxes, Folding Paperboard
2652 Boxes, Setup Paperboard
2653 Boxes, Corrugated & Solid Fiber
2654 Sanitary Food Containers
2655 Fiber Cans, Drums, Etc
2661 Building Paper & Building Board
     Mills

27   Printing & Publishing
2711 Newspapers
2721 Periodicals
2731 Book Publishing
2732 Book Printing
2741 Publishing, Misc
2751 Commercial Letterpress Printing
2752 Commercial Lithographic Printing
2753 Engraving & Plate Printing
2754 Commercial Printing, Gravure
2761 Manifold Business Forms
2771 Greeting Card Publishing
2782 Loose Leaf Binders & Blank Books
2789 Bookbinding & Related Work
2791 Typesetting
2793 Photoengraving
2794 Electrotyping & Stereotyping
2795 Lithographic Platemaking Services

28   Chemicals & Allied Products
2812 Alkalies, Chlorine
2813 Industrial Gases
2816 Inorganic Pigments
2819 Industrial Inorganic Chemicals, nec
2821 Plastics Material
2822 Synthetic Rubber
2823 Cellulosic Man-made Fibers
2824 Organic Fibers
2831 Biological Products
2833 Medicinal, Botanical Products
2834 Pharmaceutical Preparations
2841 Soap, Other Detergent
2842 Polishing, Cleaning & Sanitation
     Goods

2843 Surface Active Agents
2844 Toilet Preparations
2851 Paints & Allied Products
2861 Gum & Wood Chemicals
2865 Cyclic Crudes & Intermediates
2869 Industrial Organic Chemicals, nec
2873 Fertilizers, Nitrogenous
2874 Fertilizers, Phosphatic
2875 Fertilizers, Mixing
2879 Agricultural Chemicals, nec
2891 Adhesives & Sealants
2892 Explosives
2893 Printing Ink
2895 Carbon Black
2899 Chemical Preparations, nec

29   Petroleum & Coal Products
2911 Petroleum Refining
2951 Paving Mixtures & Blocks
2952 Asphalt Felts & Coatings
2992 Lubricating Oils & Greases
2999 Petroleum & Coal Products, nec

30   Rubber & Misc. Plastics Products
3011 Tires, Inner Tubes
3021 Rubber/Plastic Footwear
3031 Reclaimed Rubber
3041 Rubber/Plastic Hose
3069 Rubber Products, Fabricated, nec
3079 Plastic Products, Misc

31   Leather & Leather Products
3111 Leather Tanning & Finishing
3131 Footwear, Boot & Shoe Cut Stock
3142 House Slippers
3143 Men's Shoes Except Athletic
3144 Ladies' Shoes Except Athletic
3149 Footwear Except Rubber, nec
3151 Leather Gloves & Mittens
3161 Luggage
3171 Women's Handbags
3172 Leather Goods, Personal, nec
3199 Leather Goods, nec

32   Stone, Clay & Glass Products
3211 Glass, Flat
3221 Glass Containers
3229 Glass, Glassware, Pressed or Blown,
     nec
3231 Glass Products, Made of Purchased
     Glass
3241 Cement Hydraulic
3251 Brick & Structural Clay Tile
3253 Ceramic Wall & Floor Tile
3255 Clay Refractories
3259 Structural Clay Products, nec

Table 5-2 (continued)

3261 Vitreous Plumbing Fixtures
3262 Vitreous China Food Utensils
3263 Food Utensils, Earthenware
3264 Porcelain Electrical Supplies
3269 Pottery Products, nec
3271 Concrete Block & Brick
3272 Concrete Products, nec
3273 Concrete, Ready-mixed
3274 Lime
3275 Gypsum Products
3281 Cut Stone & Stone Products
3291 Abrasive Products
3292 Asbestos Products
3293 Gaskets, Packing & Sealing Devices
3295 Minerals & Earths, Ground or
     Treated
3296 Mineral Wool
3297 Refractories, Nonclay
3299 Mineral Products, Nonmetallic, nec

33   Primary Metal Industries
3312 Blast Furnaces, Steel Mills
3313 Electrometallurgical Products
3315 Steel Wire & Related Products
3316 Steel—Sheet, Strip & Bar
3317 Steel Pipe, Tubes
3321 Foundries, Gray Iron
3322 Foundries, Malleable Iron
3324 Steel Investment Foundry
3325 Steel Foundries, nec
3331 Copper, Primary
3332 Lead, Primary
3333 Zinc, Primary
3334 Aluminum, Primary
3339 Metals, Nonferrous Primary
     Smelting & Refining, nec
3341 Metals, Nonferrous, Secondary
3351 Copper Rolling, Drawing &
     Extruding
3353 Aluminum Sheet Plate & Foil
3354 Aluminum Extruded Products
3355 Aluminum Rolling & Drawing, nec
3356 Metal, Nonferrous, Rolling,
     Drawing, nec
3357 Wire, Nonferrous, Drawing &
     Insulating of, Misc
3361 Aluminum Castings
3362 Brass, Bronze, Copper Castings
3369 Foundries, Nonferrous, nec
3398 Metal Heat Treating
3399 Metal Products, Primary, nec

34   Fabricated Metal Products
3411 Metal Cans
3412 Metal Drums & Pails
3421 Cutlery

3423 Hand & Edge Tools, Except Machine
     Tools & Hand Saws
3425 Hand Saws & Saw Blades
3429 Hardware, nec
3431 Metal Sanitary Ware
3432 Plumbing Fixtures & Brass Goods
3433 Heating Equipment Except Electrical
3441 Fabricated Structural Steel
3442 Metal Doors, Sash, Trim
3443 Fabricated Plate Work
3444 Steel Metal Work
3446 Architectural & Ornamental Metal
     Work
3448 Metal Buildings, Prefabricated
3449 Metal Work, Misc
3451 Screw Machine Products
3452 Bolts, Nuts, Screws, Rivets &
     Washers
3462 Iron & Steel Forgings
3463 Forgings, Nonferrous
3465 Automotive Stampings
3466 Crowns & Closures
3469 Metal Stampings, nec
3471 Plating & Polishing
3479 Metal Coating & Allied Services
3482 Ammunition, Small Arms
3483 Ammunition, Except For Small
     Arms, nec
3484 Weapons, Small Firearms
3489 Ordinance & Accessories, nec
3493 Steel Springs
3494 Valves, Pipe Fittings
3495 Wire Springs
3496 Fabricated Wire Products, Misc
3497 Metal Foil, Leaf
3498 Fabricated Pipe & Fittings
3499 Fabricated Metal Products, nec

35   Machinery, Except Electrical
3511 Steam Engines, Turbines
3519 Internal Combustion Engines, nec
3523 Farm Machinery & Equipment
3524 Lawn & Garden Equipment
3531 Construction Machinery
3532 Mining Machinery
3533 Oil Field Machinery
3534 Elevator, Moving Stairways
3535 Conveyors & Conveying Equipment
3536 Hoists, Cranes, Monorail Systems
3537 Trucks & Tractors, Industrial
3541 Machine Tools (Metal Cut)
3542 Machine Tools, Metal Forming
3544 Special Dies, Tools
3545 Machine Tool Accessories
3546 Power Driven Hand Tool

Table 5-2 (continued)

3547 Rolling Mill Machinery
3549 Metalworking Machinery, nec
3551 Food Products Machinery
3552 Textile-Machinery
3553 Woodworking Machinery
3554 Paper Industries Machinery
3555 Printing Trades Machinery
3559 Machinery, Special Industries, nec
3561 Pumps & Pumping Equipment
3562 Ball & Roller Bearings
3563 Air & Gas Compressors
3564 Blowers & Exhaust & Ventilation Fans
3565 Industrial Patterns
3566 Speed Gear Changers
3567 Industrial Furnaces & Ovens
3568 Power Transmission Equipment, nec
3569 Industrial Machinery & Equipment, nec
3572 Typewriters
3573 Electronic Computing Equipment
3574 Calculating & Accounting Machines
3576 Scales & Balances
3579 Office Machines, nec
3581 Automatic Merchandising Machines
3582 Commercial Laundry Equipment
3585 Refrigeration & Heating Equipment
3586 Measuring & Dispensing Pumps
3589 Machines, Service Industry, nec
3592 Carburetors, Pistons, Piston Rings & Valves
3599 Machinery, Except Electrical, nec

36   Electric & Electronic Equipment
3612 Transformers
3613 Switchgear & Switchboard Apparatus
3621 Motors & Generators
3622 Industrial Controls
3623 Welding Apparatus
3624 Carbon & Graphite Products
3629 Electrical Industrial Apparatus, nec
3631 Household Cooking Equipment
3632 Refrigerators & Home Freezers
3633 Laundry Equipment, Household
3634 Electric Housewares & Fans
3635 Vacuum Cleaners, Household
3636 Sewing Machines
3639 Household Appliances, nec
3641 Electric Lamps
3643 Current Carrying Wiring Devices
3644 Wiring Devices, Non-Current Carrying
3645 Lighting Fixtures, Residential
3646 Lighting Fixtures, Commercial
3647 Vehicular Lighting Equipment

3648 Lighting Equipment, nec
3651 Radio & Television Receiving Sets
3652 Phonograph Records
3661 Telephone & Telegraph Apparatus
3662 Radio & Television Communication Equipment
3671 Electron Tubes, Radio & TV Receiving Types
3672 Cathode Ray Picture Tubes (TV)
3673 Electron Tubes & Transmitting, industrial
3674 Semiconductors & Related Devices
3675 Electronic Capacitors
3676 Electronic Resistors
3677 Electronic Coils, Transformers & Other Inductors
3678 Electronic Connectors
3679 Electronic Components, nec
3691 Batteries, Storage
3692 Batteries, Primary, Dry & Wet
3693 X-ray Apparatus & Tubes
3694 Engines, Electrical Equipment for
3699 Electric Equipment, nec

37   Transportation Equipment
3711 Motor Vehicle Bodies
3713 Truck & Bus Bodies
3714 Motor Vehicle Parts & Accessories
3715 Truck Trailers
3721 Aircraft
3724 Aircraft Engines & Engine Parts
3728 Aircraft Equipment, nec
3731 Ship Building & Repairing
3732 Boat Building & Repairing
3743 Railroad Equipment
3751 Motorcycles, Bicycle Parts
3761 Guided Missiles & Space Vehicles
3764 Guided Missiles, Space Vehicle Propulsion Units
3769 Space Vehicle Equipment, nec
3792 Travel Trailers & Campers
3795 Tanks & Tank Components
3799 Transportation Equipment, nec

38   Instruments & Related Products
3811 Engineering Laboratory Scientific & Related Equipment
3822 Automatic Temperature Controls
3823 Process Control Instruments
3824 Fluid Meters & Counting Devices
3825 Instruments for Measuring Electricity
3829 Measuring & Controlling Devices, nec
3832 Eye Instruments & Lenses
3841 Surgical & Medical Instruments

Table 5-2 (continued)

3842 Surgical Appliances & Supplies
3843 Dental Equipment & Supplies
3851 Ophthalmic Goods
3861 Photographic Equipment & Supplies
3873 Watches/Watchcases & Clocks

39   Misc. Manufacturing Industries
3911 Jewelry, Precious Metals
3914 Silverware & Plated Ware
3915 Jewelers' Material & Lapidary
3931 Musical Instruments & Parts
3942 Dolls
3944 Games/Toys & Children's Vehicles
3949 Athletic & Sporting Goods, nec
3951 Pens & Mechanical Pencils
3952 Lead Pencils & Artists' Goods
3953 Marking Devices
3955 Carbon Paper & Inked Ribbons
3961 Jewelry, Costume
3962 Flowers, Artificial
3963 Buttons
3964 Needles, Pins & Fasteners
3991 Brooms & Brushes
3993 Signs & Advertising Displays
3995 Burial Caskets
3996 Floor Coverings, Hard Surface
3999 Manufacturing Industries, nec

TRANSPORTATION, COMMUNICATION & PUBLIC UTILITIES

40   Railroad Transportation
4011 Railroads, Line-Haul Operating
4013 Switching & Terminal Establishments
4041 Railway Express Services

41   Local & Interurban Passenger Transit
4111 Local & Suburban Transportation
4119 Passenger Transportation, Local, nec
4121 Taxicabs
4131 Intercity Highway Transportation
4141 Passenger Charter Services
4142 Charter Service, Except Local
4151 School Buses
4171 Bus Terminal Services
4172 Bus Service Facilities

42   Trucking & Warehousing
4212 Trucking Without Storage, Local
4213 Trucking, Except Local
4214 Trucking With Storage, Local
4221 Farm Product Warehousing & Storage
4222 Refrigerated Warehousing

4224 Warehousing, Household Goods
4225 Warehousing & Storage, General
4226 Warehousing & Storage, nec
4231 Terminal Facilities

43   U.S. Postal Service
4311 U.S. Postal Service

44   Water Transportation
4411 Foreign Deep Sea Transportation
4421 Transportation, Noncontiguous, Deep Sea
4422 Coastwise Transportation
4423 Intercoastal Transportation
4431 Great Lakes Transportation
4441 Transportation On Rivers & Canals
4452 Ferries
4453 Lighterage
4454 Towing & Tugboat Services
4459 Water Transportation, Local, nec
4463 Marine Cargo Handling
4464 Canal Operation
4469 Water Transportation Services, nec

45   Transportation By Air
4511 Air Transportation, Certified Carriers
4521 Air Transportation, Non-Certified Carriers
4582 Airports & Flying Fields
4583 Airport Terminal Services

46   Pipe Lines, Except Natural Gas
4612 Crude Petroleum Pipe Lines
4613 Refined Petroleum Pipe Lines
4619 Pipe Lines, nec

47   Transportation Services
4712 Freight Forwarding
4722 Passenger Transportation Arrangement
4723 Freight & Cargo Transportation
4742 Railroad Car Rental With Services
4743 Railroad Car Rental Without Services
4782 Inspection & Weighing Services
4783 Packing & Crating
4784 Fixed Facilities For Vehicles, nec
4789 Transportation Services, nec

48   Communication
4811 Telephone Communications
4821 Telegraph Communications
4832 Radio Broadcasting
4833 Television Broadcasting
4899 Communication Services, nec

49   Electric, Gas & Sanitary Services
4911 Electric Services
4922 Natural Gas Transmission

Table 5-2 (continued)

4923 Natural Gas Transmission & Distribution
4924 Natural Gas Distribution
4925 Petroleum Gas Production and/or Distribution
4931 Electric & Other Services Combined
4932 Gas & Other Services Combined
4939 Utilities, nec
4941 Water Supply
4952 Sewerage Systems
4953 Refuse Systems
4959 Sanitary Services, nec
4961 Steam Supply
4971 Irrigation Systems

WHOLESALE TRADE

50   Wholesale Trade—Durable Goods
5012 Automobiles & Other Motor Vehicles
5013 Automotive Equipment
5014 Tires & Tubes
5021 Furniture
5023 Home Furnishings
5031 Lumber, Plywood, Millwork
5039 Construction Materials, nec
5041 Sporting & Amusement Goods
5042 Toys & Hobby Goods Supply
5043 Photo Equipment & Supply
5051 Metal Service Centers & Offices
5052 Coal/minerals & Ores
5063 Electrical Apparatus & Equipment
5064 Electrical Appliances, Television & Radio
5065 Electronic Parts & Equipment
5072 Hardware
5074 Plumbing & Hydronic Supplies
5075 Warm Air Heating, Air Conditioning
5078 Refrigeration Equipment & Supplies
5081 Commercial Machines & Equipment
5082 Construction & Mining Machinery
5083 Farm Machinery & Equipment
5084 Industrial Machinery & Equipment
5085 Industrial Supplies
5086 Professional Equipment & Supplies
5087 Service Establishment Equipment
5088 Transportation Equipment & Supplies
5093 Scrap & Waste Material
5094 Jewelry & Watches
5099 Durable Goods, nec

51   Wholesale Trade—Nondurable Goods
5111 Printing & Writing Paper
5112 Stationery & Supply
5113 Industrial & Personal Service Paper
5122 Drugs & Proprietaries
5133 Piece Goods
5134 Notions & Dry Goods
5136 Men's Clothing & Furnishings
5137 Women's & Children's Clothing
5139 Footwear
5141 Groceries, General Line
5142 Frozen Foods
5143 Dairy Products
5144 Poultry & Its Products
5145 Confectionery
5146 Fish & Seafoods
5147 Meat & Meat Products
5148 Fresh Fruits & Vegetables
5149 Groceries & Its Products, nec
5152 Cotton
5153 Grain
5154 Livestock
5159 Farm Product Raw Materials, nec
5161 Chemicals & Allied Products
5171 Petroleum Bulk Stations & Terminals
5172 Petroleum Products, nec
5181 Beer & Ale
5182 Wines & Distilled Beverages
5191 Farm Supplies
5194 Tobacco & Its Products
5198 Paints, Varnishes & Supplies
5199 Nondurable Goods, nec

RETAIL TRADE

52   Bldg. Materials & Garden Supplies
5211 Lumber & Building Materials
5231 Paint, Glass & Wallpaper Stores
5251 Hardware Stores
5261 Nurseries, Lawn & Garden Supply Stores
5271 Mobile Home Dealers

53   General Merchandise Stores
5311 Department Stores
5331 Variety Stores
5399 General Merchandise Stores

54   Food Stores
5411 Grocery Stores
5422 Freezer & Food Plan Provisions
5423 Meat & Seafood (Fish) Markets
5431 Fruit & Vegetable Markets
5441 Candy, Nut & Confectionery Stores
5451 Dairy Products Stores
5462 Bakeries, Baking & Selling
5463 Bakeries, Selling Only
5499 Food Stores, Misc

Table 5-2 (continued)

55   Auto Dealers & Service Stations
5511 Car Dealers, New & Used
5521 Car Dealers, Used Only
5531 Auto & Home Supply Stores
5541 Gasoline Service Stations
5551 Boat Dealers
5561 Recreational & Utility Trailer Dealers
5571 Motorcycle Dealers
5599 Automotive Dealers, nec

56   Apparel & Accessory Stores
5611 Men's & Boys' Clothing &
    Furnishings
5621 Women's Ready-to-wear Stores
5631 Women's Accessory & Specialty
    Stores
5641 Children's & Infants' Wear Stores
5651 Family Clothing Stores
5661 Shoe Stores
5681 Furriers & Fur Shops
5699 Apparel & Accessories, Misc

57   Furniture & Home Furnishings Stores
5712 Furniture Stores
5713 Floor Covering Stores
5714 Drapery & Upholstery Stores
5719 Home Furnishing Stores
5722 Household Appliance Stores
5732 Radio & Television Stores
5733 Music Stores

58   Eating & Drinking Places
5812 Restaurants, Diners, Eating Places
5813 Bars, Night Clubs (Drinking Places)

59   Miscellaneous Retail
5912 Drug & Proprietary Stores
5921 Liquor Stores
5931 Used Merchandise Stores
5941 Sporting Goods & Bicycle Stores
5942 Book Stores
5943 Stationery Stores
5944 Jewelry Stores
5945 Hobby, Toy & Game Shops
5946 Photographic Supply Stores
5947 Gift & Novelty Shops
5948 Luggage & Leather Goods Stores
5949 Sewing, Needlework & Piece Goods
    Stores
5961 Mail Order Houses
5962 Vending Machine, Machine
    Operators
5963 Direct Selling Companies
5982 Fuel & Ice Dealers, nec
5983 Fuel Oil Dealers

5984 Bottle Gas Dealers (Liquified
    Petroleum)
5992 Florists
5993 Cigar Stores & Stands
5994 News Dealers & Newsstands
5999 Miscellaneous Retail Stores, nec

FINANCE, INSURANCE & REAL ESTATE

60   Banking
6011 Federal Reserve Banks
6022 State Banks, Members of Federal
    Reserve System Insured
6023 State Banks, Not Members of Federal
    Reserve System Insured
6024 State Banks, Not Members of Federal
    Reserve System, Not Insured
6025 National Banks, Members of Federal
    Reserve System, Insured
6026 National Banks, Not Members of
    Federal Reserve System, Insured
6027 National Banks, Not Members of
    Federal Reserve System, Not Insured
6028 Unicorp Private Banks
6032 Mutual Savings Banks, Members of
    Federal Reserve System, Insured
6033 Mutual Savings Banks, Not
    Members of Federal Reserve System,
    Insured
6034 Mutual Savings Banks, Not
    Members of Federal Reserve System,
    Not Insured
6042 State Nondeposit Trust Companies,
    Members of Fed Res Sys, Insured &
    Not Insured
6044 State Nondeposit Trust Companies,
    Not Insured
6052 Foreign Exchange Establishments
6054 Safe Deposit Company
6055 Clearinghouse Associations
6056 Corporations For Banking Abroad
6059 Banking Related Services

61   Credit Agencies Other Than Banks
6112 Financing Institutions
6113 Rediscount for Agriculture
6122 Federal Savings & Loan Associations
6123 State Savings & Loans Assoc.
6124 Savings & Loan, Not Insured
    Member
6125 State Savings & Loan, Not Insured,
    nec

Table 5-2 (continued)

6131 Agricultural Credit Institutions
6142 Federal Credit Unions
6143 State Credit Unions
6144 Industrial Loan Companies
6145 Loan (Small) Lenders, Licensed
6146 Installment Sales Finance Companies
6149 Personal Credit Institutions, Misc
6153 Short Term Business Credit Institutions
6159 Business Credit Institutions, Misc
6162 Mortgage Bankers & Loan Correspondents
6163 Loan Brokers

62 Security, Commodity Brokers & Svcs
6211 Securities Brokers & Dealers
6221 Commodity Contracts Brokers & Dealers
6231 Security & Commodity Exchanges
6281 Securities or Commodities Services

63 Insurance Carriers
6311 Life Insurance
6321 Accident & Health Insurance
6324 Hospital & Medical Service Plans
6331 Fire, Sea & Casualty Insurance
6351 Surety Insurance
6361 Title Insurance
6371 Pension, Health & Welfare Funds
6399 Insurance Carriers, Misc

64 Insurance Agents, Brokers & Services
6411 Insurance Agents & Brokers

65 Real Estate
6512 Building Operators, Nonresidential
6513 Apartment Building & Residential Hotel Operators
6514 Dwelling Operators (Less Than 5 Housing Units)
6515 Residential Mobile Homesites, Operators of
6517 Railroad Property Lessors
6519 Real Property Lessors, nec
6531 Agents, Managers—Real Estate
6541 Title Abstract Offices
6552 Subdividers, Developers, Except Cemeteries
6553 Cemetery Subdivision & Development

66 Combined Real Estate, Insurance, Etc.
6611 Real Estate, Insurance Loans, Law Offices Combined

67 Holding And Other Investment Offices
6711 Holding Offices
6722 Management Investment Offices, Open-end
6723 Management Investment Offices, Closed-end
6724 Unit Investment Trusts
6732 Educational, Religious & Charitable Trusts
6733 Trusts, Except Educational, Religious & Charitable
6792 Investors, Oil & Gas Royalties
6793 Commodity Trading Companies
6794 Patent Owners & Lessors
6799 Investors, Misc

SERVICES

70 Hotels & Other Lodging Places
7011 Hotels/Inns/Tourist Courts
7021 Rooming/Boarding Houses
7032 Sports/Amusement Camps
7033 Trailer Parks For Transients
7041 Hotels, Lodging Houses for Membership Organizations

72 Personal Services
7211 Laundries, Power, Family & Commercial
7212 Garment Cleaners & Agents
7213 Linen Supply
7214 Diaper Service
7215 Coin Laundry/Cleaners
7216 Dry Cleaning Plants Except Rugs
7217 Carpet/Upholstery Cleaners
7218 Industrial Launderers
7219 Laundry/Garment Services, nec
7221 Photographic Studios
7231 Beauty Shops
7241 Barber Shops
7251 Shoe Repair Shops
7261 Funeral Service
7299 Personal Services, Misc

73 Business Services
7311 Advertising Agencies
7312 Advertising Services, Outdoor
7313 Radio TV Advertising Representatives
7319 Advertising, nec
7321 Credit Reporting & Collection
7331 Direct Mail Advertising
7332 Blueprinting & Photocopying
7333 Commercial Photography/Art
7339 Steno Duplicating Services, nec

Table 5-2 (continued)

7341 Window Cleaning
7342 Disinfecting & Exterminating
7349 Janitorial Services, nec
7351 News Syndicates
7361 Employment Agencies
7362 Temporary Aid Supply Services
7369 Personnel Supply Services, nec
7372 Computer Programming
7374 Data Processing Services
7379 Computer Related Services, nec
7391 Research & Development
     Laboratories
7392 Management & Public Relations
7393 Detective & Protective Services
7394 Equipment Rental/Leasing
7395 Photofinishing Labs
7396 Trading Stamp Services
7397 Commercial Testing Laboratories
7399 Business Services, nec

75   Auto Repair, Services & Garages
7512 Passenger Car Rental
7513 Truck Rental & Leasing
7519 Recreational Vehicle & Trailer Rentals
7523 Parking Lots
7525 Parking Structures
7531 Top & Body Repair Shops
7534 Tire Retreading & Repair
7535 Paint Shops
7538 Automotive Repair Shops, General
7539 Automotive Repair Shops,
     Specialized, nec
7542 Car Washes
7549 Automotive Services, Misc

76   Miscellaneous Repair Services
7622 Radio & Television Repair
7623 Refrigeration & Air-conditioning
     Service & Repair
7629 Electrical & Electronic Repair Shops,
     nec
7631 Watch, Clock & Jewelry Repair
7641 Reupholstery & Furniture Repair
7692 Welding Repair
7694 Armature Rewinding Shops
7699 Repair Services, nec

78   Motion Pictures
7813 Motion Picture Production Except
     Television
7814 Motion Picture Production For
     Television
7819 Motion Picture Production Service
7823 Motion Picture Film Exchanges
7824 Film or Tape Distribution for
     Television
7829 Motion Picture Distribution Service

7832 Motion Picture Theaters
7833 Drive-in Movies

79   Amusement & Recreation Services
7911 Dance Halls & Studios
7922 Theatrical Producers & Services
7929 Entertainers
7932 Billiard & Pool Establishments
7933 Bowling Alleys
7941 Sports Clubs & Promoters
7948 Race Tracks & Stables
7992 Golf Courses, Public
7993 Coin-operated Amusement Devices
7996 Amusement Parks
7997 Membership Sports & Recreation
7999 Amusement & Recreation Services,
     nec

80   Health Services
8011 Physicians, Offices of
8021 Dentists, Offices of
8031 Osteopathic Physicians, Offices of
8041 Chiropractors, Offices of
8042 Optometrists, Offices of
8049 Health Practitioners, nec Offices of
8051 Nursing Care Facilities
8059 Nursing & Personal Care Facilities,
     nec
8062 Hospitals, Medical/Surgical
8063 Hospitals, Psychiatric
8069 Specialty Hospitals, Except
     Psychiatric
8071 Medical Laboratories
8072 Dental Laboratories
8081 Outpatient Care Facilities
8091 Health & Allied Services, nec

81   Legal Services
8111 Legal Services

82   Educational Services
8211 Elementary & Secondary Schools
8221 Colleges, Universities & Professional
     Schools
8222 Junior Colleges & Technical Institutes
8231 Libraries & Information Centers
8241 Correspondence Schools
8243 Data Processing Schools
8244 Business & Secretarial Schools
8249 Vocational Schools, nec
8299 Schools & Educational Services, nec

83   Social Services
8321 Individual & Family Services
8331 Job Training & Related Services
8351 Child Day Care Services
8361 Residential Care
8399 Social Services, nec

Table 5-2 (continued)

84 Museum, Botanical, Zoological Gardens	9311 Public Finance, Taxation, & Monetary Policy
8411 Museums & Art Galleries	9411 Educational Programs, Administration of
8421 Botanical & Zoological Gardens	9431 Public Health Programs, Administration of
86 Membership Organizations	9441 Social Manpower & Income Maintenance Programs, Administration of
8611 Business Associations	
8621 Professional Organizations	
8631 Labor Organizations	9451 Veterans Affairs, Except Health & Insurance
8641 Civic & Social Organizations	
8651 Political Organizations	9511 Air, Water Resource & Solid Waste Management
8661 Religious Organizations	
8699 Membership Organizations, nec	9512 Land Mineral, Wildlife & Forest Conservation
89 Miscellaneous Services	
8911 Engineering & Architectural Services	9531 Housing Programs, Administration of
8922 Noncommercial Research Organization	9532 Urban Planning & Community Development
8931 Accounting, Auditing & Bookkeeping	9611 Economic Programs, Administration of
8999 Services, nec	9621 Transportation Programs, Regulation & Administration of
PUBLIC ADMINISTRATION	9631 Communication, Electric, Gas & Other Utilities, Regulation & Administration of
9111 Executive Offices	
9121 Legislative Bodies	9641 Agricultural Marketing & Commodities, Regulation of
9131 Executive & Legislative Offices Combined	9651 Regulation Licensing & Inspection of Misc Commerical Sectors
9199 General Government, nec	
9211 Courts	9711 National Security
9221 Police Enforcement	9721 International Affairs
9222 Legal Counsel & Prosecution	
9223 Correctional Institutions	
9224 Fire Protection	
9229 Public Order & Safety, nec	

clarification of the differences, some samples of bank objectives at work might be helpful. Here are a few activity areas in which marketing objectives may be established by the bank marketing manager:

1. Prepare for future growth and development in areas not currently served by the bank.
2. Set long-range performance requirements for profitability, earnings per share, market position, and competitive abilities.
3. Require renewed emphasis on social responsibility, community involvement, job enrichment, and technical skills growth.
4. Improve the lines of communication and make provision for more decentralization of marketing decision making.
5. Encourage innovative and productive marketing through greater synergy resulting from line/staff cooperation.

The activity areas and the nature of goals require specificity as well as quantification. If a goal is not measurable, it is difficult to determine the degree of success or failure. Although the quantifiable elements are missing, typical goals for a bank include the following:

1. To provide increased customer satisfaction (include criteria for qualitative measurement).
2. To make products and services available to a greater number of potential customers (specify numbers and time frame).
3. To expand or alter the distribution patterns of the delivery system (list types, locations, and target dates).
4. To satisfy a market need created by new technology, changing customer attitudes, or revised government regulations (identify the quantitative aspects of the action to be taken).
5. To build customer acceptance in additional markets for the bank and its products (provide the degree of acceptance in relation to the present base).
6. To cross-sell consumers from one particular product or service to the use of others (specify which customers and which products as well as volume increases).
7. To increase repeat business (to whom and which products, including quantitative results expected).
8. To increase the present volume of loans or deposits per branch (by type, amount, and by branch).
9. To increase the bank's customer base (specify which target market, the number required, and assign appropriate quotas).

The establishing of realistic objectives and goals is essential, but they should be attainable, and agreement and acceptance by those responsible for their accomplishment are crucial factors. Therefore, each objective and goal should be tested for applicability before it is finalized. The marketing manager should review each objective and goal carefully in the light of the following considerations:

1. How will the accomplishing of each objective and goal affect those responsible?
2. Have the customers' needs been identified and satisfied to the degree required?
3. Have the target markets been selected and their potential determined to be sufficient to justify performance forecasts?
4. Does the bank have sufficient human resources as well as the expertise to implement the marketing effort?
5. Has ample provision been made to provide a source of funds for

accomplishing the marketing goals?
6. What are the counteraction capabilities of competition to the objectives and goals, and what retaliation can be anticipated?
7. What are the technological and operations support requirements and their costs relative to the objectives and goals?
8. Are the objectives and goals supportive and compatible with the marketing strategy selected?
9. Are the estimated costs of program implementation and the revenue projected in attaining the objectives and goals consistent with the corporate priorities of the bank?
10. Are the objectives and goals in conflict with any laws, regulations, ethics, or bank policies and procedures?
11. Is each objective and goal sufficiently flexible to permit change or revision in the event of a change in the environment?

In bank marketing, the principal source of cohesion is the marketing strategy; strategy decisions must be made before programs can be prepared and implemented. These decisions ensure the bank's survival in the increasingly competitive environment of deregulation. To be effective, the marketing strategy must be more than an inspirational statement of objectives and goals to fulfill high aspirations; the strategy selected must not only be realistic in terms of the situation in the marketplace and the bank's resources but must provide the direction to assist the entire organization in making routine decisions that contribute to the attainment of the objectives and goals established. Everyone in the organization from tellers to directors should understand and accept the corporate task and their roles in its accomplishment.

Over the long term, the bank marketing strategy is concerned with the recognition and acceptance of the bank, its business charter, the products and services that are required, acquisitions or delivery system expansion or contraction needed, and other decisions of strategy involving resource allocation, new market entry, and potentials for growth and earnings. It is for these numerous requirements that the selection of an appropriate bank marketing strategy is such a crucial function for the bank marketing manager.

6

BANK CUSTOMER BEHAVIOR

The questions that bank marketing managers ask themselves and their associates most often are those based on why people do or do not bank with their institutions. There are reams of empirical data that indicate that people look primarily for banking convenience and secondarily for product and service. According to a 1985 study by California Communication Consultants, Inc., many consumers seek out the most convenient bank since they only require basic banking services. Although the empirical evidence supporting the rationale of convenience is overwhelming, it may be an oversimplification in one respect. Whereas convenience is the one benefit commonly sought by most bank customers, its dominance can be explained by the fact that it appears in some form on every research survey instrument concerning banking. To develop effective selling propositions and promotion programs based on what makes bank customers do what they do, there are many other behavioral characteristics that must be recognized, particularly as they are applied to specific types of customers.

Bank customer behavior is difficult to predict in advance. However, much research that has been done in the broad area of buyer behavior can be adapted by bank marketing managers. As indicated in a previous chapter, customers who have demographic, psychographic, or socioeconomic factors in common also have some predictable similarities in their use, attitudes, interest, and opinions regarding banks and their products and services. By taking note of some of the information developed by psychologists and other behavioralists, the bank marketing manager can comprehend, or at least have some familiarity with, why banking customers behave the way they do. Before reviewing the many behavioral traits of consumers, it is appropriate to understand that different customers act or react in varying ways. Thus, we need to classify the bank customer universe and become more aware of their characteristics as related to their banking needs.

BANK CUSTOMER CLASSIFICATION. The customer in a bank does not differ in the basic motivation from a supermarket shopper or a patient in a hospital; all of them have a need in common—the solving of a personal problem. The need may be routine or it may be critical; at the bank it is concerned with money, in the supermarket with food, and in the hospital with health. These needs are varied and are usually the result of an attempt by consumers to develop, maintain, or change the way they live, or as psychologists describe it, their life-styles. The bank customers' life-styles consist of their activities, attitudes, interests, and opinions that help establish personal values that eventually are reflected in the requirements and expectations that customers have for bank products and services. This method of describing the qualitative aspects of customer life-styles is called *psychographics,* and it helps determine the specific products and services used, the ways they are used, and the attitudes and opinions that prevail about a specific bank as a financial institution.

Individuals, families, and organizations have distinct life-styles, in the latter usually referred to as the *corporate culture*. Categorizations such as "yuppies," "senior citizens," "single," and "mom and pop stores," are used sometimes to describe some of the important aspects of customer life-styles. Finance-related decisions are often made out of consideration for a particular psychographic profile. For example, a yuppie may have only the liquidity for the down payment needed to purchase a Ford compact but, with a good credit base, elects instead to lease an expensive BMW. To compound the difficulty, many customers are unaware of the extent to which their banking decisions are made or influenced by their present or desired life-style even though it is a motivator of specific bank selection as well as a basic source of the criteria for perceived need and satisfaction expectations. In the behavioral sense, bank customers avail themselves of those financial products and services that they feel are necessary for their psychological bent. Thus, life-styles are often more effective as a basis for market segmentation than demographics.

Of particular significance to the consideration of life-styles is the values and life-styles (VALS) program developed at the Stanford Research Institute. The VALS approach to customer classification in general has become an invaluable tool for all marketing managers, regardless of the product involved. VALS deals with with the patterns in which people live and their requirements for their particular way of life. For bank marketing managers, this can be translated into the way money is used in the support of particular life-styles. These life-styles are the result of the total impact of economic, cultural, and social forces that affect the financial needs of each individual or organization. The VALS program classifies consumers into nine different life-styles within three basic categories. The basic categories are the following:

1. Those consumers who are motivated by basic needs.
2. Those consumers who are motivated by what others may think.

3. Those consumers who place emphasis on their needs as individuals, needs that are inner-directed rather than basic.

The first category, those driven by basic needs, includes a group comprising the aged and the poor who are struggling for survival. The second group within the basic need category includes those who are young and angry on the edge of poverty but who are striving for improvement. Neither of these groups appears to offer any immediate potential as bank customers. The second basic category is the largest, including over two-thirds of all consumers, most of whom are excellent prospects for financial services. One subcategory is a group that is traditional and conservative; another is competitive and status-conscious. The last group in this category consists of affluent professionals and leaders in business with life-styles that are materialistic and seeking fame and status. The last of the three basic categories also includes affluent consumers, most of whom are customers eagerly sought by most banks. This category consists of those consumers who are individualistic, highly participative, societally conscious, tolerant, and well adjusted.

These last two categories from VALS were the targets of an extremely successful mass communication program by Merrill Lynch. The initial commercial on television, which featured a stampeding herd of bulls, had more significance to the basic group of conservative, traditionalists because of the patriotic tag line, "Merrill Lynch is bullish on America." After analyzing its effect on consumers, it was determined that this group, although receptive to the message of the commercial, was not a large purchaser of stocks and bonds. Since the purpose of the campaign was to encourage immediate sales results, it was changed to a bull finding its way safely through a china shop. A new tag line was added: "Merrill Lynch, a breed apart." This appeal was more applicable to the group of affluents whose VALS characteristics included materialism and status consciousness. It resulted in a 2 percent increase in market share and an 800 percent increase in corporate recognition by the consumers Merrill Lynch wanted to reach.

Classification by demographics is based on the size, distribution, and structure of consumers. Such demographic variables as income structure, age shifts, geographic redistribution, and types of occupation affect banking needs and service usage patterns. Much of what is occurring in the dramatic changes in U.S. demographics is favorable to the financial services industry. For example, the income level in the United States continues to rise, and a major contributor to this is the increasing percentage of families with two income earners; obviously inflation has also played a role. Like income, the level of education continues to rise, with more than half of the population over age twenty-five having completed high school. The United States is also growing older, with nearly 50 million Americans older than fifty-five.

This group is growing at twice the rate of the rest of the population because of longer life expectancy and a lower fertility rate.

There are also shifting occupational patterns, with a decline in blue-collar workers, a rise in a new class of gray collars oriented to service industries, and computerized manufacturing and processing. These patterns are also changing with the increase in women in the labor force. Geographically, regions are growing at an uneven pace. This is occurring in the rural, suburban, and urban areas as well. The precise physical location for service availability is an important factor in selecting the particular bank customers who make up the demographic mix of greatest sales potential.

The socioeconomic classification is included by some marketers in the demographic category. However, there are homogeneous groups with respect to attitudes, values, and life-styles that are best classified on the basis of social and economic stratification. Such basic demographic factors as age and education affect social status, however, the economic variables such as type of residence, neighborhood, nature of education, and source of income have societal implications that require further classification. The basic social structure can be identified in terms of the following eight classes:

1. **Poverty class.** The most easily identified class with poverty level incomes, limited education, no jobs or menial ones at best. Members are usually from a racial minority, and marriage is generally limited to members of the same class. Those in this class are not considered to be banking prospects, but community services such as welfare check cashing, minority hiring and training, and charitable contributions are usually a requirement for the banks to fulfill their social responsibility.

2. **Blue-collar class.** The occupations of members of this class involve some degree of manual labor. Many did not complete high school so that their income and job security are low except for certain highly skilled or unionized occupations. Working wives are relatively uncommon in this class, and most social activities evolve around the family unit. Their banking potential is modest, with many members relying on money orders and cash rather than checking accounts. Considered purchases are often paid for in installments, usually through a consumer finance company or a credit union in preference to a commercial bank. This is the class targeted for lifeline checking accounts by political pressures on the banking industry.

3. **Gray-collar class.** This is a relatively new class that is evolving from the original blue-collar class. As heavy manufacturing and processing industries change to robotics and computerized controls, the labor requirements have been reduced and the remaining

force has been retrained for new jobs. This attrition has resulted in the development of higher skills and increased income levels although the social characteristics for this class continue to be those of members of the blue-collar class. The additional income has not appeared to change their banking behavior appreciably although new home purchases have increased in this class, and many have become new customers of thrift institutions.

4. **White-collar class.** Their occupations involve neither manual labor nor extensive decision making. The members are often associated with clean industries, small businesses, in an office environment. Most of them have completed high school, and many have advanced technical training including a college degree. Jobs in this class offer limited hope for advancement to another class, and those in clerical or secretarial positions may have incomes no higher than those of many blue- or gray-collar workers. However, they consider themselves in the middle- rather than lower-class stratum. As is to be expected, this class has a large percentage of working women, including wives. Its members are future-oriented, making them outstanding prospects for such basic financial services as savings accounts, transaction accounts, and consumer loans.

5. **Managerial class.** Members of this class are the decision makers in business and include not only those responsible at senior levels but department heads as well. They are well trained since most are college graduates, and, as a result, their incomes are relatively high. This class tends to be very competitive and industrious and seeks personal satisfaction as well as financial rewards. Members use a large variety of personal financial services and influence decisions regarding company banking. Those in an entrepreneurial mode require sources of capital funding as well.

6. **Professional class.** This class includes members of the various professions that require advanced education beyond the college undergraduate level. Their careers are primate, and they are very influential in local communities because of the prestige and respect accorded their professions. Members of this class are heavy users of money, particularly those making their initial entry into the medical profession. Once professionals are established they become high income generators, and they influence pockets of heavy deposits. They are investment-conscious, and nonbanking institutions are extremely competitive for their financial service business relationship.

7. **Public servant class.** This class has the characteristics of several other classes, depending upon the occupational level and the nature

of the job responsibilities. It includes office workers of local, state, and the federal governments; uniformed members of the civil and national forces; elected office holders, and so on. Although its membership is quite varied, it has been placed in a separate class because the members can have a strong effect on banking regulation as well as require basic and unique financial services involving government finance and loan subsidization or guarantees.

8. **Retiree class.** Although all of these individuals are former members of another socioeconomic class, they have certain class distinctions. They retain most of the social characteristics of their former class but develop differences because of a fixed retirement income and a geographic change of residence. In most cases their incomes are less than while employed full-time; their expenses are reduced, however. Members of this class are net providers of bank funds but are extremely sensitive to interest rates. As bank customers, they have both the time and motivation to shop for the most beneficial banking relationship.

One final consideration of the importance of the separate socioeconomic classification: It can be better appreciated when viewed on the basis of such behavioral tendencies as media reading and viewing preferences, the intensity of the search for information, the type of financial institution preferred, and the kinds and amounts of bank products and services used. These will be considered in detail in the chapters to come.

CUSTOMER ATTITUDES. Customer attitudes can be defined as the way customers think, feel, and act toward a bank; they are the result of many outside influences. Although the number of potential influences that affect customer attitudes is almost limitless, some of the major banking influences include the following, not necessarily in this order of significance:

1. Bank location, particularly its convenience
2. Nature and quality of products and services
3. Interest rates and fee structure
4. Bank contact personnel
5. Bank facilities and resources
6. Bank lobby atmosphere
7. Bank reputation
8. Advertising and promotion credibility
9. Posttransaction service and satisfaction

Numerous research efforts by such organizations as the A.B.A. and McKinsey as well as the author have reinforced the conclusion that banking convenience is a crucial consideration. There is also some evidence that indicates that friendly and efficient service is equally important and that customers are always willing to pay, under certain circumstances, for good service. Retail establishments in general have found that the proper location strategy is one of the most important factors for consumer acceptance. For example, many consumers acknowledge their taste or service preferences for Burger King or Wendys, but the fact that McDonalds outsells both of them by a wide margin can be traced to its overwhelming location advantage in number of outlets; food and pricing do not appear to be as significant for market share. The same may be said for banks and their locations. If they are well situated and in a sufficient number of places, the prevailing attitude of customers may be that they are the most convenient. The number of Citibank and Chase Manhattan retail customers as opposed to those of some of the other well-known banks in New York City may attest to the validity of the positive influence of banking services' being available at convenient locations.

From a bank marketing perspective, the proper location of the bank delivery system warrants special attention. If numbers are not possible because of legal restrictions or dominant competitors, a specific location advantage is essential. Such advantages are obtained through the following variables:

1. Banking customer potential (within two-mile radius, two blocks if location is urban)
2. Pedestrian flow
3. Traffic flow
4. Parking convenience
5. Egress/ingress
6. Site improvements (ATM, drive-up, walk-up facilities)
7. Visibility, signing, ambience
8. Retail neighbors

In a sense, bank marketing managers have the continuing task of altering customer attitudes from unfavorable or apathetic to favorable. It is important to be aware that attitudes cannot be observed directly and that they are difficult to change. A bank customer attitude always implies a relationship between the customer and the bank, so that the more positive the attitude or the more negative it tends to be can become a crucial element in the way the customer behaves toward the bank.

Favorable attitudes about a bank are formed in a variety of ways. One of these is the result of whether the customer perceives equal or greater value in the service received by one bank over its competitors. Another is the positive effect of persuasion by communication. This can be done through the personal sales effort of tellers, platform officers, or calling officers; by informative advertising and innovative promotions; and by word-of-mouth referrals from friends and business associates. Extended contact with the bank and its people also forms attitudes based on the nature of the experiences. The risk in this kind of attitude reinforcement exists when favorable attitudes are built up over a long period of time, only to be destroyed or neutralized by an isolated contact with a tempermental teller or an inattentive platform officer.

Bank marketing managers may not have the assigned responsibility for altering customer attitudes, but there is no other function in a banking organization that requires the knowledge or has the resources necessary to deal as effectively with some of the current problems in consumer attitude. Customers today have overcome the traditional barriers to changing banks. They have less loyalty and are no longer intimidated by bankers, and the inertia that prevented unhappy customers from closing their accounts has been reduced substantially. After many years of favorable attitudes, the general public is now harboring opinions that may be difficult to reverse. For example, in a 1985 Roper poll reported in *Forbes* 46 percent of those contacted had the attitude that credit cards were more bad for the user than good. In the opposite category of more good than bad, credit cards were ranked even below nuclear energy.

Since the deregulation process began, some influential consumer groups have maintained that it now costs more to keep money in a checking account because of minimum balance requirements and fee penalties below minimums. These groups also complain that it takes longer than necessary for checks to clear. In spite of industry explanations to the contrary, Congress and the state and federal regulators are listening to these complaints. The groups criticize the industry's fee structure and insist that fees for overdrafts are usurious. Such complaints affect customer attitudes negatively, and the marketing effort must be directed to counteract this situation of growing negative attitudes. Since unfavorable changes in attitude are among the quickest ways to lose customers, managing attitudes become an important responsibility of the public relations function. Banks lose good accounts when they cannot continue to fulfill the expectations of their customers. It is axiomatic that it is six times more expensive to attract new customers than to retain old ones.

BANKING BEHAVIOR. Since customers are the final link in the ebb and flow of money, it is important to understand why they behave the way they do in a banking environment. Unfortunately, customers have more than the power to make and execute the banking decision. They have the power to force changes in pricing, bargain aggressively or passively for quality and service, play competitive financial institutions against each other, or to seek substitutes in nonbanks as they did originally through money market funds and cash management accounts. They possess effective bargaining powers on both the liability and asset sides of the ledger. If they are large depositors or large users of well-collateralized loans, their cost of service may be lower and their relative importance to the bank greater. If the products offered by the bank are standard or relatively undifferentiated in form or rate, the customer is usually more rate-sensitive: there are alternative banks available and one can be played against another. If, on the other hand, the credit is complicated and the collateral somewhat illiquid, it may make switching banks more difficult. In such a case, the bargaining power of the customer is lessened.

One of the principal factors in bank customer behavior is the process of decision making. Edward Furash observed that such decisions have emotional and personal risks because of the fear of making a poor financial decision. He cited that consumer financial behavior is not always rational because no product is more personal and emotional than money. Many of today's corporate treasurers feel that the commercial banker knows less and less about the problems and processes that the corporate financial executive must deal with. The individual consumer is also becoming less tolerant. Both of these prime customers switch banks more on the basis of a behavioral decision than a purchase decision; in spite of the hassle, customers move quite often defensively rather than always opportunely.

For many business banks, corporate treasurers and chief financial officers (CFOs) represent the ultimate corporate customer. These customers are primarily concerned with a bank's responsiveness to their financial needs. All CFOs behave according to different sets of requirements that are applied in unique internal environments. Depending upon the nature of the corporation, these customers can seek a total relationship with product and service linkage or be selective through several banks on a fee basis. The former tend to be companies that are marketing-driven with good operating margins and heavy internally generated cash flows. The latter are heavy users of capital and in a stage of high growth. They are often involved in cash-intensive new markets in order to sustain growth. Small businesses borrow for working capital; however, many also borrow just to keep their credit line active. They resent indifferent treatment on the main banking floor and are most interested in products and services similar to those offered to individuals—a high-volume transaction account and unsophisticated loan services.

Bank customers must make banking decisions that affect the enhancement or maintenance of their life-style. As a result, they behave according to the behavioral characteristics of their particular life-style. Critical to every banking decision is financial problem identification; without identification, a decision is not sought by the customer. The process for financial problem identification is illustrated in the model in Figure 6-1. Both the bank and the customer have primary eras of interest in the decision-making process.

Problem identification is the heart of decision making and its most difficult aspect to accomplish. To help in the process, customers as well as bank marketing managers should be familiar with the types of problems to be encountered. There are four types that deal with personal or company finances—routine, emergency, anticipated, and evolving. Routine problems are those of a recurring nature such as seasonal cash flow. They can be solved very simply by the use of a bank product such as a credit card or by a more complex service such as asset-based lending. Emergency problems are unexpected and require an immediate solution. Personal or company revolving lines of credit can be used to solve these problems without bank interjection or liquidation of assets. Anticipated problems are those expected or planned for, but without an immediate need for remedial action. The best solution to these problems is a good credit rating and liquid collateral. Evolving problems are those that are unexpected but do not require any emergency or ongoing solution once they occur. They are to be solved in due time, and they provide the best opportunity for bankers to demonstrate their expertise and creativity since time is available for recommending the best solution.

There are some traditional life-styles that affect customer behavior, depending upon the stage in life the customer has reached. These stages can be classified behaviorally as follows:

1. Young singles
2. Young marrieds
3. First nest
4. Full nest
5. Empty nest
6. Older singles
7. Retireds
8. Survivors

The financial behavior of young singles is unlike that of any of the other stages. Earnings are relatively low, but discretionary income is high. Their finances are committed to automobile purchase, mate search and selection, and basic equipment and furnishings for their first home, usually rented. Their use of savings and insurance products is limited, and they are

Figure 6-1. Financial Problem Identification Process Model

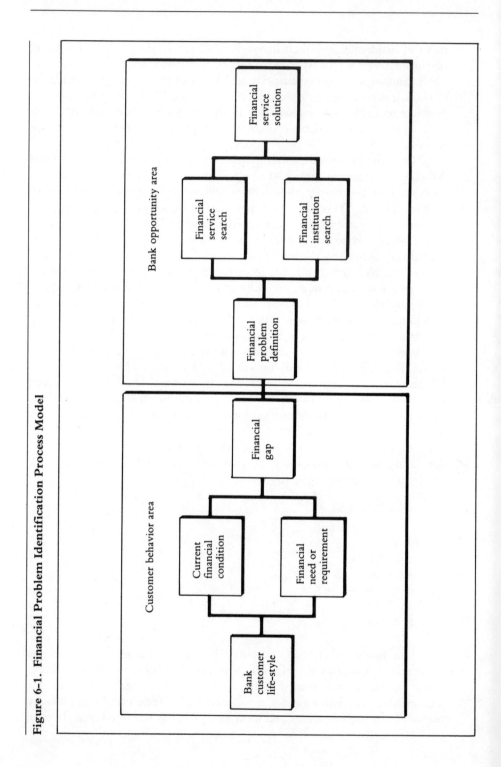

particularly susceptible to peer group influences. Young marrieds are usually in fair financial condition since both are probably employed. They have a relatively high combined earnings and disposable income, and they continue to spend most of their income on cars, clothing, vacations, and other leisure time activities. The bank services utilized include transaction accounts, often separate; a small goal-oriented savings account; and probably beginning IRAs for both. Those in this stage are heavy users of ATMs.

The first nest stage consists of married couples with their first child. The medical expenses for childbirth as well as the costs of baby supplies and appropriate furniture for baby and new parents reduce or eliminate the couple's savings. This often results in their first medium-term bank debt other than an auto loan or a lingering credit card balance. They may experience a sharp drop in combined income if the wife quits work. They often move into their first home, which accounts for their first long-term debt. This is the beginning of the stage in life in which they will become net funds users and will remain that way for many years. In the full nest stage, the youngest child is six or older. One or both parents' careers are advancing, and family income is improving with each year. Finances are used for convenience goods and luxury appliances. Bank savings accounts are beginning to carry modest balances for emergencies or education, or for whatever goal is set. They have IRAs with growing balances and participate in company or 401(k) retirement plans. They begin to think about self-direction of these balances.

When the children leave home and are no longer dependent upon their parents financially, the couple reaches the empty nest stage. They are fairly satisfied with their financial position, and their savings continue to rise as their net income increases. At this time, the wife resumes a career if she has been out of the work force while the children were at home. The couple uses home improvement loans, makes stock and bond investments, investigates trust services, and spends a portion of their income on vacation travel and recreation. These couples provide a very important source of funds for banks; they are no longer net users of funds. The older singles stage is made up of the divorced and those who never married. Some remarry and revert to one of the other nest stages. However, those who remain in this stage behave similarly to those in the empty nest and offer excellent banking potential. The exception to this are those who are divorced and are forced to earn income for survival.

The retired stage is characterized by a fixed income that has been reduced as a result of not having full-time work. Finances are used for travel and health expenses primarily. Assets remain stable through income generated by part-time work or through the sale of the old family home and the purchase of a smaller residence in a more pleasant climate. This provides for new banking affiliations as the retireds move away from their original communities. This stage is also an excellent source of funds. The final stage consists of the survivors. These are widows or widowers, whose income remains fixed and may be reduced further because of costly health expenses and the need for security. Women exceed men in numbers and depend upon the financial services industry for counsel and asset protection. In many cases they are beneficiaries of bank-administered trusts, but their discretionary income is usually limited.

Bank marketing managers can use the Customer Behavior Matrix (Table 6-1) to relate social classes with stages of life-style. The matrix helps identify promising market segments or niches on the basis of their behavioral tendencies. Understanding their behavioral traits permits the development of products and services to match the specific needs of special customer groups. By identifying such groups, additional marketing research can be initiated to determine the essential marketing guidance for effective communication appeals in sales and advertising, bank promotion techniques, and inadequately served consumer segments and niches. Although identified as marketing research, it could be described with equal accuracy as consumer research or behavior analysis.

MARKETING RESEARCH TECHNIQUES. Information concerning customers and prospects is an integral part of the total bank marketing information system (BMIS). In addition to customer research, a bank marketing manager requires information related to bank product and service development, market segment and niche potential, effective sales methods, and other areas of concern. The type of information for use by the bank marketing manager usually falls into one of four investigative areas and includes the following specific marketing information requirements:

1. Research related to customers
   Demographic information on retail customers
   Psychographic information on retail customers
   Socioeconomic data on retail customers
   Type of business by SIC for commercial customers
   Deposit and loan balances
   Number of products and services used
   Account growth and longevity
   Profitability of all major accounts
   Seasonal banking patterns
2. Research related to bank products and services
   New product development
   Improvement of present products and services

Table 6-1. Customer Behavior Matrix

Social classes	Young singles	Young marrieds	First nest	Full nest	Empty nest	Older singles	Retired	Survivor
Poverty Welfare recipient Unemployed Racial minority Limited education								
Blue-collar Laborer Low-income Union member High school only								
Gray-collar Retrained Medium-income Union supporter Trade school								
White-collar Clerical Secretarial Working wife Technical training								
Managerial Decision maker College-trained Department head Sr. management								
Professional Advanced education Career-oriented Affluent Influential								
Public servant Government worker Service member Office holder Regulator								
Retiree Fixed income Rate-sensitive Second career Reduced expenses								

New applications of present products and services
Competitive position of bank services
New packaging of bank products
Product or service names for differentiation
Pretesting new or improved products and services
Product and service preferences by customers
Service elimination or simplification
Costs and profitability of products and services
3. Research related to markets
Designation of primary and secondary market areas
Analysis of consumer markets (segments and niches)
Analysis of commercial markets (by SIC)
Determination of relative profitability of markets
Analysis of branch location potential
Estimation of potential loan and deposit volume
Estimation of potential for fee-based services
Market analysis by calling officer sales areas
Delineation of sales territories/account assignments
Establishment of calling officer quotas
Competitive conditions in the market
Analysis of general business potential in the market
General economic forecasting (local and national)
4. Research related to communication
Sales performance measurement
Calling effort costs
Sales training effectiveness
Selection of advertising media
Testing of communication messages
Testing of awareness of advertising
Testing for effect of communication on customer attitudes
Analysis of competitive advertising

The marketing research process is a sequential method of identifying problems and opportunities affecting the bank's marketing effort, designing research instruments for gathering the information relevant to the marketing function, and analyzing the data collected to determine viable targets and courses of action. There are two sources for research data; one is designated as primary and the other is identified as secondary.

Primary research is concerned with the collection of data from original sources. It can be used to determine customer attitudes and opinions about specific bank services or facilities. It can also be used for measuring bank performance internally, for such activities as training effectiveness and advertising impact, and for gathering information on calling officer contact efficiency. Other primary research provides information on account balances, loan application volume, and branch lobby activity such as teller transaction volume and customer traffic. Several techniques are used for primary research, and most are based on the traditional survey method—mail questionnaires, personal interviews, or telephone surveys. Another particularly useful technique for banks is the professional shopper. These trained research specialists can be used to open and close accounts, apply for loans, and seek operational contact with bank personnel. Unfortunately, employee relations may suffer somewhat because of the covert nature of this technique; the effect on morale may outweigh the advantages of collecting data in this way.

Secondary research data were originally collected for another purpose than specific bank use, by the media or by an external organization such as a government agency or industry association. Secondary sources should be investigated for relevant data before turning to primary research; the latter is usually very costly. Some excellent sources for secondary research data were listed in Chapter 3.

To implement the marketing research process, there is a set of recommended procedures. From a practical point of view there are eight desirable steps in the application of research to the marketing function:

1. Ask well-structured questions that are likely to develop appropriate responses with pertinent information.
2. Devise in advance hypotheses that can be tested to answer the questions selected.
3. State any assumptions that have been made relative to the marketing problem.
4. Derive the logical consequences of any assumptions that are made.
5. Design marketing research techniques that will test the validity and logic of the assumptions.
6. Test the research techniques for relevance to the problem and reliability in the results.
7. Conduct the research and interpret the data collected.
8. Evaluate the worth of the conclusions and the fidelity of the marketing research technique used.

With the completion of the market research project it is necessary to prepare a report that includes a detailed analysis of the research findings and conclusions or recommendations. This report should be used to support any marketing proposals by substantiating or reinforcing recommended courses of action. There are several considerations involved in the report, including the following:

1. Involve both senior and line management of the bank by seeking their opinions about the data and the analysis.
2. Recommend specific courses of action based on the report rather than emphasizing the obvious with a general conclusion that customers will save, borrow, or use services less or more.
3. Provide information that is practical, timely, and highly relevant; avoid pure scholarship and heavy theory.
4. Establish some measure of marketing research efficiency on the basis of cost relative to the information obtained and its potential for use.
5. Present information in the logic of the action recommended rather than in the logic of the way the data were collected.
6. Avoid publishing research reports that were conducted primarily for internal political reasons; they lessen the credibility of marketing research.
7. Reject research that is technically inadequate because of poor research instruments, incomplete data, or thinness due to an inadequate commitment of funds.
8. Do not allow the research report to make the marketing decisions; information from markets is only one of several sources for use in gathering data for the decision making.
9. Let the report stand on its own but make certain that it is received with appropriate concern by senior bank management as a supportive document for marketing recommendations.

Most banks do not have internal marketing research capability. They rely on their advertising agency or an outside research firm. Except in rare cases, advertising agencies are less qualified to conduct marketing research than the bank itself. Because of this, bank marketing managers should call on a professional firm for primary research; secondary research can be conducted by the personnel in the marketing department. In either case, bank marketing managers should become familiar with some of the key terms used in the research process. This will help them understand and evaluate any proposals made by outside research sources.

Marketing Research Terms

Attitude research. Concerns those efforts that range from defining an attitude to designing the instruments for measurement.

Attitude scale. A device for measuring the degree of the feeling that an individual associates with the issue or object in question.

Audience (cumulative). The rate at which the audience grows with each additional media exposure as expressed in total numbers.

Audience (repeat). The number of readers or viewers who are in the medium's audience more than once.

Block sampling. A procedure for area sampling drawn from a listing of all blocks in an urbanized area.

Block statistics. Data from the U.S. Census Bureau that consist of selected information on housing and population for individual blocks in each urbanized area.

Brand loyalty. The degree of consistency in the preference for a particular brand. In banking, brands are applied to identify the institution or its generic products and services.

Call-backs. Repeated attempts to contact and interview survey respondents who were not available initially.

Carry-over effect. The propensity of an advertisement to be seen or recalled for extended periods after its initial appearance.

Closed-end question. A question that offers the respondent a choice of alternative responses that are specified in the survey.

Coding. Numbers assigned to verbal responses in surveys to facilitate computer processing and analysis.

Concept testing. Measuring the viability of new ideas in product and service design, communication message content, or bank marketing approaches; this precedes product or market testing.

Control group. An equivalent group of subjects to measure against a test group for determining the effectiveness of the test.

Correlation analysis. Technique for determining the existence of a relationship between two sets of data either positively or negatively.

Correlation coefficient. A measure of the magnitude of the relationship between two sets of data as expressed in the equivalent of a positive or negative percentage.

Cross-tabulations. Examining the responses to one survey question in terms of responses to another.

Depth interviews. Unstructured interviews to permit the respondent greater latitude in selecting the nature of the discussion.

Factor analysis. Procedure for determining the extent to which measures of different variables are describing the same phenomenon.

Frame. The listing of the members of the population from which the survey sample is drawn.

Gross rating points. The sum of the TV ratings for each of the programs on which the bank's commercial is carried.

Index numbers. Measure of the magnitude of change of a variable in relation to a specified base value of the variable; the consumer price index is a good example.

Judgment sampling. Selecting a sample based on an expert's personal assessment that the one chosen is representative of the population universe.

Life cycle. The classification of households in their various stages of development.

Matched samples. Selecting two or more groups of individuals in a way that assures that they are alike according to specified characteristics; random sampling is less biased.

Motivation research. Techniques that adapt psychological testing to determine the behavioral patterns of respondents.

Nonresponse. The degree to which the interviews with respondents are not completed.

Nonsampling errors. Errors in data from causes other than the random selection of the respondent sample.

Open-end questions. Survey questions without response alternatives that allow respondents to answer in their own words.

Paired comparisons. Offering respondents a choice between two items for preference judgment or comparison.

Panel research. Repeated measurements of the same respondents to observe any changes over time.

Pass-along readership. The number of readers who may see the medium in addition to the initial subscriber or purchaser.

Pilot test. Investigating the workability of a research project in advance by reproducing it in a smaller, less costly version.

Probability. A measure of the likelihood that a given event will occur according to a previously determined ratio of occurrence (objective) or one's personal belief (subjective).

Probability sampling. The assignment of known probabilities of selection to the universe and the random selection of the sample.

Quota sampling. A method in which the frequency distribution of respondents with respect to some variables matches the variables similarly in the population universe.

Random digit dialing. A procedure for conducting telephone surveys through random dialing so that new and unlisted numbers are included.

Random numbers. A table for use in numerical order selection that prevents any relationship of occurrence between numbers.

Recall (aided). A form of advertising research that prompts the respondent by the use of a leading question.

Recall (unaided). A question seeking recall by limiting the cues or promptings provided to the respondent.

Regression analysis. Basis for prediction using the given values of one variable to estimate the related values of another.

Response error. Variations in responses based on perceptions of truth or lack of reliability.

Sample surveys. Data obtained from a relatively small number of respondents representing the universe for use as inference only.

Semantic differential. A combination of controlled word association and scaling procedures to determine the word association and intensity of the respondent's opinion or attitude.

Unweighted data. Survey findings that have not been adjusted for the varying probabilities of selection.

Wear out. The rate at which the usage of an advertising campaign loses its effectiveness.

Weighted data. Data that have been adjusted for unequal probabilities of selection.

7

BANK PRODUCTS AND SERVICES

In the past, success in banking was often equated to growth and size by customers and competitors, and according to some bankers, the asset side of the ledger was foremost in any measurement so that loan products and services held the key to peer respect. Recently, the regulators have been requesting that banks improve their margin of safety by increasing their capital ratios. As a result, some banks have been selling off their loans and are seeking new sources of income. Many banks are making only those loans with high yields, or they are developing new products and services that produce fee income but do not appear on their balance sheet as assets. Thus, for the first time, bank marketing managers have internal restrictions that may inhibit the marketing of traditional financial products and encourage the development or revision of products and services to suit both the institution and its changing market.

There are other circumstances that also impact the products and services offered by banks. Operating expenses are growing rapidly, and net interest margins are under pressure because of the environment of deregulation and competition. With profit margins shrinking, banks are faced with the choice of increasing the volume of present product lines or expanding the lines further and selling more to each bank customer. The latter product strategy appears to offer the greater opportunity for marketing success because it is less costly to sell an additional service to present customers than to sell the same service to new customers. To assess this option properly, a thorough analysis of the potential volume of present products and services should be completed by the bank marketing manager. In addition, expansion of product lines and discontinuing of superfluous products and services should also be considered. For example, not all banks have the customer base or expertise to offer discount brokerage services or to establish an export trading company; both are now permitted by law and have a special customer appeal. However, very few banks can justify either from a marketing standpoint.

Contrary to what many bankers believe, most financial services are not considered to be essential; most are categorized as only useful, and some are considered luxuries. An in-house survey of subscribers by *Better Homes and Gardens* indicated an almost unanimous agreement that auto and home insurance were the most essential financial services. Credit cards were the only noninsurance financial product in the top four services mentioned. In spite of their widespread use, credit cards were deemed to be less important to a family's financial well-being. Whether or not these customers consider the need to make efficient and frequent bank transactions as essential as insurance, it may be that banking services are taken too much for granted. One startling statistic in this regard, however, is that only 65 percent of the U.S. population are estimated to have checking accounts, according to the A.B.A.

A luxury or a necessity notwithstanding, those who sell financial products must have a strong servicing ethic. One prime consideration is to develop product integrity that implies substantiation and delivery of all product and service claims and promises. In the airline industry, as in banking, the principal service is often a commodity, and product differentiation is to be found in the supplementary services such as personnel attitudes, baggage handling, ticketing convenience, meals, and refreshments. The quality aspect of banking service can be found in two areas—technical expertise and the human attributes of bank contact personnel. Technical expertise includes not only providing a good match between product benefits and customer requirements but having product readily available. Human attributes consist of accessibility, timely response, and genuine concern for customers. Survey after survey indicates that customers want the standard package of consideration—convenience of time and place as well as access to their money, products that are easy to comprehend, and bank employees who are courteous, knowledgeable, and willing to demonstrate that they care about their customers.

One aspect of product and service determination is the fact that banks are in the business of risk management. Products and services are developed with the tacid understanding that risks in banking must be managed as in any other business; risks can be identified, considered, and managed. As with any other business, there are driving forces in the business of banking. Foremost is the classic rationale, providing an adequate return on equity for the shareholders. Another force is the operating policies of the bank as shaped by public policy. Once these are in control, the bank can exploit business opportunities through the medium of products and services. Such products and services, however, must be related to business risk and reward. From a product and service standpoint there are several types of risk:

> **Funding risk.** Can uninsured liabilities be readily renewed? ($1 million Certificates of Deposit)
>
> **Asset quality risk.** Are assets collectable at collateral value? (MAI appraised value)

Control risk. Is there a threat of financial liability from operations other than lending? (insurance, brokerage, REITs)

Interest rate risk. Will earnings be lessened by mismatching? (short-term deposits versus long-term mortgages)

Overhead risk. Are support costs excessive? (Bank-owned computers instead of contracts with outside service bureaus)

Strategy risk. Is support technology adequate? (ATMs, POS, Videotex, Teletext, etc.)

Capital risk. Is new capital available on favorable or nondilutive terms? (Increasing loan volume and declining capital ratios)

An additional consideration is the form a product or service may take. Theodore Levitt of Harvard considers product form to be in one of three classes—the form that is expected by customers, a form that augments the present form, or a form that seeks to tap the potential. Levitt advocates that marketing or product managers move beyond the minimal set of specifications that customers accept for product or service differentiation to an analysis of whether the profitability and share of market can be enhanced by either the form with augmented benefits or one with greater potential benefit. Augmentation is normally performed on existing product lines or services to remain competitive. Potential-seeking form is associated with new products and services for innovation by market leaders. However, form is a tributary of the bank product mainstream; thus, it is essential to examine the numerous product and service categories prior to an analysis of the appropriate form by the bank marketing manager.

From a macro perspective, financial services are considered to be in one of three categories—credit, investment, or insurance. In certain instances such as a certificate of deposit used as collateral for a personal or commercial loan, the product or service may overlap into two categories, credit and investment. Those who borrow against a life insurance policy are also involved in two categories. Overlaps notwithstanding, one category is always primate on the basis of its initial or principal use. Each category is represented on the complete product and service menu of commercial banks. However, for marketing purposes, the three macro categories require subsets in order to review them and their marketing potential from a micro viewpoint.

PERSONAL DEPOSIT PRODUCTS AND SERVICES. Money is used as a medium of exchange and also as a store of value in the conduct of living. Money, in the form of deposits, is the principal source of funds or raw material for banks to use for manufacturing credit or making appropriate investments. The interest received from loans and investments provides the major source of bank revenue. The contribution of the marketing effort is to generate deposits by paying an explicit rate of interest to depositors or by paying an implicit return in the form of customer convenience, reduced fees, promotional premiums, or additional services not readily available from competitors. Some of the deposit-related products and services targeted to individual customers are the following:

1. **Demand deposit accounts.** The deposits in these accounts are legally subject to negotiable checks or to direct transfers, both of which facilitate the exchange of money between payee and payor. These checking deposits make up the major part of the nation's money supply; to emphasize the importance of checking accounts, personal and business, the currency in circulation is only a relatively minor part of the money supply. The elimination of Regulation Q and its restriction on interest payment for deposits has had a dramatic impact on demand deposit marketing. In some instances, bank customers have become more satisfied with accounts that provide exceptional services rather than explicit interest. Some of these implicit substitutes for high interest include free checking, ATM access, nonfee credit cards, and free check supply. However, the pure demand deposit account has been proliferated by other interest-earning versions.

2. **Negotiable orders for withdrawal (NOW) accounts.** This original version of an interest-bearing demand deposit account was designed to circumvent the Banking Act of 1933, which prohibited banks from paying interest on demand deposits. The NOW account was augmented later by the Super-NOW account. Both paid varying rates of interest and were subject to regulated minimums. In 1986 the restrictions on rate and minimum balances for these demand deposit accounts were lifted. Bank marketing managers can now operate in the free marketplace to generate demand deposits based on marketing advantage.

3. **Automatic transfer service.** The customer can request the transfer of funds between accounts. This was particularly attractive before demand deposits were permitted to earn interest. Banks transferred customer funds automatically between an interest-bearing savings account and a non–interest-earning checking account as funds were required to cover checks received by the bank for payment. This automatic service is now relatively obsolete although transfers by telephone between accounts is common on an as-requested basis.

4. **Direct deposit service.** Customers who receive periodic payments from large funds disbursers such as major employers or the Social Security Administration can authorize the bank to receive payments and to credit them directly to their account. This offers customers the benefit of automatic deposit without the problems of mail delay or lost or stolen checks. Similar service is the automatic payroll service offered to commercial firms.

5. **Check truncation service.** Instead of producing a monthly statement that also contains cancelled checks, this service microfilms the checks during processing and stores them on bank premises. If a subsequent need arises for a copy of the check, it can be obtained from the bank for a nominal charge. The advantage of such a service to the bank is obvious; to customers, this service can reduce checking account fees and eliminate lost checks or the need for check storage at home.

6. **Automatic bill payment service.** Customers provide the bank with a list of their charge account relationships, which can include all credit cards, loan and mortgage payments, taxes, and so on. These bills are paid directly by the bank to the appropriate payees when due by debiting the customer's checking account and crediting the payee's business account. Payment is made only after telephone authorization by the customer. Charges for this service are usually less than the cost of postage for the customer if the bills were paid at home by check.

7. **Money market account.** This transaction-type account for individuals and partnerships was designed to permit banks to compete with the money market funds offered by nonbank financial institutions. It pays a relatively high rate of interest and is a pseudoinvestment account that also offers liquidity to the customer. Three third-party checks can be written each month as well as three in-bank transfers. It is a very popular bank product for those customers who wish to invest risk-free under the umbrella of an FDIC insured account while still preserving immediate access to funds upon demand.

8. **Check guarantee card.** This serves as a guarantee to retailers and other recipients of check payments that the bank will honor a customer's check regardless of the funds on deposit. There is usually a specified limit of one hundred dollars or two hundred dollars. However, merchant customers of the bank consider this service to be most helpful since it not only guarantees that the check won't bounce, a tremendous source of losses to merchants each year, but also serves as another means of check verification by indicating the number and location of the customer's bank account.

9. **Passbook savings account.** The primary appeal of this product is convenience. It offers a lower rate of interest and has become less important with the introduction of interest-bearing checking accounts such as the NOW account. This account is also offered as a statement savings account by those banks who have eliminated the use of the traditional passbook. In some areas, however, old-line customers continue to demand deposit and withdrawal entries in their passbook. To compete successfully in the statement or passbook savings market, banks must now offer more than convenience by adding other benefits that compensate for the low interest rate of this type of account. Some of these benefits might include free companion checking accounts or a waiver of the annual fee for credit cards if a minimum savings account balance is maintained.

10. **Specific-purpose savings accounts.** These special accounts are used primarily for promotional purposes by featuring a wide variety of rationales for saving such as the payment of income taxes (April Tax Club), financing of vacations (Vacation Account), or other obvious savings goals such as a "Stork Account," "Rainy Day Account," or the traditional "Christmas" or Hanukkah Club" for cash for holiday shopping. In these accounts, customers save for a particular reason, and any interest earned is a secondary consideration to disciplined saving.

11. **Certificate of deposit.** For those customers who are interest-sensitive, this nonnegotiable savings instrument is offered in fixed maturities from 30 days to 5 to 10 years. Interest is paid by check or deposited on a monthly or quarterly basis. When requested, the interest may be accumulated and compounded to maturity. Rates are based on market forces of supply and demand and may be tied in with the prime rate, the Treasury bill rate, or another index such as the Donoghue Average. Although interest costs fluctuate over time, funds raised through such deposits may be more permanent as core deposits, particularly with an automatic rollover feature. Unless the amount is large and is categorized as "hot money," these deposits tend to remain because they are relatively liquid and FDIC insured up to $100,000 against loss. Some individual customers of higher net worth may choose "Jumbo" certificates, which are issued in amounts over $100,000. To banks, the larger certificates are excellent sources of funds but cannot be considered core deposits; they may follow a higher rate to another financial institution or be subject to disintermediation to buy securities.

12. **Lifeline account.** Deregulation has spawned a need to offer no-frills checking accounts for low-income customers. Rising sales

expense for attracting bank deposits through higher interest has made it necessary that customers begin to pay for many of the services that once were free. Congress has reacted to the complaints of poorer constituents who feel that fees and minimums are too high. There is a threat of legislation to protect these customers; some banks have volunteered new, low-cost checking accounts that are structured with such specifications as a $100 minimum balance, no monthly fee, a ten-check-per-month limit, or a requirement that transactions be conducted through ATMs instead of through in-branch tellers. Such accounts have the potential to become profitable in time; low-income customers such as students or others entering the work force may ultimately use other bank products and services as they progress.

13. **Service barter account.** Selected bank services can be priced individually according to an interest percentage related to a specific level of deposits. This level can be either a monthly minimum or an average balance. Customers contract with the bank for the services they desire and receive such services free or at a discount in lieu of deposit interest. This form of extra service payment can also be structured by using a compensating deposit balance for each service instead of a specific price based on a percentage of interest earned.

CONSUMER LOAN PRODUCTS AND SERVICES. The growth in demand for consumer credit has been phenomenal with dramatic increases each year. In 1985 it was reported by *U.S. News and World Report* that individuals owed more than $500 billion on installment loans, without including the debt for home mortgages. This debt can be translated into a scenario in which a person who earns $45,000 a year is estimated to have $9,000 in auto loans, credit card balances, and personal loans; the average monthly payments for such debt is over $300 a month, again without mortgage payments. This high debt has resulted in an increase in the consumers' dislike of such bank fees as service charges. According to a Conference Board survey of six thousand families, almost half disliked credit card and bank service charges; only three other consumer services had higher negative ratings—hospital charges, lawyers' fees, and the cost of movie tickets. Incidentally, the pricing of used cars was 10 percent more favored than credit card charges.

The successful marketing of consumer loans is not dependent solely upon uncovering prospects in person at the branch level, some make a telemarketing effort through telephone solicitation or by direct mail. Once uncovered, a prudent and responsive credit applicant analysis system is vital to process customers quickly and safely. The two types of credit evaluation are judgmental and empirical. *Judgmental evaluation* relies on the consumer loan officers' experience and insight and considers income and collateral as primate, although character as defined through credit history and nature of employment are also judgmental factors. When time and heavy volume are essential to the loan marketing effort, an empirical analysis or a credit scoring system may be more appropriate.

To provide for processing in a volume, a *credit scoring system* (Table 7-1) can be developed by using statistical techniques such as regression or discriminate analysis to identify predictor characteristics associated with both good and bad customers for credit. The data are based on the credit records of customers in the bank's own credit files. The consumer demographic and psychographic characteristics are weighted so that credit applicants can be judged on the statistical likelihood of their becoming either good or bad personal credit risks. Factors that may be used to develop credit scoring systems include the following:

Own or rent	Telephone at home and work
Bank savings account	Time at present address
Bank checking account	Zip code of residence
Age	Age, make, and model of car
Marital status	Geographic area of United States
Age difference between spouses	Finance company reference
Number of dependents	Savings and loan reference
Time with employer	Monthly rent/mortgage payment
Time with previous employer	Income
Type of employment	Debt to income ratio
Trade union membership	Ownership of life insurance
Other credit references	Location of nearest relative
Industry in which employed	Level of formal education

A relatively new development in the marketing of consumer loans involves shopping guides for credit. Banks and other credit sources are listed in local periodicals, which also list their loan charges for specific products and services. One company, Mortgage Reporting Service, Inc., of Jenkintown, Pennsylvania, publishes a weekly listing of mortgage rates in Pennsylvania and New Jersey. Customers purchase the guides in bookstores for $20; annual subscribers such as builders, realtors, and lenders pay $375 a year. In 1985 the Federal Reserve Board completed an experiment in comparative shopping for consumer loans by collecting interest rates on personal, auto, mortgage, and second mortgage loans that were published by newspapers in the test area. Consumer groups want the project to be expanded nationally. Such activity is an indication of the growing competi-

Table 7-1. Sample Credit Scoring System (Indicating Relative Weights)

	Points		Points
A. Residence		**F. Time with employer**	
Owns/buying	10	Under 1 year	3
Rents	2	1–3 years	4
All other	6	3–5 years	5
No answer	2	Over 5 years or retired	6
B. Residence zip code		No answer	3
Zip code A	6	**G. Bank references**	
Zip code B	5	Checking only	10
Zip code C	4	Savings only	10
Zip code D	3	Checking and savings	15
No answer	3	Loan and checking or savings	7
C. Time at present address		Loan only	2
Less than 6 months	3	No answer	2
7 months–2 years	4	**H. Retail credit**	
2 years–7 years	5	Credit cards and department	
Over 7 years	9	stores	10
No answer	3	Major credit cards only	10
D. Occupation		Department stores only	7
Clergy	4	None	2
Artist/writer	4	**I. Income**	
Executive	6	$0–15,000	4
Driver	3	$15,000–30,000	5
Manager	4	$30,000–50,000	6
Homemaker	5	Over $50,000	10
Laborer	3	**J. Monthly Payments**	
Military (enlisted)	4	$0–100	8
Military (officer)	6	$100–300	6
Professional	6	$300–500	4
Retired	4	Over $500	2
Teacher	4	No payments	10
Student	3	No answer	2
Clerical	4	**K. Derogatory credit ratings**	
Unemployed	2	No investigation	0
Sales	4	No credit record	0
All other	4	Two or more derogatory	−5
No answer	3	One derogatory	−2
E. Age		All positive ratings	4
Under 45	1		
Over 45	5		
No answer	1		

tiveness and consumer concern for loan charges. To increase a bank's presence in such a market, there are several key products and services to be considered by the bank marketing manager.

1. **Personal loans.** This is a broad loan category that can be merchandised and promoted according to its end use, for example, vacation, income tax, education, or bill consolidation. They can be structured for repayment in installments or by a single payment at maturity. Some opportunities for innovation include delayed payments, skip payments, interest-only payments, or other variations of amortization that may have consumer appeal.

2. **Credit cards.** The market for standard bank credit cards is basic and is now considered to be a product with certain service requirements such as ATM compatibility that all banks are expected to provide to their customers. This has resulted in a race of product discrimination through marketing innovations identified by such descriptions as gold, silver, or platinum. Competitors in the marketplace are multiplying and include such old-line travel and entertainment card leaders as American Express and Carte Blanche, to the various bank-type credit cards issued by Merrill Lynch, Sears, the thrifts, credit unions, and so on. It has been estimated that the standard Visa and Master Card holders will decline from the current level of 125 million to 102 million by 1990. The average credit cardholder has seven cards and the cost of advertising and promotion to add a new cardholder is forty dollars compared with only ten dollars a few years ago. Growth is anticipated in the premium card segment, however, since prestige cards offer larger lines of credit and more complimentary services. *Business Week* reported that credit card customers use premium cards 50 percent more often and charge an average of 150 percent more than the standard bank credit card customers. Most banks have found that larger lines of credit encourage larger outstanding balances, which in turn generate more bank revenue. These increased profits will invite more competition, which may well lead to a reevaluation of credit card pricing. Technology improvement is not confined to the color of the plastic card. "Smart" cards that contain microchips that can compute as well as store data are now being marketed on a limited basis. These will be the credit cards of the future, offering many information and identification services that are peripheral to personal banking and go beyond the credit function.

3. **Debit cards.** This product permits customers to gain immediate access to their deposit accounts. Its initial use, which requires more marketing emphasis, is its ATM applications. This usage is primi-

tive in a sense since the potential for the debit card is to serve as an activator of a point-of-sale device in retail stores. This device serves as a card-reading computer terminal that is on line with the merchant's cash registers. The terminal allows customers to transfer funds directly from their checking accounts to the merchant's bank account on a real-time basis. This aspect of the debit card usage will require an aggressive and highly persuasive marketing effort since most bank customers do not recognize the benefits of electronic funds transfer when it is compared to the loss of float. Initially, the debit card has been most successful when used with those retailers who emphasize discount-for-cash transactions such as gas stations or are cash-only outlets such as food stores. Unfortunately, the development of electronic funds transfer at the retail level has been slow since it has not been determined whether the banks or the retailers are to be responsible for the cost of POS terminal purchases and installation. In the meantime, consumer acceptance and usage has been less than expected.

4. **Personal line of credit.** This widely used product offers greater convenience and wider latitude to bank loan customers. Once the credit line has been approved, customers do not need to reapply each time they use the funds. The credit can be used for whatever purpose the customer wishes and, since it is a revolving line, it may be repaid at any time. Repayment does not reduce the ability of the customer to borrow funds in the amount of the original line of credit. A slight variation of this product can be offered by establishing a specific reserve amount behind the customer's checking account balance. If the checking account is overdrawn, funds are automatically transferred to cover the amount of the check. This particular adaptation of the personal line of credit requires a minimum reduction in principal and an interest payment each month, however.

5. **Vehicle loans.** Until the automobile manufacturers began to use bargain interest rates as sales promotion tools, loans for passenger cars and trucks accounted for almost half of bank installment loans to individuals. Now banks depend more upon the financing of used automobiles for their vehicle loan volume. Those vehicles over five years old are not usually financed by banks, however. Maturity terms are being extended on new car financing to periods as long as sixty months as a result of competitive market pressures. In addition to passenger cars and trucks, bank marketing is directed to promoting the financing of motor homes, recreational vehicles, campers, boats, van conversions, and trailers. The leisure market can be a key target for vehicle financing.

6. **Residential mortgage loans.** Those customers for this product are seeking long-term financing on one- to four-family residences. The marketing effort can be directed toward conventional loans that are not government-insured or those insured by the Federal Housing Administration (FHA) or the Veterans Administration (VA). For many years, banks abdicated this business to the thrifts. Once in the residential lending business, banks offered only mortgage loans that had a first lien on the property. With the rapid appreciation of housing values, home equity loans, or second mortgages, have been offered, using the growing equity of homeowner customers as collateral. There are many legal ramifications for bank managers to become aware of, including consumer protection and community reinvestment laws such as the Fair Housing Act, the Equal Credit Opportunity Act, the Home Mortgage Disclosure Act, and the Community Reinvestment Act, to name a few. Marketing managers must review their marketing program proposals with legal counsel to assure compliance with these acts. To differentiate product, banks have developed several variations of the standard residential mortgage loan. Most are based on changes in the method of pricing or repayment. Some of these variations include *adjustable rate mortgages* (ARMs), which change interest rates each year on the basis of a predetermined rate or one tied to an index such as the prime rate or Treasury bill rate. *Graduated-payment* or *interest-only mortgages* are adaptations that provide for lower monthly payments during the early years when the borrower's income is lower. *Reverse annuity mortgages* are provided for elderly persons who wish to draw down their home equity as a source of income. *Rollover mortgages* are written for short terms only, with an option of a balloon payment of the remaining principal at the end of the term; another option for this type of residential mortgage is to refinance it for another rollover term at current interest rates. There are many opportunities for innovative real estate loans. Real estate loans usually involve the commitment of large sums over an extended period, so proper credit analysis is an essential factor in the successful marketing of residential mortgages.

7. **Mobile home loans.** This special type of housing loan is increasing in importance for use by retirees and vacation home owners. It is usually provided on a shorter-term basis. Most states classify mobile homes as vehicles, thus excluding them from consideration for mortgage lending. Banks usually provide financing indirectly through a mobile home dealer network rather than marketing the loans directly to bank customers. The marketing effort for this product must be directed to the various mobile home dealers.

8. **Single-payment loans.** These loans are marketed to customers who provide a certificate of deposit (CD) or savings account balance for collateral. The maturity of the CD-secured loan coincides with the maturity of the certificate of deposit. The savings account is placed on hold to prevent any withdrawals below a prescribed minimum that are in excess of the loan balance. Terms usually do not exceed thirty-six months, and payment is made in total at maturity.
9. **Stock-secured loans.** This loan product is provided for upscale customers using common stocks listed on the New York, American, or over-the-counter exchanges. This product is not to be confused with margin accounts used for stock purchases, which have specific percentage restrictions. Banks may lend a greater percentage on securities in possession than on those purchased on margin. The normal term for stock-secured loans is thirty-six months or less. Marketing of this product is highly selective.
10. **Bank employee loans.** Although not necessarily a responsibility of the bank marketing manager, personal loans to employees can be made available at preferred rates as a fringe benefit. The marketing manager whose responsibility includes employee relations as part of the public relations function will be concerned with this product.

COMMERCIAL DEPOSIT PRODUCTS AND SERVICES. Deposits for commercial, industrial, institutional, and government organizations also rely heavily on money as a medium of exchange. They must maintain deposit balances for the ebb and flow of payables and receivables. One of the most crucial areas for a sustained marketing effort is in the generating of deposit balances from large businesses. Large deposits are always necessary to meet the demands of business for credit. Thus, bank marketing managers must seek this critical funding by providing the products and services to attract the deposits. If classified by ownership, deposits can originate from private, public, or interbank sources. Although falling under the general category of commercial deposits, *private deposits* are those sourced from individuals, partnerships, corporations, or other private institutions. *Public deposits* come from all levels of government; those from the federal government are classified as Treasury tax and loan accounts. *Interbank deposits* are those of foreign banks, mutual savings banks, or correspondent balances from other commercial banks. Each of these sources of funds requires specialized marketing techniques.

1. **Demand deposit accounts.** This is the basic account for a commercial banking relationship. Target customers include all commercial customers from large corporations to small mom and pop businesses to national, state, and local nonprofit institutions or government agencies. Because banks currently have some restrictions on the payment of interest for demand deposits of business firms, they compete primarily on the basis of services provided. Pricing of loans can be related to the level of demand deposits maintained in the bank; compensating balances are provided to qualify for favorable borrowing terms. This is the most utilized of all bank products.

2. **Check clearing service.** This is one of the most essential services in conjunction with demand deposit accounts to provide the funds necessary in the conducting of business. Bank marketing managers can measure the excellence of the service by the time required for clearing checks so that funds can be made available to the commercial depositors at the earliest possible moment. The electronic funds transfer systems involving automated clearing help reduce clearing time; the resultant savings in the cost of idle or unusable funds can become an important source of income or cost reduction for commercial customers.

3. **Bank wire service.** This service facilitates the direct transfer of funds on a real-time basis among participating banks. It can be used as a marketing tool to improve service for commercial customers who require large funds to be available on short notice in areas outside their immediate headquarters.

4. **Funds collection service.** Commercial customers are not permitted to use uncollected funds for transactions or short-term investments. To speed up the collection process, large firms establish deposit accounts with several banks in appropriate geographical locations throughout the country. A post office box, or *lock box* as it is called, is rented near each bank so that local checks remitted can be picked up several times each day by the designated banks and deposited for immediate processing. The important marketing advantage is that funds spend less time in the mail for remittance from the commercial customer to the bank; time is saved at both ends of the remittance process. Each local bank collecting checks records the transactions daily and initiates the clearing process, often clearing many of the checks quickly through the local clearinghouse. This service is an integral part of the cash management service provided for commercial customers. It is also necessary for sweep accounts since the concept requires maximum availability of funds for overnight investment.

5. **Certificates of deposit.** As corporate treasurers manage their cash flows, the companies have potential cash balances that are greater than needed in a non–interest-bearing demand deposit account. As an alternative to establishing a sweep account, which is primarily for overnight investment, these treasurers often use negotiable certificates of deposit that are issued by large money center banks in large denominations. Local banks compete with nonnegotiable versions; however, bank marketing managers should be aware of the potential for this negotiable product to erode the demand deposit base unless the alternative is marketed aggressively. Principal targets for a negotiable certificate of deposit include not only large commercial firms, but pension funds, substantial nonprofit organizations, and government units as well. In addition to nonnegotiable certificates, other competitive products are other money market instruments such as commercial paper and short-term Treasury and federal agency securities.

COMMERCIAL LOAN PRODUCTS AND SERVICES. Marketing a commercial loan, like any other product or service, requires a viable selling proposition. The marketing effort is conducted through commercial loan officers or calling officers who specialize in the uncovering, qualifying, and selling of commercial banking prospects as well as the continued servicing of present commercial customers. These bank representatives implement the line marketing effort, and they must be technically adept to deal with basic loan marketing considerations such as pricing, compensating balance requirements, service barter opportunities, account profitability analysis, detailed cash flow forecasting, and use of protective loan covenants. Calling officers must be well indoctrinated in the three bank lending situations that govern the nature of the marketing effort. These are based on the purpose of the loan, the source of repayment, the risk inherent in the situation, and the structure of the loan. The key commercial lending applications are loans for asset conversion, cash flow, or asset protection.

1. **Asset conversion loans.** In conducting business it is seldom that the flow of funds into the company from sales parallels the outflow of payables to keep the business going. In some cases this deficiency is seasonal or occurs during a period of inventory build-up. Loans in this category provide short-term, temporary financing based on the conversion of assets in the form of payback from the cash collected when the account receivables from the sale of inventory are liquidated. This is the most traditional form of bank commercial

lending and includes loans secured by accounts receivable and inventory. Repayment is dependent upon the completion of the asset conversion cycle. These loans are generally considered unsecured, and the bank's best protection against loss is the ability of the firm's management to complete the conversion cycle as planned, as well as the liquidity of the assets being financed.

2. **Cash flow loans.** This product is marketed to finance a firm's permanent or long-term capital needs. These include such loan purposes as providing a permanent level of working investment, capital expenditures, or other investment activities related to the business. These loans are usually made for terms up to seven or eight years; all loans over one year are considered long-term debt. The financing of plants and equipment is expected to produce additional working assets that can be converted to cash for loan repayment. Permanent levels of working investment are required to increase the borrower's sales volume, and it can be expected that these sales will result in additional retained earnings to repay the term loan. Competition for this business can be expected from insurance companies, pension funds, government agencies. and public bond offerings that offer terms up to forty years.

3. **Asset protection loans.** This is primarily a short-term product used to provide financing that satisfies a relatively permanent need for funds. This requirement for permanency usually exists in a situation in which companies have a stable level of current assets but the assets revolve. In essence, the bank finances a continuing stream of asset conversion cycles that causes the loan to be "evergreen" because it is rolled over continuously. Calling officers should seek prospects for this product from those companies who do not generate sufficient cash flow to amortize a substantial term loan. Obviously, the bank must be confident that the prospect has the ability to repay the "evergreen" loan, if necessary, from the liquidation of the assets being refinanced each time. The competence and integrity of the company's management are critical considerations in the marketing process. Key sales prospects include wholesalers, importers and exporters, finance companies, commodity dealers, and security brokers—where the business acts as an intermediary between buyer and seller, supplier and manufacturer, saver and investor, and so on.

4. **Commercial real estate loans.** This is a special type of commercial business loan that cannot be categorized as being asset or cash flow lending. It involves industrial, commercial office, and retail construction projects. Traditionally, commercial banks have provided interim construction loans before long-term permanent fi-

nancing is obtained from insurance companies, savings and loans, pension and trust funds, or government agencies. Interim construction loans are relatively short-term and are provided to allow the builder or developer to fund the initial costs of construction before financing the completed project over a long term. Loans on the raw land prior to its development are not considered attractive for bank financing because of the lack of liquidity in the collateral. There are exceptions to this, however, based on the financial strength of the borrower. Banks that market interim construction loans must be prepared to monitor the progress of the construction after determining the feasibility of the proposed project and the ability of the developer or builder to perform. This will require special technical expertise. In the event that permanent financing is considered for smaller commercial real estate projects such as medical offices or smaller income-producing properties, the calling officer should prepare a thorough commercial real estate prospect analysis. A suggested format for the initial prospect qualification analysis is provided in Table 7-2 to assist calling officers in their marketing effort.

5. **Export financing.** Bank customers involved in international trade have special product and service requirements related to financing imports and exports that differ from those of the domestic marketplace. A company that exports is concerned with business risk, which includes not only the terms of the sale but an assurance of payment by the buyer. An overseas buyer also has some concerns. He must be guaranteed performance of the terms of sale regarding delivery as well as the quality of the goods. Banks, as intermediaries, can provide not only the instrument for buyers not willing to pay for goods before delivery, but for the interim financing until the goods are resold. As part of an export financing product, banks can provide additional services to facilitate insurance as well as the foreign exchange and funds transfer requirements. Some specific products and services to be marketed to prospects engaged in import and export include letters of credit, bankers acceptances, lines of credit, direct commercial bank credits, and preexport financing. This is another area of bank marketing that requires a high level of technical expertise.

Whether domestic or international, the marketing of commercial loans is based more on an effective personal calling effort than on mass communication techniques such as advertising. Sales contact by calling officers, customer referrals, and additional business from present bank customers are the keys to marketing effectiveness. One difficulty that bank marketing managers will discover in developing a productive calling effort

Table 7-2. Commercial Real Estate Prospect Analysis

Calling Officer: _____

Prospect: _____

Address: _____ **Phone:** _____

Document review	(check)
Audited financial statement (company)	_____
Personal financial statement (guarantors)	_____
Other banking relationships	_____
Credit evaluations of previous projects	_____
Credit check of general contractor	_____
Pro forma operating formulas (project)	_____
Dun & Bradstreet Report	_____

Proposed credit

Amount. _____ Rate. _____ Fees. _____

Purpose. _____

Type of loan. _____ Maturity. _____

Repayment terms. _____

Sources of repayment. _____

Collateral. _____

Guarantor. _____

Other conditions. _____

Description of company. _____

_____

Description of project. _____

_____

Repayment analysis. _____

_____

Cash flows

Lease payments (_____ × per sq. ft.) $_____

Expenses   _____

Cash flow

Summary of operation

Profitabiity (return of equity, net profit margin) _____

Liquidity (current ratio)   _____

Leverage and solvency (total debt to net worth) _____

Strengths: _____

_____

_____

Weaknesses: _____

_____

is making certain that the calling officers be familiar with the basic technical requirements of the various products available to commercial loan prospects. The Commercial Loan Marketing Matrix (Table 7-3) provides a guide for calling officers to use in the preparation of their sales calls. The various specifications that appear in the matrix are only suggestions. A special matrix should be prepared for the individual bank in keeping with its credit policies and procedures.

TRUST PRODUCTS AND SERVICES. In the past, banks were the principal domiciles for trust accounts. However, an extended period of lackluster investment performance and strong competition from independent investment advisors and other money managers has required a more aggressive marketing effort by banks to seek and retain trust business. This effort, plus improved investment performance, has generated renewed interest in the trust capabilities of commercial banks. One study revealed that in the period from 1982 through 1984 bank commingled trust funds outperformed mutual funds, insurance company funds, and even investment advisors. Banks have begun to market trust services more aggressively because of the desirability of fee income to offset narrowing loan interest spreads. To improve profitability, banks have increased their trust service pricing, segmented their services, targeted market niches with greater potential, and improved their investment expertise. Most banks have decided to specialize in only one of the traditional areas of trust services. They feature personal, corporate, or employee benefit products as well as emphasize the relatively new and growing category of individual retirement products such as SEPs and 401(k) accounts.

1. **Personal trust services.** These services for individuals include the settlement of estates; the administration of personal trusts; the performance of agencies such as custodian, managing agent, or attorney-in-fact; and service as guardians or conservators of estates. The use of such marketing innovations as the living trust in place of the probate process has been a particularly effective product to attract new customers. Other trust departments continue to be the principal competitors, and investment performance remains as the most important differentiating factor for customer appeal. Pricing does not appear to be a sensitive issue with individual trust customers.
2. **Corporate trust services.** These products fill the need for an unbiased intermediary to avoid possible conflicts of interest between corporations and their shareholders, bondholders, or the investing public. These services involve the holding of the mortgage against

Table 7-3. Commercial Loan Marketing Matrix

	Well-established firm	Zero-growth company	Real estate development	Start-up enterprise	Speculative proposition	Community service projects
Credit criteria						
Current bank customer	Opt	Req	Opt	Req	Req	Opt
Appropriate financial statement	Req	Req	Req	Req	Req	Req
Competent senior management	Req	Req	Req	Req	Req	Req
Stable industry	Req	Req	Req	Req	Req	Req
Minimum Dun and Bradstreet rating						
Types of loans						
Unsecured term loan	OK	No	No	No	No	No
Secured term loan	OK	OK	OK	OK	OK	OK
Accounts receivable financing	OK	OK	No	No	No	No
Interim construction financing (with take-out)	OK	OK	OK	OK	OK	OK
Revolving credit line (secured term)	OK	OK	OK	OK	OK	OK
Commodity loans	OK	No	No	No	No	No
Capital loans	No	No	No	No	No	No
Working capital loan (secured term)	OK	OK	OK	OK	OK	OK
Estate loans	OK	OK	No	No	No	No
International loans	OK	No	No	No	No	No
Collateral and maturity						
General (all loans)	Req	Req	Req	Req	Req	Req
Convertible into cash	Req	Req	Req	Req	Req	Req
Conservative margin	Req	Req	Req	Req	Req	Req
Lender's rights before loss in value	Req	Req	Req	Req	Req	Req
Scheduled repayment	Req	Req	Req	Req	Req	Req
Protected promise (contract)	Req	Req	Req	Req	Req	Req
Detailed documentation	Req	Req	Req	Req	Req	Req
Unsecured term loan (up to 90 days)	OK	No	No	No	No	No
Excellent balance sheet	Req	—	—	—	—	—
Excellent earnings statement	Req	—	—	—	—	—
Officer/owner personal guarantee	Opt	—	—	—	—	—
Personal banking relationship	Opt	—	—	—	—	—
Appropriate insurance	Opt	—	—	—	—	—
Secured term loan (3–48 months)	OK	OK	OK	OK	OK	OK
Equipment (% of market value)	85	75	60	60	60	75
Finished goods inventory (% of market)	60	60	60	60	60	60
U.S. Govt./agency securities (% of value)	90	90	90	90	90	90
NYSE/ASE listed securities (% of market)	75	75	75	75	75	75
"A" rated municipal bonds (% of market)	60	60	60	60	60	60
Mutual funds (% of market)	75	75	75	75	75	75
Parts inventory (% of market value)	50	50	50	50	50	50

Table 7-3 (continued)

	Well-established firm	Zero-growth company	Real estate development	Start-up enterprise	Speculative proposition	Community service projects
Money market/savings accts (% of balance)	90	90	90	90	90	90
OTC traded securities (% of market)	60	60	60	60	60	60
Stock in closed corporation	OK	No	No	No	No	No
Commercial RE—local (% of appraisal)	75	75	75	75	75	75
Commercial RE—not local (% of appraisal)	60	60	60	60	60	60
Life insurance (cash value)	OK	OK	OK	OK	OK	OK
Commodity futures	OK	No	No	No	No	No
Officer/owner personal guarantee	OK	Req	Req	Req	Req	Req
Officer/owner validity guarantee	OK	—	—	—	—	—
Personal banking relationship	OK	Req	Req	Req	Req	Req
Rate futures insurance	OK	Req	Req	Req	Req	Req
Residential RE mortgage (% of appraisal)	65	65	65	65	65	65
Appropriate insurance	OK	Req	OK	Req	Req	Req
Accounts receivable financing (3–12 months)	OK	OK	No	No	No	No
Assigned accounts (90 days or less) (%)	80	80	—	—	—	—
Officer/owner personal guarantee	OK	Req	—	—	—	—
Personal banking relationship	OK	Req	—	—	—	—
Appropriate insurance	OK	Req	—	—	—	—
Interim construction financing (3–12 months)						
Full pay-out upon completion	OK	Req	Req	Req	Req	Req
Prior take-out commitment	OK	Req	Req	Req	Req	Req
Officer/owner personal guarantee	OK	Req	Req	Req	Req	Req
Personal banking relationship	OK	Req	OK	Req	Req	OK
Appropriate insurance	Req	Req	Req	Req	Req	Req
Revolving line of credit (see secured term loans)	OK	OK	OK	OK	OK	OK
Commodity loan (1–6 months)	OK	No	No	No	No	No
Bonded/field warehouse receipts	Req	—	—	—	—	—
Working capital loan/1–6 months (secured loan)	OK	OK	OK	OK	OK	OK
Estate loan (1–12 months)	OK	OK	No	No	No	No
Guaranteed by estate	Req	Req	—	—	—	—
Estate banking relationship	Req	Req	—	—	—	—

Loan pricing formula

Interest income (rate × amount × time)
+ Value of balances [MFR × balances × (1 − reserve required) × time]
+ Fee income (rate × amount)
= Gross contribution to income

Table 7-3 (continued)

	Well-established firm	Zero-growth company	Real estate development	Start-up enterprise	Speculative proposition	Community service projects
$\text{Yield} = \dfrac{\text{Gross contribution to income}}{\text{Average loans outstanding}}$						
Pricing						
General (all loans)	Req	Req	Req	Req	Req	Req
Use prime rate as base	Req	Req	Req	Req	Req	Req
Commitment fee desirable	Opt	Req	Req	Req	Req	Req
Specific rate change date (90-day maximum)	Req	Req	Req	Req	Req	Req
Unsecured term loan	OK	No	No	No	No	No
Rate (prime +)	2–4	—	—	—	—	—
Commitment fee (points)	1–2	—	—	—	—	—
Application /credit review fee ($)	200	—	—	—	—	—
Secured term loan	OK	OK	OK	OK	OK	OK
Rate (prime +)	1–2	2–3	2–3	3–4	4	2–3
Commitment fee (points)	1	2	2–3	2–3	2–3	1
Application/credit review fee ($)	100	100	100	200	200	100
Accounts receivable financing	OK	OK	No	No	No	No
Rate (prime +)	2	2	—	—	—	—
Commitment fee (points)	1	1	—	—	—	—
Accounts review fee (charged at cost)	Yes	Yes	—	—	—	—
Interim construction financing	OK	OK	OK	OK	OK	OK
Rate (prime +)	3	4	3	4	4	3
Commitment fee (points)	1	1–2	2–3	2–3	2–3	1
Application/project review fee ($)	250	250	250	250	250	250
Revolving line of credit	OK	OK	OK	OK	OK	OK
Rate (prime +)	2–3	4–5	4–5	4–5	4–5	2–3
Commitment fee (points)	1	1–2	1–2	2–3	2–3	1
Application/credit review fee ($)	100	100	100	200	200	100
Commodity loan	OK	No	No	No	No	No
Rate (prime +)	3–4	—	—	—	—	—
Commitment fee (points)	1–2	—	—	—	—	—
Application/verification fee ($)	500	—	—	—	—	—
Working capital loan	OK	OK	OK	OK	OK	OK
Rate (prime +)	2–3	4–5	4–5	4–5	4–5	2–3
Commitment fee (points)	1	1–2	1–2	2–3	2–3	1
Application/credit review fee ($)	100	100	100	200	200	100
Estate loan	OK	OK	No	No	No	No
Rate (prime +)	2–3	3–4	—	—	—	—
Commitment fee (points)	1	1–2	—	—	—	—
Application/legal review fee ($)	500	500	—	—	—	—

which bonds are issued by a corporation and the enforcement of the provisions related to the mortgage. Banks can also handle the registration and transfer of ownership of registered securities, enforce or supervise insurance requirements, execute various releases, and administer sinking funds. Other responsibilities include those of stock registrar, transfer agent or dividend dispersing agent. There is little nonbank competition in this product and service area. It is a fee-based service in which data processing efficiency is an important selling advantage.

3. **Employee benefit services.** The banks provide management of funds generated from employee benefit plans of organizations. The funds are usually invested in a combination of bonds and securities, depending upon the investment objectives of the customers. Corporate and individual pension plans are established to offer retirement income and tax benefits. These trust services include trust accounts with the bank's having full control over fund management and custody accounts for which the bank performs record-keeping duties; in this case, the bank only buys and sells securities as directed by an investment manager. The bank may also offer investment management and advisory services as well as serve as administrators of the plan and prepare the necessary tax or other government reports. From a marketing standpoint, employee benefit services are experiencing tremendous growth with over 400,000 plans currently in existence covering 36 million private and 16 million government workers. It is estimated that 50,000 new plans are being formed each year. Competition is extensive with insurance companies, brokerage firms, and mutual funds active in the marketing arena with banks and trust companies.

4. **Individual retirement services.** Recent legislation has provided for trust investment vehicles that allow individuals to establish their own tax-deferred pension plans. Accounts such as IRAs, Keoghs for self-employeds, simplified employees pension, and 401(k)s for employer-employee participation provide for yearly contributions. These have a maximum amount and are tax-deductable in the year of contribution. Much of this funding is invested in banks' certificates of deposit or invested by means of self-direction by the account holder into higher risk investments. Self-directed accounts usually seek greater opportunities for appreciation and dramatic growth in the fund. These accounts are the most competitive of the trust-related products and are offered by the thrifts, credit unions, insurance companies, brokerage firms, mutual funds, as well as banks. The customer base for these products, particularly IRAs, is an expanding one; over 60 percent of the U.S. households do not

have IRAs. The recent eligibility of all workers, including the provision for nonworking spouses, and the faltering faith in the Social Security system, makes these products a high priority for bank marketing emphasis. This product has been subject to legislative review by the Congress and because of the recent tax reform action by Congress appears to have a political dimension that may effect its terms and conditions in the future.

INVESTMENT PRODUCTS AND SERVICES. As deregulation continues and the marketplace becomes more crowded with competitors, the investment area of financial services will become more attractive to banks; customers will also become more susceptible to bank marketing appeals. For the present, the investment products and services marketed through commercial banks are somewhat limited. However, this situation is changing. Basically, there are only two distinct investment services available—cash management and security brokerage services—although self-directed IRAs can also qualify, technically. There are many types of investments available through commercial banks in addition to the many securities for investment through stock exchanges. Some of the more common instruments that can be marketed through banks are shown in Table 7-4.

1. **Cash management services.** In today's economy, cash has become a valuable earning asset for many bank customers with appropriate cash flows. In order to maximize earnings from idle cash, banks and other financial service institutions have provided for the collection, concentration, and disbursement of funds for customers. Earnings are generated for customers by reducing float time through more efficient collection procedures, concentrating the cash into a single account so that payments can be made through a tightly controlled disbursement process, and by investing any excess cash not required immediately for payables into interest-earning instruments. This service is based on the principle of rapid, more efficient collection through strategically located lock boxes in local post offices. Once collected, the funds are subjected to a zero balance accounting service that permits sweeping the consolidated account nightly to obtain excess cash for investment. Cash management services have both domestic and international application; however, competition for these fee-based services is keen. The initial Merrill Lynch effort providing such a service to individuals has been a tremendous marketing coup. Now, most major life insurance and brokerage firms offer this service; banks were late in responding but are now becoming factors in the market as well.

Table 7-4. Investment Products

Type	Term	Minimum order	Form	Interest payment	Security	State income tax liability
Direct U.S. government obligations						
Treasury bills	Up to 1 yr.	10,000	Book entry	Discount	Direct U.S. government debt	Nontaxable
Treasury notes	1–10 yrs.	1,000	Book entry; bearer or registered	Semiannually		
Treasury bonds	10–30 yrs.					
U.S. government agencies						
Federal farm credit banks	6 months	5,000		At maturity	Federal agencies	Nontaxable
	9 months		Book entry			
	1–15 yrs.	1,000				
FNMA (Fannie Mae)	Various	10,000		Semiannually	Quasi-government agency	Taxable
Federal Home Loan Bank					Federal agencies	Nontaxable
GNMA (Ginny Mae–Pass Through)	Avg. life 12 yrs.	25,000	Registered	Principal and interest monthly	Federal agency government guaranteed	Taxable

Money market instruments	Maturity	Denomination	Form	Interest	Backing	Tax
Commercial paper	1–270 days	100,000	Bearer or registered	Disc. or interest-bearing, paid at maturity	Unsecured promissory notes of corporations, rating on request	Taxable
	30–270 days	25,000				
Bankers acceptance	1–180 days	100,000			Backed by credit of bank accepting the instrument	
FNMA discount notes	30–360	50,000	Bearer	Discount	Quasi-government agency	
SALLIE MAE discount notes	5–360	100,000			Federal agency	Nontaxable
FREDDIE MAC discount notes	30–360					
FHLB discount notes		150,000				
FFCB discount notes	5–365	50,000				
Repurchase agreement	1–30 days	250,000	Book entry	At maturity	U.S. government federal agency	Taxable
Tax-free issues						
Municipal bonds	1–30 yrs.	5,000			Taxing power of issuer, or revenue from project	Usually nontaxable in state of issue
Short-term tax-exempt, notes	Up to 1 yr.	25,000	Bearer	Interest-bearing	Depending on type of note, some are fully guaranteed by U.S.	

2. **Discount brokerage services.** This is a relatively new area for banks and, with few exceptions, has not been highly profitable. The major problem appears to be that banks have been limited to trade execution and can not underwrite or offer investment advice. In addition, they have not marketed the service effectively. There are three types of accounts that banks are permitted to offer—a cash account for customers to buy stocks, bonds, and mutual funds shares in the normal manner through recognized exchanges, a margin account subject to the requirements of Regulation T, and an option account to exercise "puts" and "calls." Some discount brokerages owned by banks are now underwriting new issues on a limited basis, the legality of which is being challenged. This controversy over the right of banks to engage in more than the discount area of the brokerage function is expected to be resolved by Congress or in the courts so that banks may eventually participate in the same manner as full-service brokerage firms. Until that time, bank marketing managers should prepare for full service by building a customer base with the limited discount brokerage services.

INSURANCE PRODUCTS AND SERVICES. This is viewed by marketing-oriented commercial banks as an area for service expansion. The profit potential is considered to be greater than that of many of the traditional depository services. It is also apparent that banks already have an effective distribution network in place to offer insurance services, literally over the counter. By augmenting the frequent personal contact with branch customers, as well as through their extensive automation and computerized customer information sources, insurance sales through banks are expected to be cost-effective. As it is within the insurance industry itself, the key to volume is an effective marketing effort. For the moment, all that banks offer is a minimum product line based primarily on credit life insurance. They also offer insurance for lost credit cards and have travel accident policies tied in with credit card usage.

1. **Personal insurance products.** These products include auto, home, and life insurance for bank customers. Of particular marketing importance are the retired and upscale customers since they purchase more insurance than other market segments. For example, the affluent niche changes residences and automobiles more often than the general public, providing a steady market. The ability of branch personnel to market these products is limited; however, they can be trained to sell basic insurance products. To market

insurance products, those employees holding major marketing contact positions should be licensed with appropriate state agencies.

2. **Commercial insurance products.** These products include a wide variety of risk coverages since every business needs some form of insurance. Some of the more common types are casualty, workmen's compensation, key man, and liability insurance. Bank calling officers should be trained to recognize insurance prospects among their present customers as well as prospects uncovered when calling on potential customers. A sales follow-up with a trained insurance specialist will provide an effective marketing effort.

SPECIAL PRODUCTS AND SERVICES. As bank marketing strategies are directed toward particular segments or niches, the product differentiation effort becomes more crucial. There are numerous special products and services being offered, and more will be developed as the marketing effort intensifies within the financial services industry. Some of these services are traditional; others are the result of deregulation or the recognition of a marketing opportunity.

1. **Correspondent banking services.** This requires a network of mutual relationships between financial institutions that involves a variety of services; they are usually provided by a larger bank to a smaller respondent. These services permit both institutions to gain access to other geographical regions and expand the services available to their customers. Some of the services include check clearing, cash letters, loan participation, credit references, Federal Reserve balance requirements, funds transfers, foreign exchange, letters of credit, and operations support with computers from the correspondent's system. For all but the few large multinational banks, a correspondent relationship is necessary for international business.

2. **Equipment leasing service.** The leasing of capital equipment has become an important source of financing for business and professional customers. Leasing can be applied for such items as company aircraft, computer systems, ocean vessels, automobiles for private or company use, or factory machinery and equipment. There are tax credit options that affect leasing and must be considered when pricing the service. Most banks limit the scope of their participation in large capital equipment and prefer to finance independent equipment leasing companies or smaller local leasing operations involving automobiles and office furnishings. Some

banks also limit their exposure to lease syndications. For marketing, larger banks appear to be the best suited for this service since margins are thin and a high level of expertise is required to mitigate risk. Aggressive marketing action is necessary for developing presence in this specialized market.

3. **Personal banking service.** This is a competitive service that uses personal selling in a hands-on mode to obtain new customers and to retain present ones. Through the emphasis on personal recognition and care, customers develop a strong relationship with bank personnel, making it less likely that customers will change banks. Personal banker, as a designated title and function, is a position that requires training. Those who fill the job must have a thorough knowledge of product, credit skills, sales abilities, tact and diplomacy, and a continuing understanding of the best way to serve customers.

4. **Courier services.** This is a service of convenience for commercial customers. The bank provides a courier service to pick up or deliver deposits or other banking-related items at the customer's place of business and returns them to the bank for deposit or processing. This can be provided by arrangement with an armored car service or by a bank-owned courier fleet. This is an excellent service to offer in barter for demand deposit balances. Almost any business with large cash accumulations is a prospect for this service.

5. **Home banking service.** This permits customers to pay bills by using a deposit account debit and then transmitting the funds electronically to a designated creditor. As part of the service, banks provide a detailed list of those merchants, such as retail stores, utilities, and other local service organizations, who participate in the electronic system. Customers use their television receiver or computer cathode ray tube (CRT) to view account balance statements and to review recent banking transactions. Citibank has expanded its regular home banking service to permit data from the regular checking account to be fed into a complete finance program that sorts the customer's expenditures automatically into 120 categories for tax or budgeting purposes. Chase Manhattan has added a stock quotation display to their service and has a feature that permits the customer to buy or sell securities through Chase's discount brokerage operation. The possibilities for home banking should stimulate the imagination of innovative bank marketing managers, although recognizing the limitations against the physical exchange of currency.

6. **Telephone inquiry service.** This extended-hour telephone service provides customers with a convenient source for information about bank services and interest rates, as well as detailed account information. For example, balance inquiries and funds verification are the two most common questions that customers ask in the branches. Others involve check clearance and explanations of service charges. These and other operational queries can be handled over the telephone without a costly or time-consuming visit to a bank branch office. It is not only more convenient for customers but less costly to the bank.

7. **Off–balance sheet services.** Some banks are emphasizing products and services that do not appear as assets on their balance sheet. Among the most prevalent of these are standby letters of credit that produce fee income without an actual use of funds. These standby letters of credit are used often in international transactions as a guarantee that a company will pay an invoice. Operationally, these letters are carried as a contingent liability rather than an asset. There appears to be an expanding market for standby letters of credit; at Citibank, the outstandings for this product in 1985 was almost $20 billion. Another off–balance sheet service that generates fee income is interest rate swaps. This is a relatively new and growing service that involves two customers—one wishing to pay a fixed interest rate and receive a floating rate, and the other desiring to pay a floating rate and receive a fixed interest rate. This swap of interest rates may also involve two customers' wishing to exchange floating rate cash flows based on different indices. Both involve the exchange of interest payments in either case but without an exchange of the underlying liability, asset, or principal amount. This is another highly technical service, but it offers an opportunity for specialized niche marketing.

8. **Interest rate futures.** This is another relatively sophisticated service and requires a highly qualified marketer. The service involves the trading of interest rate futures contracts to reduce the customer's risk of higher interest rates caused by a mismatch of asset and liabilities maturities. This service offers customers the option of placing a ceiling on loan interest rates during a period of rapidly rising interest rates. As corporate treasurers become more familiar with it the market will increase accordingly.

9. **Export trading company (ETC).** With the approval of Congress, banks can now invest in export trading companies to provide customers in small and medium-size businesses with exporting expertise that is affiliated with the bank. This has opened up

important new sources of financing for the historically undercap-italized U.S. export industry. In conjunction with the Export-Import Bank program, loan guarantees will be provided for export trading companies. Up to this point, bank activity in ETCs has been disappointing and is centered primarily in countertrade (barter). The marketing effort should be directed to small U.S. trading firms, export management companies, or manufacturing and service firms considering growth through international trade.

10. **Investment banking services.** Some of the large money center banks are providing the services of investment banks. The Glass-Steagall Act prevents banks from underwriting corporate debt and equity, but they can engage in mergers and acquisitions and Euromarket underwriting. It is estimated that over 25 percent of most money center banks' earnings are now coming from investment banking services. These services are ideal for marketing by large banks because they already have strong relationships with potential investment banking service customers; they are usually the same clients being called on by the bank's calling officers to promote the sale of other commercial banking services. It is anticipated that the major banks will continue to expand in this service area.

The most critical elements in any bank marketing effort are the products and services the bank offers to the marketplace. The competitive environment and the age of deregulation places increased emphasis on new product development as each bank seeks new and different segments of the market while trying to retain its present share. The banking industry is characterized by many traditional products approaching obsolescence while substitute products and services with more attractive benefits are being offered by nonbank financial institutions. This dynamic marketing environment offers a challenge to bank marketing managers and their implementers, bank product managers. The financial services area will require new product development and the most innovative product management to keep abreast.

8

PRICING BANK PRODUCTS AND SERVICES

Like other aspects of the banking industry, the pricing of products and services is undergoing radical change. Because of deregulation and increased competition, interest margins have narrowed, as has profitability. As a result, each bank has had to reevaluate its sources of profit and its pricing policies. Loans are now being priced more competitively and services that formerly were provided free of charge are being unbundled and priced according to cost or market and are generating fee income when possible.

The changes in pricing requirements have also resulted in the need for more information related to the costs and ultimate profitability of specific products and services. Product costs provide only some of the information necessary for marketing managers to make pricing decisions. There are other considerations such as customer value perception, competition, and the specific bank marketing objectives as related to product and service volume. As more nonbanks enter the banking arena, they bring an acute awareness of the consumer perceptions of value that affect pricing decisions. This awareness has been developed through many years of consumer marketing; it is a dimension of pricing that marketing-driven banks are now recognizing as one of the important factors in addition to actual costs.

When purchasing products and services, consumers attempt to establish a relationship between price and value: *Price* is what consumers pay and *value* is what consumers pay for. Low price and high value are not usually bedfellows because the largest share of market is not usually obtained by the company that offers the least expensive product or service. On the contrary, market leaders are normally value leaders. The key to pricing is customer perception of value, and the key to value perception is need satisfaction. An informal law of marketing states that consumers are willing to pay more for whatever they define as value. In this regard, they actually measure value, but do so according to their unique specifications.

The sole determinant of the value of a product or service is consumer perception, which may or may not represent true value. Value must be established as being consistent with price, and several components of the selling proposition for bank products and services are used to provide the proper customer value mix. For example, products and services can be bundled into a single package such as free checking with a minimum balance savings account. Premiums can be offered such as reduced consumer loan rates to employees if the employer uses the bank's automatic payroll service. Convenience can be provided in many forms such as extended lobby hours, ATM network membership, or personal off-premises banking courier services.

PRICING CONSIDERATIONS. The bonds of tradition and pressures of time often lead bank marketing managers to emulate market leaders in their efforts to establish a realistic price. Decisions made under these circumstances are fraught with risk and do not necessarily take into account certain essential pricing considerations. In banking, as in many other industries, there is always a relationship between the price of a product and the consumer demand for its purchase and utilization. Once a price has been established, there needs to be some estimate of the way the price will affect customer demand. Too often such estimates assume that demand will not be affected. However, there are some basic economic concepts that can be applied to demonstrate the relationship between price and the quantity of product or service demanded. For example, higher prices always result in a demand for excellent service. In this situation, demand is elastic because the quantity demanded is usually greater than the rate of price change. If the reverse is true, as is often the case in ordering a supply of checks, price does not affect the volume of demand to any significant degree; price can be said to be inelastic for supplies of printed checks. Thus, elastic demand can be considered as price sensitivity and inelastic demand indicates customer insensitivity to price.

Elasticity has additional dimensions. There is elasticity within the marketplace as well as elasticity within an individual bank. Market elasticity indicates the way the market reacts in total to a change in pricing by all competitors; the inflow of deposits to banks from money market funds once their rates became more attractive is a good example. Bank elasticity measures the willingness of customers to move their accounts from one bank to another solely on the basis of price: price-sensitive retirees follow deposit interest rates closely, and it has been estimated that their margin of price sensitivity or muskrat range is between 25 and 50 basis points. (The term *muskrat range* refers to the propensity of this rodent family to migrate to new nesting areas once their population exceeds a certain number.)

Bank marketing managers should be familiar with the degree of elasticity associated with markets as well as with the bank. Elasticity will be greater in the marketplace—

1. where only a small percentage of potential customers buy the product or service, causing a lessening of primary demand (discount brokerage).
2. where a high rate of growth is anticipated in a particular market segment (IRAs to first nesters).
3. where the rate of usage can be increased by a substitute or new product or service (money market accounts).

Bank elasticity in the marketplace will be greater—

1. where the product or service represents a high percentage of the customer's budget (home mortgage).
2. where the customer perceives that the risk of poor quality between competitors is low (FDIC deposit insurance).
3. where the price change exceeds the norm in the market considerably (high check overdraft charges).
4. where many competitors offer comparable services and convenience (credit cards).
5. where the method of charging for services is not clearly understood (trust services).
6. where price sensitivity is built up through heavy price and premium advertising (toasters for new accounts).
7. where customers have more than one banking relationship in the same market (household versus business accounts).
8. where population attrition or immigration is high because of growing or declining communities (checking account gains and losses).

Proposed pricing can be examined on the basis of its probable effect on elasticity of demand by forecasting sales volume at each price level contemplated. The formulae are relatively uncomplicated:

(Old Price) × (Old Quantity) = Old Total Revenue
(New Price) × (New Quantity) = New Total Revenue

If the new revenue exceeds the old revenue, the demand is elastic. If the increase in revenue does not offset the price change, the demand is inelastic. Bank marketing managers usually look toward increased demand as a source of increased profitability. If an attempt is made to increase demand in the market as a whole, it is considered a *primary pricing strategy;* if it is directed toward acquiring additional demand from competitors, it is a *selective pricing strategy.* In either case, there are several other influences on price sensitivity or elasticity.

1. **Availability of alternatives.** The more substitutes that are available, the greater the opportunity for switching banks.
2. **Importance and frequency of use.** Some financial services are not considered sufficiently critical to cause price to be a major consideration in customer dissatisfaction.
3. **Awareness of difference in price–value relationship.** There must be a recognizable shortfall between price and value before customers change banks.
4. **Variety of product and service use.** Those used widely are more elastic (for example, credit cards with check guarantee, ATM network compatibility, and use for credit purchases in retail stores). Providing more services for less cost stimulates usage and justifies selection of one credit card over another.
5. **Product and service switching time.** Adverse reaction to price changes is seldom evident immediately if the product or service, such as trust or cash management, requires a lengthy conversion time to change banks.
6. **Nonprice benefits.** These include prestige, convenience, bank personnel attitude, and other factors not necessarily associated with price.

The pricing considerations of most concern to bank marketing managers involve customers and competitors. Customers make a value analysis of the selling proposition of the product or service being offered. Value is perceived on the basis of the reliability of the bank as it performs the various financial services, convenience of its delivery system, financial information and advice provided, and degree of deposit security offered. The aggregate of these various benefits plus the price constitutes the selling proposition of the bank's line of products and services. Although convenience continues to be the most significant competitive advantage as indicated by consumer research, price is becoming more of a factor as financial service competition begins to establish banking services as a basic commodity for which value is measured more by pricing considerations. As a case in point, the bank's transaction account has several dimensions to its pricing, which include more than the amount of interest earned. Table 8-1 on transaction account pricing indicates the numerous charges and sources of interest payment associated with most transaction accounts offered by banks. This worksheet can be used to assist bank marketing managers in their analysis of the competitive environment for this generic product that is the key to most banking relationships.

The competitive considerations in pricing are changing as nonbanks enter the marketplace. There is a proliferation of transaction accounts, and other sources such as money markets are providing for the borrowing needs

Table 8-1. Transaction Account Pricing

Type of Account	This Bank	Bank A	Bank B	Bank C	Bank D	Thrift A	Thrift B	Credit union
Minimum balance								
Monthly service charge								
Interest rate Standard Below minimum balance								
Annualized yield								
Method of interest Compounded daily Compounded monthly Compounded quarterly Paid monthly Paid quarterly On collected balance On ledger balance								
Interest computation 365 days 360 days								
Cancelled checks Returned Truncated								
Check supply charge Basic Deluxe								
Per-item charge								
Stop payment charge								
NSF/overdraft charge								
Dormant account Charge Months to be dormant								

of customers as well. The rate of growth of traditional demand deposits has slowed, and they are less viable as a dependable source of bank funds. The development of share drafts by credit unions, NOW accounts, and various other forms of transaction accounts offered against margin accounts by brokerage firms has challenged the formerly exclusive province of bank checking accounts so that pricing has become a major promotion tool in the marketing of new transaction accounts. The large companies and institutions are bypassing commercial banks in favor of the commercial paper market. The larger firms have also improved their cash management capabilities, resulting in less use of this important banking service. As a consequence, commercial banks have now increased their dependence upon the retail credit market, a market that is very price-sensitive. Finally, to make pricing decisions, it is important for the bank marketing manager to understand the various components of the price-setting process. The three main components of concern are pricing objectives, pricing methods, and pricing strategies.

PRICING OBJECTIVES. As in pricing or demand elasticity, bank pricing objectives are concerned either with the marketplace externally or with the bank internally. Pricing objectives for the market deal with the specific impact that is to be registered against customer demand in total. Internal objectives for the bank may use price as a key product or service ingredient for obtaining growth in assets or liabilities, an increase in share of market, profitability in terms of return on assets or earnings per share, liquidity to permit more flexibility in resource commitment, and stability to reduce fluctuations in deposit and loan volume.

In terms of customer-oriented pricing, objectives and goals can be established to acquire new customers from new arrivals in the marketplace and present customers from competitors or from those consumers not currently using the product or service. Retention of present customers is a defensive profit objective, but it does provide an opportunity for profitability because of reduced sales costs to reach these existing customers. Increased demand by current customers through the cross-selling of other services can be encouraged with price concessions. Price can also change the usage patterns of customers and reduce the cost of operations support. For example, pricing concessions for the use of ATMs for routine transactions rather than using in-branch personal teller service offers a pricing advantage while reducing costs.

The specific pricing objectives to be considered by the bank marketing manager are usually the most logical in the eyes of senior management. These include those dealing with profitability targets on an annual basis that measure return on investment, return on assets, or earnings per share. If the corporate objective is growth-oriented, profit objectives have to consider increases in sales volume or share of market. Another pricing objective is concerned with market stabilization, which is used to discourage price cutting and to desensitize customers to price; this is usually an option only open to market leaders. One objective that will be utilized more frequently as competition heats up is pricing to help maintain price leadership. This objective not only discourages the market entry of nonbank institutions, but makes expansion on a national basis more costly; a side benefit of this objective may also be encouraging exit from the market of marginal, nonbank competitors. The last pricing objective is directed to increasing the visibility of specific products and services. Pricing can help build a wider customer base and create more immediate bank product interest and consumer familiarity.

The use of some of the various pricing methods to accomplish pricing objectives is another element in the pricing decision-making process that requires identification and analysis before the adoption of specific prices. The methods now available to bank marketing managers are far more numerous in this age of deregulation and competition than they were during the previous era of relatively nondiscriminating banking. The free market is hard at work so that the methods of pricing now fall into two major categories—traditional pricing methods used for many years and opportunistic pricing methods being adapted by banks from similar methods developed and used by other industries, including those in financial services that now compete with banks.

TRADITIONAL PRICING METHODS. The concept of basing prices on cost was developed originally for the manufacturing sector, where the cost of labor and the value of finished goods were relatively easy to measure. In these industries, variable costs tended to exceed fixed costs. In banking, the opposite is true: inventories of finished goods are nonexistent and labor costs vary widely with different banking transactions. Thus, costs are difficult to determine precisely. In spite of this difficulty, banks have traditionally based their pricing decisions on costs, using three methods—average costing, analysis of cost versus volume versus profit, or incremental costing.

In average costing, banks depend upon the annual functional cost analysis of banking services compiled by the Federal Reserve. This valuable reference source provides comparative cost data for a variety of banking functions and reports them according to specific volume levels to make up for differences in the size of banks. The raw data are provided by banks throughout the country that participate in the annual study. The total cost reported consists of both direct and indirect allocations, with direct costs applied only to the individual service. Those indirect costs that cannot be traced to individual services are allocated by relative share on a logical basis. Once all costs have been allocated to the various services, the total cost is divided by the number of transactions to obtain the average cost per transaction. When a major change in volume is anticipated by the marketing manager, either of the other two traditional methods is more appropriate than average costing.

There is a relationship between profitability and volume. This becomes a key consideration in pricing when excess capacity is a factor in the bank. Obviously, if a bank can increase branch transaction volume without increasing the overhead, any savings in cost become profit. The key to such a relationship is referred to in business as *economies of scale*. In such a situation in which increased volume is readily obtainable through a price reduction, such a pricing method can result in economies through increased volume that in turn affect profit margins favorably. To analyze the profitability potential of a price change by using this method, the following formula is suggested: Profit equals price minus the variable cost per transaction times the volume minus the fixed costs. To recommend any price change, the result contemplated should exceed the current profit level. To analyze alternate pricing levels, the following procedure is recommended:

1. Identify both fixed and variable costs.
2. Identify the minimum acceptable profit level.
3. Identify the price levels being considered.
4. Determine the volume required to reach the profit level at each price being considered.
5. Assess whether the volume is obtainable at each price.

The recommended formula for determining this is the following:

$$\text{Required volume} = \frac{\text{Fixed cost} + \text{Profit level}}{\text{New price} - \text{Variable cost}}$$

However, there may be some negative side effects with greater volume. For example, customer service may suffer with longer teller lines, greater loan volume may require more risk, and increased customer bases through volume often result in smaller deposit or loan balances, which are more costly to service on a per-account basis.

The third method of traditional costing involves the incremental costs associated with changes in volume. These are fundamental in the pricing of new products and services and to marketing managers' attempts to predict the impact of a change in price and volume of present services. The incremental costs are the differences in costs added through new product introduction or other significant changes in present volume. Costs due to a change in volume include all variable costs; however, in some instances, an increase in volume of existing products and services can be handled without additional expense. In new product introduction, the incremental costs are the net changes in all bank costs as a result of the new service. However, a new product or service may well be able to share existing bank resources without adding much additional cost. These costs are also affected by account size; it is less costly to service large accounts or those with limited usage. This situation has fostered more selective pricing methods to encourage larger deposit balances or fewer transactions. The last important consideration in incremental costing is the cost of funds. This cost becomes an incremental cost to the extent that additional funds must be raised to support new asset-based products or services when greater sales volume is the marketing objective.

OPPORTUNISTIC PRICING METHODS. As an adjunct to cost pricing in the traditional sense, many banks are using cost-plus pricing, which adds a specific percentage mark-up on top of the operating expenses and the cost of funds. This cost-plus or mark-up method has no apparent relationship to value, and it may understate the price acceptance level of consumers. If so, this may cause the bank to miss an opportunity for increased margins. An example of cost-plus pricing can be found in loan rates, using the following formula: Interest income (rate times amount times time) plus the value of earnings of balances plus fee income equals the gross contribution to bank income. The efficiency of the pricing method can be measured in terms of yield by

$$\text{Yield} = \frac{\text{Gross contribution to income}}{\text{Average loans outstanding}}$$

For the more esoteric, prestigious, or complicated products, consumer value pricing is recommended. Customers for these products and services are relatively price-insensitive and place more consideration on perceived value than on price alone. For example, a personal checking account at Morgan Guaranty has more value to certain market segments than one at less cost at Chase or Citibank although the latter two have more resources and are more readily accessible for service. The method identified as competitive pricing is related to value provided, but it generally involves only the most generic products. In this method, the price is determined by the cost or market leader among competitors. A case in point is the prime rate. There are four or five money center banks in New York City who establish the prime rate, and the remainder of the industry throughout the country adjusts their prime rate accordingly.

Industries other than financial services have provided additional pricing methods that have been adapted by banks. For example, skimming pricing is based on a relatively high price to maximize short-term profits; fees for interest rate futures offered by very few banks can be priced accordingly, particularly in a rising interest situation. Skimming can also be used when targeting high-value customers or when introducing new, innovative products. The opposite of skimming is low-ball pricing. It is used when aggressive marketing action is contemplated to increase share of market or to hold market share against new entrants. This is a very short-term method whereby products and services are sold at cost or at a slight loss. Penetration pricing is a middle course between skimming and low-ball pricing. It is used to achieve an increased share of market quickly. In the marketing situation favorable to this method there is a large untapped potential. The bank must posses sufficient resources to support high volume that is characteristic of the results obtained with penetration pricing. Another favorable situation is one in which competitors are relatively few or are slow to react.

In addition to these, there are several other opportunistic pricing methods. Obviously, pricing for an opportunity that results from economic or other circumstances outside the bank's control is another viable method. A good example of this is a situation in which the availability of credit is tight. However, pricing to take advantage of a lender's market may have harmful long-term effects since it may invite customer defection to other banks that may be using penetration pricing methods to encourage switching banks. Another method of use in certain circumstances is loss leader pricing. This method can serve as an excellent cross-selling device by building branch traffic with a basic service that is priced below market at cost. To recover the loss, this method must result in the sale of a companion product at the same time. An example of this is a low-cost auto loan tied in with credit life insurance. Defensive pricing methods are used to prevent loss of market share or to discourage market entry by competition. This differs from low-ball pricing in that it is used over a longer period of time by banks who have been in the marketplace for many years and possess a large, stable customer base. It is more of a retaliatory action than one designed for increasing share such as penetration or low-ball pricing, which are used mostly for that purpose. The last of the opportunistic methods is demand-oriented pricing. This method fluctuates according to either total market or specific customer demand. The auto loan market is often driven by this method by setting lower interest requirements during periods of weak new car demand and higher prices when demand is strong. The credit arms of the major automobile manufacturers such as GMAC adjust interest rates to match sales demand and inventory levels. Strong competitors like GMAC and Ford Credit affect bank pricing levels for auto loans.

PRICING STRATEGIES. The strategies available to the bank marketing manager make selection difficult because the strategies favored most frequently by senior management are bank- rather than customer-oriented. They usually prefer pricing related to cost or levels set by competitors. Such pricing strategies may leave the bank vulnerable to the possibility that customers will not pay the price established. One solution to a lack of appreciation of the realities of the marketplace by senior management is to initiate a value-based strategy. In this strategy, the marketing effort is supported by pricing that is acceptable to high-value-seeking customers. These are the ones who are most likely to buy when unusual value is perceived. Low prices often suggest to this niche that the quality of service may be questionable.

There are certain dimensions to a value-based pricing strategy. The first depends upon the value that is added beyond the intrinsic price. This includes such variables as convenience, service efficiency, delivery system quality, and egocentric appeals. Some consumers appear to be willing and eager to pay more for such value, and they look for the price-value relationship primarily in terms of banking convenience. Convenience is measured in several ways and even includes the extent of the product and service selection and the number of alternatives available. This is best represented by the breadth of the product line and the value added as perceived by the customer. Some banks may have a relatively narrow product and service line in total, but it may be sufficiently broad to serve the needs of a particular niche without qualifying as a full-service bank. One example of a high-value-added and a relatively narrow-product-line bank is the Bank of California with limited services for upscale customers. Bankers Trust is another example; both of these banks have sold most of their retail branch system. Citibank and Chase are relatively low-value-added banks offering broad product lines. Morgan Guaranty is a high-value-added bank with a relatively broad product line for its particular customer base. Most thrift institutions are examples of low-value-added sources with narrow product lines.

There are other pricing strategies of importance such as those that price products as substitutes for others on the market or those that are complementary to other products or services offered by the bank. A substitute pricing strategy is designed to be consistent with certain marketing objectives. For example, pricing the credit card attractively to certain market segments allows it to be used in the place of small personal loans that are more costly to administer. Home equity loans offer a substitute for refinancing the original home mortgage, which may be at an interest rate below the current market. Another compatible marketing objective is to use a pricing strategy that reaches those segments who would not otherwise buy any of the substitute products or services; certificates of deposit rates tied in with Treasury bill rates may appeal to some bank customers who consider passbook savings as offering interest rates that are too low. They may also prefer acquiring a CD to the procedure for purchasing Treasury bills. A shift to other products or services can also be encouraged to reduce bank operating costs; the debit card and POS terminals may require a greater capital commitment, but large savings will accrue in the cost of processing checks when direct debit is not possible.

Complementary services may be priced to increase profits or to increase sales volume. If a new product or service enhances the value of one that already exists, such as self-directed IRAs that use discount brokerage services, there may be an opportunity to seek a higher fee for either or both services. There are many complementary services to improve the marketability and price of checking accounts. These include overdraft protection, ATM access cards, direct payroll or retirement deposit, and automatic bill payment. Products such as checking accounts that are considered basic or lead to the use of other services may require price incentives to build a customer base for cross-selling other complementary products that bind the customer to the bank. Such key products are promoted aggressively in retail banking. In commercial relationships, the complementary products and services to checking accounts include direct deposit, account reconciliation, and pension and profit-sharing accounts. These continue to be underutilized, however. Complementary products are best priced in a package or, in banking terms, bundled. Bundling offers a group of services for a single price instead of setting separate prices for each one. For example, a credit card, debit card, and check guarantee card can be combined into one plastic card with a single annual fee.

Some bank marketing managers have discovered to their regret that many products and services either are neutral or attract only low-balance accounts. Pricing neutral services requires a strategy of its own. For example, overdraft questions and balance inquiries are associated more frequently with low-balance customers; giving away free checks without per-item charges or minimum balance requirements stimulates more transactions rather than reducing costly account activity. The trend in banking is toward unbundled products and services in order to be certain that each one pays its own way. Thus, the pricing of some neutral services has changed. Banks have repriced overdraft charges and have reduced or eliminated the free float time between use and payment of credit card charges. Other services such as returned checks and pay-by-phone charges have also been increased to cover costs and profitability. Another advantage of such a pricing strategy is that it removes the undesirable situation in which the income from some customers subsidizes the services provided to others.

PRICE POSITIONING. Coincident with the pricing strategy selection is the price positioning determination. As commercial banks become better known by type of customer and product menu rather than by size alone, the way the bank is positioned according to its pricing methods and strategies is another important point of differentiation. Here are some of the possibilities for bank positioning relative to pricing.

1. **Prime rate traditionalist.** Still links price primarily to risk and maturity factors.
2. **Relationship pricer.** Seeks proven client relationships with loan or deposit price incentives.
3. **High-volume discounter.** Works with thin spreads, either as a funds gatherer or as a credit allocator.
4. **Low-volume entreprenuer.** Wide spread risk taker who knows his borrowers well.
5. **Product value pricer.** Views the value of the product or service to a customer as the key pricing consideration.
6. **Prestige pricer.** Specialized banking with premium pricing for both product quality and service exclusivity.
7. **Product price bundler.** Packages services and prices them in total rather than by item.
8. **Bargain basement pricer.** Achieves market share or product penetration by low pricing and mass marketing.

IMPLEMENTATION OF THE PRICING DECISION. In reaching the pricing decision, the bank marketing manager must also determine the degree of pricing freedom that exists in the current marketing situation. The basics in pricing freedom consist of the amount of value of the product or service as perceived by the target customers. Next, the relative intensity of the local banking or financial services industry should be considered. Once these factors are estimated, the marketing manager should review the product line and the market in terms of both value perception and competitive stature. If the product or service is judged to be of high value and against little competition, the price can be established independent of sales volume. If the product has a relatively low value and competition is prevalent, the supply and demand forces at work cause the price to be driven by volume rather than by value. If it has high value and stiff competition, then a competitive pricing strategy prevails. If the value is unknown or not firmly established in the minds of consumers, as is the case of new products, price becomes an independent variable regardless of competition.

When implementing a pricing decision, there are several adjustments that can be made in the pricing structure. They may or may not require changing price, although a change may be used to increase the perceived price-value relationship. For example, extending a loan maturity at a current rate or establishing an interest rebate plan based upon deposit balances can offset the customer reaction to increased pricing. Discounts are also a price mechanism for all businesses. Banks can use this method in such areas as merchant discounts on credit card sales draft processing once certain volume levels are achieved. Consumer premiums and sales incentives are forms of added value that do not disturb the basic pricing structure. Careful analysis should be made of each account over a predetermined size. The sample account analysis form in Table 8-2 can be used for a review of both customer profit contribution and pricing levels by each calling officer. This not only serves as an important measurement of the commercial marketing effort but also provides a pricing control mechanism.

A specific procedure or process for relating cost to price is usually necessary to satisfy senior management in spite of the many new methods available that are based on factors other than costs exclusively. However, the realities of cost of funds and administration can never be ignored. Thus, bank marketing managers may wish to establish a procedure for price analysis and planning based on costs. In price-cost planning, it is necessary that the current pricing structure be analyzed after developing appropriate pricing data. A specific pricing strategy is selected with respect to cost and competitive considerations. Once the strategy is selected, sales and profit forecasting is required and compared with the cost targets. As a result, a final price-cost plan can be developed with price change options, cost reduction alternatives, or a combination of both. A suggested procedure or process flow for a price-cost analysis and plan is listed next for use by the bank marketing manager.

1. Define the existing price structure.
2. List prices by major bank competitors.
3. Calculate the current gross profit margins.
4. Identify products for immediate price-cost consideration.
5. Establish cost experience curves.
6. Establish price experience curves.
7. Establish historical sales volume levels.
8. Forecast future sales volume levels.
9. Assess competitive marketing situation.
10. Establish bank profit objectives.
11. Select pricing methods.
12. Select pricing strategy.
13. Estimate costs based on sales forecast.
14. Estimate profitability based on price-cost spread.
15. Design procedures for cost control.
16. Implement price changes.

Several variables including cost are essential in establishing prices for products and services that will deliver the margins necessary for profitability. The proper or most advantageous price floor varies with each bank. This is necessary because all banks have different operating capacities for

Table 8-2. Customer Profit/Pricing Analysis

Customer name. _____

Account officer. _____ Period. _____

Flow of funds

Average loan balance		_____
Demand deposit balance	_____	
Time deposit balance	_____	
Less reserve requirement	_____	
Total deposits	_____	
Less investment funds supplied	_____	
Net funds used	_____	

Account income

Interest income on loans		_____
Earnings on total investable deposits		_____
At money market rates	_____	
At cost of funds rates	_____	
At rate of return on bank portfolio	_____	
Fee income		_____
Total income		_____

Account expenses

Account maintenance	_____	
Loan administration	_____	
Interest on time deposits	_____	
Cost of other services	_____	
Trust	_____	
Payroll	_____	
Cash management	_____	
Courier	_____	
Insurance	_____	
Letters of credit	_____	
Other	_____	
Total expense		_____

Account spread

Income	_____	
Less expense	_____	
Account spread		_____

each product and service. However, regardless of which profit method or strategy is adopted, bank marketing managers should recognize that not all lines of products and services can be marketed using the same method or strategy of pricing, and not all will be equally profitable. Such diverse elements as competition and customer demand may require that the prices of some products and services be set close to the price floor; others may have a relatively large price-cost spread. Another note of caution for marketers is the fact that not all customers are equally profitable. This phenomenon is due to usage patterns and varies even though they use the same service through the same delivery system.

Bank marketing managers should also be aware of some pricing problems in the commercial loan marketing area. Lending officers in many banks have sufficient discretionary pricing authority to influence the overall bank profitability significantly. Therefore, bank marketing managers must establish account objectives for the major accounts of each calling officer. These objectives must tie in directly to the profit objectives of the bank. The management of commercial customer relationships is best handled through formalized procedures such as the customer profit/pricing analysis in Table 8-2. The marketing control processes such as this must be supported by an excellent information compiling and organizing capability. To make bank profit objectives meaningful, customer account performance must be monitored continuously.

IV

BANK MARKETING ACTION

9

BANK DISTRIBUTION

Bank distribution is best defined as the key marketing function between the bank and its customers that provides the utility of product availability and service convenience. Its major components are logistics, or the technical support requirements provided by the bank's backroom operations, and the delivery systems, the channels used by customers to obtain bank products and services. The process of distributing products and services is usually considered in terms of direct costs to the bank. However, looking at distribution only as an issue involving costs for the delivery of services does not acknowledge it as one of the principal strategic weapons available to bank marketing managers. Poor distribution coverage and reduced productivity can be responsible for losses in customers as well as sales volume. Hence, bank distribution provides the critical linkage between operations and customer service.

BANK DISTRIBUTION ENVIRONMENT. At the present time, deregulation and competitive pressures have altered banks' distribution environment. In the past, delivery systems were usually centered around a permanently located "brick and mortar" office, a branch providing personal service. Within these structures the business of banking was conducted during fairly rigid time periods on a one-on-one basis. The new environment for the delivery of financial services has recognized for the first time that there are many facits of consumer behavior that affect the process. These include the convenience provided by time as well as place, the level of customer service expectation, the cost of products and services, and the type of personal contact customers desire. At the same time, pressures on profit margins, rising operating costs, and the increasing capital-intensive nature of the banking business have made it necessary for banks to lower their noninterest expenses, to increase the productivity of delivery systems, and to make the time and place factors of convenience more competitive with those of other financial services institutions.

Competitive delivery systems from nonbank financial institutions are the most compelling sources of pressure for banks to alter their past reliance on the traditional branch office, almost to the exclusion of other channels. For example, insurance companies are augmenting their personal sales efforts and heavy direct mail solicitation through their traditional insurance agency delivery systems to other forms of mass marketing such as telemarketing. They are also trying to lower costs of sales in the process of altered delivery. Money market funds are using mass communication media to solicit customers at relatively low cost-per-thousand advertising message exposures instead of using brokers and calling officers for more costly personal contact. The use of toll free 800 telephone numbers and postage paid return envelopes is now responsible for the great majority of customer transactions; direct office contact in person by customer is negligible. The financial supermarket concept is being pursued aggressively by Sears through their Financial Service Centers. These centers are staffed during extended store hours with representatives of Allstate, Dean Witter, Coldwell Banker, and, in California, the Sears Savings Bank. In addition, they have plans for a consumer bank in many of their stores nationally based on the nonbank bank loophole in current banking regulations.

There are several misconceptions affecting bank distribution environment that bank marketing managers should recognize. The Management Analysis Center (MAC) has identified some of these after extensive research in the banking industry. One misconception is that by adding products to the current delivery system, profitability will be improved since direct costs will be spread over a broader range of product sales. More product is not necessarily better as some banks can attest after adding discount brokerage services. Another industry myth concerns the technological explosion. Some automation specialists would have banks abandon almost all manualization in favor of machines. The personal service branch office will always be required in some number to serve those customers who require—or think they require—hands-on service. One last misconception is the one that new customers offer banks more opportunity for profitability than present ones. It is almost an inviolate marketing law that repeat sales are less costly, and, therefore, more profitable, than those made initially to new customers. In spite of this law, some financial services institutions seek customers from other supposedly greener pastures, whereas the most successful firms put their major marketing effort toward the cross-selling of present customers.

BANK DELIVERY PROVINCES. The distribution environment for commercial banks is centered primarily in four delivery provinces: near where the customer works, near where the customer shops, in the home or office, or through communication media. Using the latter, banking is conducted by telephone, by coaxial cable, or by mail, rather than by a personal visit. These delivery provinces are subject to the following variables that affect the relative effectiveness of each province. They, in turn, determine which type of delivery system or channel is used predominantly by a specific type of financial institution to reach the desired segment of the marketplace.

1. **Demographic forces.** These include changes in population mix that indicate an aging trend, a change in affluence, a higher level of education, or presence of more women in the work force.

2. **Technological innovations.** These result in the improved use of computerized information systems, more efficient sales transaction procedures, and improved communications (Videotex, Teletext, and Cable).

3. **Operating flexibility.** This has improved banking convenience with seven-day, twenty-four hour facilities, a dramatic growth in nonpersonal service, and decreased customer resistance to changes in traditional operating methods.

4. **Competitive pressure.** The type of financial service institution in each market can indicate which delivery system is most appropriate. The various financial services include those discounting services (Bank of America's Charles Schwab), those withdrawing from full service and specializing in certain services only (Bankers Trust), those full-service banking institutions who are adding even more services (Citicorp), and those providing national franchising (First Interstate).

5. **Inevitable competition.** Although only in the early stages of competitive growth, there are other sources of financial services that are developing whose ultimate delivery systems may require strong bank counteraction. These include those circumventing traditional banking regulations (nonbank banks), those with a limited array of bank-related services (insurance institutions offering only IRAs or asset management), those in off-bank premises locations not engaged in bank-related services (grocery and convenience stores).

6. **Marketing positioning.** The two key dimensions of positioning, service value and product selection, are also important considerations in the delivery provinces. These include high value–broad product line (Morgan Guaranty), low value–broad product line (Citibank), high value–narrow product line (Bankers Trust), and low value–narrow product line (Sears Savings Bank).

7. **Bank merchandising adaptability.** Each delivery province can be identified further by a preferred approach to informing customers and prospects. These include using mass communication

media for reaching large market segments, using specialized media for individualizing products and services, or initiating bank actions that emphasize quality of service rather than particular products through customer contact personnel or in-branch displays.

DELIVERY SYSTEM PERFORMANCE REQUIREMENTS. In the past, all delivery systems for financial services were designed to provide a uniform and relatively high level of service. Now, many undedicated high-service delivery systems include more low-cost, low-service channels such as direct mail, telephone, ATMs, or personal service banking agents such as couriers for the relatively uncomplicated products and services that are easily sold to a broad customer base. The more complex products and services are sold through the more costly, high-service-oriented channels such as the personal service branch and individual, more knowledgeable, investment counselors. The latter channels are more productive when participating in marketing programs that are designed to satisfy customer need instead of competitive pricing.

In redefining its distribution performance requirements for the total institution, Citicorp, the parent of Citibank, devoted several years to the exploration of new delivery channels while the banking deregulation process progressed. It concluded that Citicorp would function as a national distribution company for financial services by offering a full line of products with an emphasis on service and price trade-offs. As part of the requirements for its financial services subsidiaries, Citicorp decided to establish a broad, national delivery system that would implement the most cost-effective distribution or logistical methods to replace the high cost of traditional personal banking offices. One of the fundamental concepts of the approach of Citicorp was to employ new channels such as on-line interactive networks, banking by mail, by phone, and at the point of sale. One version, the self-contained banking kiosk, takes up less than five hundred square feet and contains two ATMs and an office for a customer sales and service representative. This satellite of a personal banking branch can be installed in two weeks in a high-consumer-traffic area for one-third the initial investment of a typical personal service branch, maintain it for one-fourth of the normal branch operating costs, and, if the location is not sufficiently productive, move it to a better location. Citicorp has decided that one of the essential requirements for a delivery system is off-premises, personal banking that breaks the local as well as national geographic barriers to the branch banking concept of convenience of time and place to suit individual customers.

Another delivery system requirement concerns the specific physical location of the channel. Banking customers usually evaluate the channel locations by some of the following criteria:

1. **Location.** The location of the channel installation in relation to egress and ingress. It should be consistent with the individual customer's driving or walking patterns for work or shopping. Ample parking is mandatory, and access should offer some protection from extremes in weather as well as ample lighting for personal safety.
2. **Product and service inventory.** The basic banking products and services should be readily available, as well as any special products particularly appropriate for the market segment served from the location.
3. **Type of delivery channel.** As customers become more vertical in their behavioral characteristics, channel preferences have also become more fragmented. For example, older consumers are less trusting of ATM transactions, fearing that the wrong button would wipe out the record of their balances. Young professionals, on the other hand, utilize the personal service branch less frequently because of time constraints.
4. **Merchandising.** The specific price-value relationships of the basic product line and the service support being offered through the channel, including the bundling, packaging, and display of customer benefits.
5. **Bank transaction process.** The ease and convenience provided for banking transactions, including information available, method of personal contact, employee attitudes, and the reliability of operations support equipment.
6. **Advertising and sales promotion.** The decor and image of the channel as reinforced by mass communication techniques to the degree that consumer peer group identification with the particular location is egocentric, attractive, and highly acceptable.

These location criteria are always evaluated on a comparative basis with other bank channels in the same, approximate location. Many are unacceptable, or neutral, for reasons that may be of little consequence to any but the particular customer making the comparison. For example, the rationale for selecting one installation over another can be based on such minor irritants as narrow parking spaces, poor heating or air conditioning systems, uncomfortable lobby seating, lack of free coffee, poor writing instruments, or any of a dozen other minor differences. Regardless of the various idiosyncrasies, the choice of a particular channel is a complex process involving the evaluation criteria, the perceived characteristics of competing channels, the consumer comparison process, and the ultimate determination of those most and least acceptable. Prior to the selection of channel type and its specific location, bank marketing managers should obtain shopper or worker profiles based on both demographic and psychographic data.

DISTRIBUTION STRATEGIES. The various types of delivery channels provide different levels of service from machine execution to hands-on professional assistance. Each transaction has certain servicing characteristics and ranges from the routine to the complex, and from local, to regional, to national availability. Unfortunately, since all transactions have some relationship with money, customer emotions also run the gamut from the passive to the hyperactive. There are times when keys can be pushed and others when hands must be held. The most successful strategy continues to be one that offers less extensive transaction options for faster service, yet matches most of the needs of the local target customers with a relatively popular product line. Cost considerations suggest that, except in the most unusual circumstances involving high-value-added banks, the channels with less extensive characteristics and less dedication to many products will be lower in cost to remain in operation. However, in the race for bank and service differentiation, alternative approaches that provide multiproduct availability and transaction characteristics permitting the selection of personal or machine service at the same channel location may be selected. This is quite prevalent in traditional branches with twenty-four-hour ATMs installed through the outside walls of personal branch offices.

The preceding criteria are all applicable and must be considered as a prelude to the actual selection of the particular distribution strategy (Table 9-1). It is obvious that the distribution strategy must be consistent with the bank marketing strategy. However, it should not be confused with the type of delivery channel available. Channels to be used are always determined after the distribution strategy has been selected. Since the distribution strategy depends upon both logistical requirements and delivery channel availability for implementation, it is basically a decision arrived at through an analysis of the physical location and the scope of the bank's operation. In general, six distribution strategies can be used:

1. **National delivery.** This strategy is usually one requiring heavy capitalization by financial service institutions with low debt-to-equity ratios as in the case of nonbanks. All must have excellent product management capabilities; planning and marketing expertise are essential. Large customer bases are necessary to support the lengthy logistical structure. There are very few institutions who can qualify for this strategy. These firms may include some of the money cen-

Table 9-1. Distribution Strategy Selection

	Current bank strategy	Other strategies in market	Opportunity for strategy
National delivery Heavy capitalization Rigid cost accounting Outstanding management in depth Strong R&D capability Outstanding marketing expertise Separate strategic planning unit Reliance on economies of scale Leading correspondent bank Loan syndicator Acquisition-driven Wide corporate identity Major depository institution Decentralized management Broad customer base			
Regional delivery Strong capitalization Emphasis on cost controls Excellent senior management Some R&D capability Concentrated marketing effort Effective corporate planning Correspondent bank Loan syndicator Too costly to acquire Strong regional presence Second-tier depository institution Centralized management Broad customer base Very competitive to nationals			
Statewide delivery Moderately well-capitalized Efficient cost control system Strong middle management Limited product differentiation Heavy channel density In-depth market coverage Small unit bank correspondent Acquisition target Decentralized control Good political leverage Rural and urban representation Medium loan syndicator Highly visible leadership			
Urban-suburban delivery Adequate capitalization Selected channel locations Centralized management Strong community involvement			

Table 9-1 (continued)

	Current bank strategy	Other strategies in market	Opportunity for strategy
Respondent bank Horizontal organization Limited financial expertise Acquisition- or merger-minded Local investors Modest marketing effort Limited product line Reliance on network participation Commercial and retail emphasis Loan participant			
Satellite cluster delivery Adequate capitalization Few full-service centers Limited-service satellite channels Centralized management Lower asset base Special customer niches Vertical organization Strict cost controls Machine-driven channels Limited financial expertise Reduced product line Selected market coverage Respondent bank Heavy retail emphasis Acquisition target Unique architecture			
Independent unit delivery Minimum legal capitalization Small closely held ownership Single unit in network Limited organization and expertise Limited marketing effort Respondent bank Acquisition target Limited customer niche Recently established			

ter giants such as Citibank, Bank of America, Security Pacific, and Chase, as well as American Express, Sears, and J. C. Penney. It is obvious that the key players in this delivery strategy are already preparing for channel entry and are seeking acquisitions aggressively outside their primary market or specific line of business.

2. **Regional delivery.** The basic requirements for regional predominance are also drawn by strong capital support and excellent senior management. The resources of banks using this strategy, although not as extensive as those distributing on the national level, are still considerable. The marketing effort must be interstate, and they must be prepared to compete head to head with the nationals through aggressive marketing, rigid cost controls, and a very broad and loyal customer base. Some of the best regionals include Wachovia, Wells Fargo, Chemical, First Interstate, and Mellon. Their distribution strategy concentrates on serving regions that comprise several contiguous states. Banks using this strategy are usually too large to be acquired because of the investment required. Thus, these banks rely on a series of acquisitions to reinforce their position in the market and to solidify a parochial customer base against the eventual competitive onslaught by national delivery financial institutions.

3. **Statewide delivery.** The number of banks using this distribution strategy are restricted by the number of states permitting branch banking. They are also limited to one or two per state, with the exception of California and New York, where they are more numerous. Some banks in the unit banking states of Illinois and Texas meet the strategy specifications of capitalization and political leverage but cannot provide rural as well as metropolitan representation physically because of state branch banking restrictions. The true statewide strategy requires in-depth market coverage through a multichannel network in small rural communities as well as in the urban business centers. Strong middle management is essential to sustain the heavy channel density. Banks selecting this strategy include Valley National, Rainier, Barnett, Marine Midland, Bank of Virginia, and North Carolina National Bank.

4. **Urban-suburban delivery.** This strategy uses in-state locations that are very selective. Capitalization is only sufficient to support a relatively limited product line and moderately knowledgeable staff. The investors are usually local, and the stock is traded over the counter with limited trading activity. Channels are only located in areas of considerable banking potential, both business and residential, to reach a specific target market through a modest marketing effort. These banks rely on network and correspondent bank par-

ticipation to enhance banking convenience; their principal competitors in the statewide category offer channel density throughout the same market. Management is highly centralized, with a thin, horizontal organization structure. These banks are heavily involved in the community, and their target market is a niche rather than a broad customer base. They are a third-tier depository and are in the large middle group in size of assets. Every metropolitan center over 250,000 in population has three or four banks adopting this distribution strategy.

5. **Satellite cluster delivery.** In an effort to provide market coverage at less cost, some banks mix full-service channels with those offering limited service. There are cost savings that can be realized by clustering several satellite branches around a full-service, supportive "mother hen." The satellite channels achieve cost savings because they are machine- rather than labor-intensive. Product and service referrals are sent to the mother branch since the satellites provide only basic banking services, and principally retail rather than commercial. In most cases, the satellites are only glorified ATMs with one customer service representative in attendance. The lower deposit base and highly vertical organization are characteristic of this distribution strategy. In an effort to achieve additional cost savings, market coverage is selective, and the institution is spartan, featuring no-frills facilities. Such low-margin services as safe deposit boxes and merchant night depository are eliminated. Most, however, offer some form of drive-up service.

6. **Independent unit delivery.** This strategy is one associated with small, independent banks and limited to one or two branch offices. Those states such as Missouri, Colorado, Texas, and Illinois with unit banking only also have large unit banks such as Republic in Dallas, Continental of Illinois, and First National of Chicago. These large banks usually qualify as having a regional delivery strategy. However, unit banking states as well as those permitting branch banking have numerous independent units. It is estimated that the majority of the fourteen thousand U.S. banks fall into this distribution strategy. Most of these banks have the minimum legal capitalization and have a small, closely held ownership by local businessmen. Because of limited resources, the organization and depth of expertise are shallow. Some of these banks have been formed recently for the primary purpose of attracting buyers once the charter has been obtained and a fair customer base has been established. In branch banking states, these banks offer a less costly alternative to expansion by larger banks through the *de novo* process.

The distribution strategy selection requires an analysis of the various characteristics associated with each of the six types of strategy. Bank marketing managers can use the distribution strategy selection worksheet (Table 9-1) to help determine the current strategy of their bank. Once identified, the strategy can be compared with the strategies of the other banks in the market. Completing the analysis allows opportunities for an improvement or change in distribution strategy to be identified. Any distribution strategy selected, before final implementation, should be reconciled with the bank's transaction characteristics, product and service lines, as well as with the types and costs of the various delivery channels needed for the strategy.

TYPES OF DELIVERY CHANNELS. By defining distribution components as part logistics and part delivery channels, it is apparent that the latter is the critical area of customer contact. The point of delivery is where transactions are not only completed, but are contemplated in the first place. Thus, delivery channels are an inseparable part of the consumer's banking decision-making process. Traditional channels are being replaced or augmented by new types of delivery. In spite of marketing opportunities created by deregulation, competitive cost pressures, and new delivery technologies, some banks have continued to try to sell different products through the same old channels and often by the same contact personnel. Bank marketing managers should resist the temptation to achieve cost savings by pushing new products and services through existing channels. Sound marketing reasoning will point out the folly of such a course of action:

1. Additional products delivered through channels in common often suffer because products turn out to be too dissimilar.
2. The type and level of service necessary for the expanding range of financial products do not require the same degree of personal attention, financial guidance, or technical expertise.
3. Whether based on a mass body of consumers or a specific vertical niche, the particular characteristics of the target market are seldom similar in terms of financial sophistication, risk tolerance, or buyer behavior.
4. Calling officer or branch contact personnel vary widely in their training requirements, sales skills, or basis for compensation and motivation.
5. The convenience issue continues to be so critical for customers that any compromise in terms of less efficient delivery will not be acceptable.

6. The initial cost savings may be offset by declining sales volume and the eventual loss of economies of scale.

The explosive growth in communications and the technological advances in the delivery of financial services have made bank marketing managers realize that they no longer need to rely solely on the traditional "brick and mortar" branch offices. In addition to the delivery system currently in place and operating, new, nontraditional methods of delivery are also available to be activated. Customer acceptance has combined with savings in labor to make many of the new methods cost-effective and volume-generating. Several traditional and nontraditional delivery channels can be adapted by the bank marketing manager for use in planning effective courses of action (Table 9-2).

1. **Personal banking delivery channels.** These traditional branch banking offices were the original home of full-service banking. This free standing structure of grandeur, resplendent in the marble decor, mahogany fences, and thick pile, has now evolved into a modern, well-lighted, functional structure with computer terminals at every teller station, automatic balance inquiry, twenty-four-hour cash dispensers, and other technological triumphs. The branch of the past, rooted in one location from the beginning and never to be closed in spite of neighborhood decay, now can be shut or moved away. The personal service branch is now available in a variety of forms: as integral units or lease departments inside mass merchandising stores such as K-Mart or as full-fledged departments in Sears. Small versions of storefront banks are located within neighborhood shopping centers with walls in common with adjoining retail stores. Other machine-driven efficiency units such as minibranches, kiosks, and satellite offices are also being used extensively. Rural or mountainous areas where population is sparse, such as many areas in northern California, are served once or twice weekly by recreation vehicles converted into mobile banking offices. Those consumers working in plants or in large office complexes are also served on a limited basis by mobile banking carts or by couriers after hours who pick up or deliver while providing a limited number of special products or services. In some areas, remote drive-up facilities are located some distance away from the basic banking structure and provide extended-hour service.
2. **Automatic teller machine (ATM) delivery channels.** There has been phenomenal growth in the number of ATMs and ATM transactions. By 1985, IBM and Diebold, ATM manufacturers, reported that nearly half of U.S. bank customers have used ATMs

Table 9-2. Delivery Channel Analysis

Census tract. _____ Zip code. _____	This Bank	Bank A	Bank B	Bank C	Bank D	Thrift A	Thrift B	Credit Union
Personal banking Freestanding office In-store office Store front office Minibranch (kiosk) Satellite office Mobile truck Mobile office cart In-person courier Drive-up								
ATM Freestanding In-store installation In-branch accessory Exclusive use Shared use Cirrus Tyme Pulse Plus Money express Instant teller Master teller Visa travel network The exchange Nationet								
POS Exclusive Shared								
Home/office banking Videotex Pronto Compuserve Citibank financial Video financial (VFS) Viewtron Spectrum Trintex Telephone access								
Telemarketing Telephone sales Direct mail sales Account information								

and that more than 25 percent use them for most of their bank transactions. *The Wall Street Journal* has estimated that over 60,000 transaction terminals are currently in use and that over 100,000 will be in use by 1990. By substituting ATM access for personal service branches, those banks adopting a national distribution strategy such as Citibank will be able to market more effectively on an interstate basis with ATM networks. In an effort to cut costs, banks are also encouraging customers to use ATMs instead of costly bank tellers. Some are also providing less costly lifeline checking accounts to lower-income customers by incorporating ATM usage as a partial requirement for the account.

Because of the capital investment necessary to provide in-branch or free standing ATM installations by a single organization, shared equipment provides some relief from the extensive capital requirements. Shared ATMs in the form of membership in ATM networks are now being provided by numerous independent companies and consortiums. However, there are individual bank marketing requirements in network membership as the complexities of interchange across local, regional, or national geographic areas grow and the options increase. Few bank marketing managers fully understand and appreciate the esoteric nature of a shared ATM marketing environment. As customer usage expands, the interchange position of the bank relative to competition, as a net provider of ATM service or as a net user of the service, becomes an important consideration in the success of an ATM marketing effort. Network membership is now readily available from many sources. Those banks with their own ATMs can add their machines and locations to any system they join.

3. **Point of sale (POS) delivery terminals.** As part of an electronic network similar to ATMs, banks are connected directly to merchants to make real-time credit available for merchandise sold. Charges are debited from the accounts of customers that both the bank and the merchant have in common. The POS not only verifies the validity of the bank debit card of the customer and the PIN code identification, but processes the transaction while determining whether there are sufficient funds to cover each purchase. A well-designed POS system is more convenient than personal check approval, but since customers lose personal check float time and checking accounts are free or very low in cost, the fee that can be charged for a POS debit is very limited. In addition, most retailers are reluctant to pay any more for a POS transaction than they are able to realize in the savings for check processing at their bank. Nevertheless, the benefits of tighter inventory control through in-

terface with their own computer system, the close monitoring of sales, and timely data capture are now possible. Therefore, POS terminals are being accepted and installed at a growing rate, primarily by leading cash-oriented retailers such as gas stations and convenience stores, including large retailers such as Exxon, Mobil, Seven Eleven, and Circle K. To be economically feasible, a POS network must generate extremely high transaction volume. This obviously requires strong marketing support by both banks and retailers through mass communication media and aggressive promotion at the point of purchase.

4. **Home and office delivery channels.** The mass off-premises banking market concentrated in homes and offices requires a special technology such as a personal computer via a modem through the standard telephone system or a videotex terminal. The number of home or office banking customers is quite small, but it is growing as the hardware and necessary software become more widespread in offices and residences. In a 1985 survey, the *American Banker* estimated that a total of forty-four thousand customers and small business owners were using personal computers to conduct their basic banking from the home or other remote location. A number that small is not sufficiently encouraging to attract many banks; however, some industry pioneers have invested heavily in the service. Chemical Bank with its Pronto service and Bank of America have made their entrance early and are committed to providing home banking services. Chase, Manufacturers Hanover, and Citibank are beginning to market their home banking services aggressively as well.

If home banking can be combined with at-home shopping faster market growth can be anticipated. It has been estimated that 45 percent of U.S. consumers would subscribe to an at-home shopping service and that 25 percent would use the service regularly. These figures are not startling when the increasing use of shopping by mail is considered. The number becomes even more exciting to marketers when considering the capability of providing every home in the country with such a service. Just to participate in a modest share of this business opens a banking potential for exploitation that should whet the appetite of bank marketing managers. For the moment, however, the growth in home banking is steady, if slow, because of the hardware requirements. The service menu is also restricted, with many banks' limiting the services offered to funds transfer, bill payment, and account balance information. However, from a strategic marketing standpoint, bank marketing managers must determine whether to become involved in home and office banking at present or to wait for at-home shopping to pave the way.

5. **Telemarketing delivery channel.** Some bank marketers consider telemarketing to be a selling technique and a more efficient method for reaching banking prospects. However, because telemarketing seeks customers and delivers product as a result of the solicitation, it is better classified as a delivery channel. This delivery channel has grown substantially in usage as the personal contact between banks and their customers is lessening, not only because of cost considerations, but through a decline in the perceived need by customers. Telemarketing provides a complementary adjunct to the personal sales activity and is more effective for inquiry response, sales lead qualification, extension of the effectiveness of the mass communication effort, and replacement of traditional in-branch retail banking. It permits the application of cost-effective telecommunication techniques to reach specific target markets on a timely, one-on-one basis.

As a delivery channel, telemarketing provides a bridge between the impersonal ATM contact and the need for a personal exchange of product information and customer requirements regarding financial services. Many customers demand personal interaction for some products or services such as IRAs that are complex because of tax implications, earning options, time commitments, and control over the type of investment to be made. In addition, telemarketing provides a potential for price advantage; the delivery of products and services through telemarketing, by telephone or direct mail, costs substantially less than face-to-face delivery. This savings can be passed on as a rate or cost advantage. With personal service continuing as the major factor in maintaining customer loyalty, telemarketing provides a delivery channel that treats every consumer as an individual.

With such a wide choice of delivery channels, bank marketing managers should examine each delivery option before determining which offers the most effective means for delivering product to target customers. Within a market, customer needs vary widely from the suburban residential neighborhoods to the urban commercial areas. Therefore, a delivery channel analysis should be made for each census tract or zip code in the bank's marketing area. The delivery channel analysis form in Table 9-2 has been provided for this purpose. Once the analysis is completed, the bank marketing manager can better determine which channels to select for specific marketing action.

10

PERSONAL SELLING

In spite of the dramatic growth of the banking segment of the financial services industry over the past 20 years, sophisticated management of the personal sales effort has often been lacking. Bank marketing managers have become professional managers in many areas but have seldom applied sound management principles to the important selling function. The competitive nature of the industry now requires that banks direct their personal selling effort with the same degree of professionalism applied to the credit and operations functions.

There are several differences between selling and managing. For example, the bank calling officer's primary responsibility is to develop and service accounts, and the marketing manager's chief responsibility is to develop and maintain the selling effort. Customer contact personnel in the branch offices have responsibilities that are higher in priority than personal sales. Any sales activities are secondary to the branch operations function. These people report to branch managers or operations supervisors and have no direct organizational linkage to the bank marketing manager. Whereas branch personnel work as a team, the calling officer usually does the job alone. Thus, the marketing manager must accomplish a successful sales effort through others as individuals or through the branch delivery system.

The most productive salespeople are self-starters, loners in a sense, who are primarily interested in themselves, their customers, and the bank, often in that order. The sales management function must be directed toward developing talented individuals and those with primary responsibilities other than sales into a productive team without inhibiting the entrepreneurial spirit of each calling officer and without interfering with the operations functions of branch customer contact personnel. The bank's sales effort is complicated further because the bank marketing manager is often a member of the senior management team and has other responsibilities in addition to the one-on-one administration of individual calling officers or the cascading of directions through organizational channels to the branch office system. The bank marketing manager must plan and organize the personal selling function and then coordinate and control the effort on a synergistic, bankwide basis.

There have been misunderstandings about the difference between sales and marketing. Even though sales has been categorized as a key component of marketing, some traditional bankers have been reluctant to add the "sales" terminology to accepted banking jargon. They have been willing to add "marketing" as a functional identification, but designations such as *calling officers, customer service representatives, account officers, loan officers, and account executives* continue to be used instead of *salesmen* or *salespersons*. Notwithstanding, sales remains as a key component of marketing and is acknowledged to be so by most bank customers in the conduct of their respective lines of business. In fact, in the most successful business organizations, personal sales is one of the three major areas of marketing activity—the others being mass communication and sales promotion, which will be discussed in detail later in chapters 11, 12, and 13.

As a major marketing component, sales has some specific responsibilities. Sales emphasizes the needs of the seller. Those engaged in the personal selling function must be preoccupied with the needs of the bank for additional revenue. They must sell products and services that generate income immediately. Marketing on the other hand, is concerned with the bank's customers. It develops and delivers those products and services that satisfy the needs of the customers. Sales sells what marketing provides; marketing provides what sales can sell. Writing in the *Harvard Business Review,* Theodore Levitt concluded that selling is finding customers for what you have, and marketing is making sure you have what customers want.

It remains the province of the bank marketing manager to provide product leadership and to be concerned with the emerging technologies and their effect on future financial products. This particular responsibility is often delegated to product managers who serve on the staff of the bank marketing manager. The sales management function provided by those supervising the calling effort as well as some of the more resourceful branch managers is concerned with the responsibility for distribution leadership. These individuals must be aware of the marketplace and its immediate effect on sales. In a sense, marketing is strategic and sales is tactical.

Personal selling, as opposed to mass communication or sales promotion, involves direct contact between the seller and the prospect or customer. In banks, personal selling is either deliberate or indirect. Deliberate personal selling is accomplished primarily by calling officers or by customer service representatives in the branch offices. Some bank directors or advisory committee members also exert direct sales pressure on business associates. Indirect personal selling is the result of employees who cross-sell in addition to other primary duties. All customer contact personnel such as tellers, telephone operators, safe deposit attendants, and guards have an element of personal selling in their jobs. Whether deliberate or indirect, there are several accepted methods of selling:

1. **Stimulus-response selling.** This is a memorized sales presentation that is well rehearsed to present various strong selling arguments that have been designed only to elicit a single response that is an agreement to buy. It is used for training inexperienced personnel to sell uncomplicated products and services, or for selling by professional telemarketers. The technique is often too impersonal for banking and is considered a form of high-pressure selling that is not very effective for most bank products and services.
2. **Need assessment selling.** This is used to encourage customer response in situations in which the customer may not be completely aware of the specific nature of the financial problem. The customer is permitted to do most of the talking so that the bank's salesperson can respond accordingly after demonstrating good listening skills and isolating the problem.
3. **Formula selling.** This is a mechanistic and relatively inflexible sales method that has a specific sequence in the sales presentation that invites occasional responses from prospects or customers. These responses provide the necessary cues for advancing through each selling sequence. It is also used for less experienced bank personnel or for more complicated products and services.
4. **Problem-solving selling.** Many prospects or customers are most receptive to sales presentations when they are faced with a personal or business-related financial problem. The role of the bank representative is to serve as a counselor or consultant by providing expertise and making specific recommendations. This method is particularly effective with new customers or prospects as a prelude to long-term banking relationships.
5. **Relationship selling.** This is the ultimate in financial services selling since the customer relies almost exclusively on one bank and one customer representative for all bank products and services. In this situation the bank's representative is accepted as the individual customer's personal banker or as a trusted financial consultant to the principal or the chief financial officer of a business organization.

Personal selling is an essential function for financial services. Because of the high emotional dimension of money, very few bank products and services can be classified as presold by mass communication or as products that are accepted generally as being necessary. For example, most national brands of consumer convenience products such as food, cosmetics, and drug items are purchased by self- or limited service. Other products such as capital goods, automobiles, and major appliances require personal selling because, as with most financial services, many of these are complex and are being marketed to customers with a limited knowledge of the product. Even checking accounts require some degree of personal selling. They are increasingly complex because of varying account balance minimums, service charge schedules, and usage limitations that require a personal exchange between buyer and seller. It is because of these complexities that personal selling has several areas of activity that must be considered by the bank marketing manager in the implementation of a successful personal selling effort.

THE PERSONAL SALES FUNCTION. Many banks are not organized properly to provide a productive selling effort. Some bank personnel attach prestige and self-esteem to those relationships with large corporations that emphasize the more sophisticated products and services. This false sense of superiority works to the detriment of smaller customers who require only the basic services. A bank selling culture of this kind often results in a high turnover in calling officers since the desirable career path may be perceived to be one that advances quickly through a series of small customers to sales responsibilities of larger size and complexity. The common error in this scenario is that small-size customers using a minimum of products and services can be made most profitable by expanding the extent of their banking relationship. The emphasis on relationship selling, or in-depth salesmanship, results in stronger, higher-revenue-generating customer ties regardless of company size or individual net worth.

In order to encourage relationship selling, bank marketing managers should develop a selling sequence that provides a uniform and highly efficient flow of sales from the initial product to subsequent products and services offered by the bank. Depending upon the general sales target, there are three models suggested for establishing a relationship selling sequence for calling officers and other customer contact personnel. One model is used for corporate banking, a second for small-business or light-industrial customers, and a third model for personal banking. Each model has an initial series of products and services that have been identified as the most frequently used by customers during their first relationship with a bank. These initial products and services must become the basis for expanding additional relationships with the bank through universally used products and services. These have been identified as the demand deposit account for business customers and the basic transaction account for individuals. From these universally used accounts, banking relationships are expanded with some of the other products and services indicated in the suggested relationship selling sequence models in Figures 10-1, 10-2, and 10-3. It can be seen that each model has two additional major product or service relationships—cash

Figure 10-1. Relationship Selling Sequence (Corporate Banking)

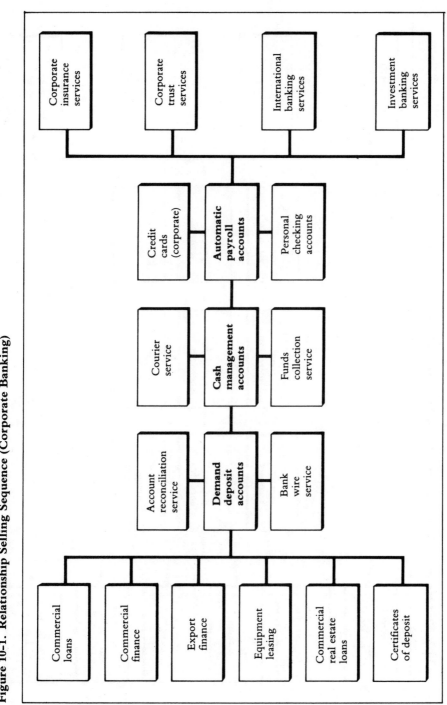

Figure 10–2. Relationship Selling Sequence (Small Business–Light Industrial Customers)

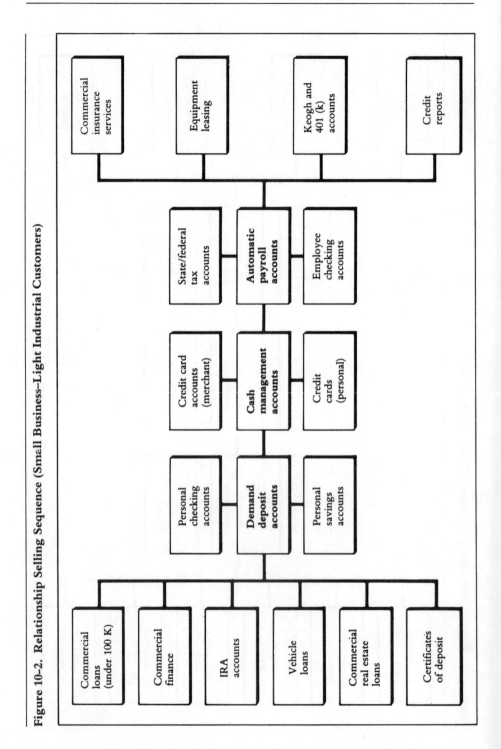

Figure 10-3. Relationship Selling Sequence (Personal Banking)

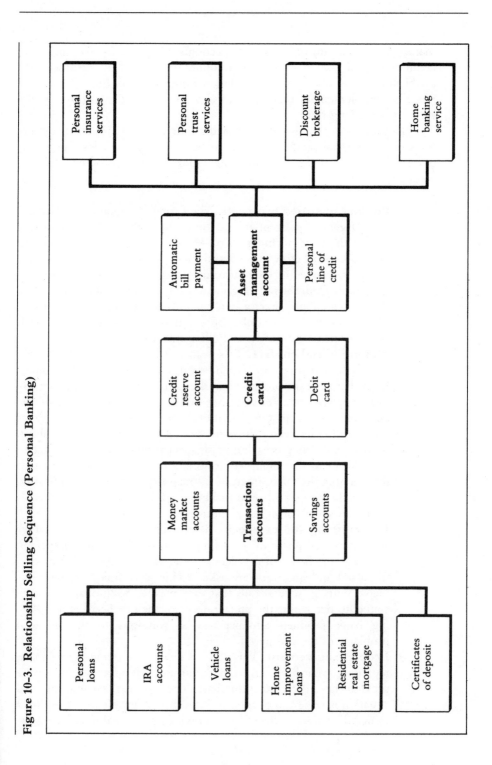

management and automatic payroll accounts for business customers and credit cards and asset management accounts for individual customers. By establishing these three common relationships, the bank can offer a wide range of complementary products and services to keep the customer in the bank over the long term.

Regardless of whether the personal selling effort is planned or opportunistic, there are several basic steps to be taken by the sales representative in the course of the customer solicitation for bank products and services:

1. **Finding qualified prospects.** The formal designation of primary sales targets is an essential function of the bank marketing manager during the sales planning stage. However, each prospect must be well qualified before any commitment of sales time and expense. Prospect sources include customer referrals, media-generated inquiries, or from the use of standard prospect lists from such sources as the telephone directory, Dun and Bradstreet's computerized company lists, local chamber of commerce rosters, and others from specialty firms such as R. L. Polk and F. W. Dodge.

2. **Making initial contact.** This is an important step in selling since most sales situations are dependent upon the initial rapport established between the prospect and the calling officer or customer service representative. First impressions are critical because of the emotional issues surrounding money. It is in this first meeting that buyer and seller personalities may meld satisfactorily and establish mutual confidence as each investigates the other informally, face to face. Clues to the selling environment can be discovered through determining the major interests of the prospect and other indicators such as the type of office furnishings and the general characteristics of the prospect's business or industry.

3. **Determining the prospect's needs.** This is the working rather than the social phase of the selling process. The bank salesperson identifies the financial problems of the prospect as the business is discussed and questions are asked. This phase may not be completed without several calls that may involve additional bank personnel to determine the precise needs of the prospect before offering bank products and services as solutions to the financial problems of the prospect.

4. **Problem agreement.** This phase is devoted to obtaining feedback regarding what has been learned and understood as a result of the previous need determination phase. The prospect's current financial situation is reviewed openly, and the specific problems are outlined in detail. If not uncovered in a previous phase voluntarily, an au-

dited or reviewed personal or company financial statement must be obtained. This is a critical requirement for loan-related products or services.

5. **Solution agreement.** Once the financial problem and specific need have been identified and understood by the prospect and the bank representative, the recommendations are presented and an agreement is reached to establish a relationship with the bank. In sales parlance, this is known as "closing the sale" or "asking for the order." Since there are always several facets of a selling proposition, it is necessary to discuss such items as pricing, maturity, and any major covenants at this time to prevent surprises during the formal acceptance phase that follows.

6. **Formal acceptance.** This phase is often conducted on bank premises for commercial relationships and almost always for individual customers. Bank presence is more convenient for handling such documentation requirements as account signature cards, loan agreements, collateral assignments, check selection, and other administrative matters. This is also an excellent opportunity for the introduction of the customer to key bank personnel who are in support of the relationship.

7. **Relationship expansion.** The last phase is one that is on-going and coincidental with the after-sale servicing of the initial product or service. As the customer is served, bank sales as well as servicing personnel should be conscious of the opportunities for cross-selling such as those indicated in the relationship selling sequence models. Additional products and services not only increase bank revenue but make it cost-effective to spend more time in learning more about the customer's line of business and ways additional products can help.

It is essential when following these seven sales steps that bank calling officers and contact personnel develop a thorough knowledge of bank products and services. This knowledge is necessary for the application of bank resources most appropriately to satisfy the needs of the customer. It helps communicate the ability of the bank through the individual representative to solve specific financial problems more professionally than the competition. By understanding product, the bank officers increase the personal confidence and conviction that are necessary to present and demonstrate the superiority of the bank's products and services. Lack of knowledge becomes readily apparent to customers and prospects when a product is described without reference to customer benefits or a plausible explanation of the way the service operates to deliver the promised benefits. It is also necessary that a cause and effect relationship between a service and its benefit features be established before customers will accept claims made for the selling proposition by the bank representative.

SALES TRAINING. One of the keys to increasing sales is to make bank salespeople more effective through training. Formal training in credit and operations has long been the capstone for developing professionalism among bank personnel. It has been estimated that direct sales representatives such as calling officers make only fifteen personal calls to customers each week and that the majority of these calls are primarily social, wasting time rather than producing sales, facilitating service, and directly benefiting the customer. Effective sales training for banks includes instruction in bank products, competitive information, pricing structures, prospecting skills, customer qualifying, counteracting objections, customer support options, and proven sales closing techniques. These are the major subjects to be covered in training sessions.

There are two generally accepted philosophies of training bank sales personnel. The first is the one that customer contact not be permitted until the individual has been fully trained, not only in the knowledge of the bank and its products and services, but also in productive selling techniques. Other banks prefer to have sales personnel prove their natural and technical ability and desire to sell on the department or branch level before the bank invests in costly training programs for them. Regardless of which philosophy prevails in a particular bank, the need for training never ends with the completion of the initial program. Bank calling officers and other contact personnel require refresher courses continuously.

Most bank sales training programs, because of the perennial shortage of experienced salespeople, are broad in scope and may include the following general topics:

1. **Product and service knowledge.** This training includes the advantages and disadvantages of each product as demonstrated with features that comprise the complete selling proposition. An understanding of competition as well as specific opportunities for product application must be provided in depth in the training program for sales personnel.

2. **Target market knowledge.** Closely allied with the need for product knowledge is familiarity with the specific targets designated by the bank marketing plan for product application. Target market training should also include prospect identification and qualification on the basis of specific customer need as well as some of the common financial problems to be encountered in the selling effort.

3. **Sales policy and procedure knowledge.** The terms for both as-
set- and liability-based products must be understood, as must the
procedures for implementation and control. These policies and procedures include not only the ones established by the bank, but any
legal or regulatory considerations as well. In addition to policy and
operational procedures, details on qualification, pricing, maturities,
and availabilities are also desirable.
4. **Sales techniques.** This training should include becoming familiar
with the selling process from the preparation phase to the sales
close. Role playing is often used for training purposes and has
proved to be an excellent training technique for recognizing such
key cues as when to listen, how to overcome sales objectives, and
how to respond to competition. The natural inhibitions of bank
personnel require that heavy training emphasis be placed on the
behavioral aspects of salesmanship.

The overriding training objectives in the competitive situation facing
banks are those that suggest more emphasis be placed on the techniques of
selling. From a behavioral point of view, there are three areas that are crucial
for the development of successful salespeople. The first is to improve listening skills in order to comprehend the description of the financial problems by the prospect. Next, the bank officer needs to increase interaction
skills as an aid in sensing the prospect's predisposition about the way a
banker is expected to behave and to react accordingly. Last, the basic communication skills must be improved so that the various characteristics of
verbal exchanges and nonverbal cues can be interpreted properly to increase
selling effectiveness.

Sales training should attempt to correct or prevent many of the weaknesses that have been associated most frequently with sales representatives.
As reported in *Sales and Marketing Management,* the following criticisms of
sales personnel were identified:

Poor planning of time and effort
Lack of effort, motivation, and aggressiveness
Failure to call and develop prospects
Uncooperative attitude
Insufficient product knowledge
Poor self-conduct
Lack of selling ability
Poor sales judgment
Poor customer service
Little attention to detail
Improper handling of expenses

Inexperience
Misuse of support facilities
Lack of persuasiveness
Failure to evaluate sales potential
Failure to follow policy
Inability to follow procedures
Poor account administration
Poor communication skills
Impatience
Failure to apply training
Poor use of merchandising techniques
Lack of follow-through
Poor decisions
Lack of full-time sales effort

The selection, training, and motivation of direct sales personnel, as represented by the bank's calling officers, are essential activities in which the bank marketing manager must be involved. In the selection process there are several characteristics and qualifications identified with productive calling officers. Some general qualifications are good health, energy, and vitality. Calling officers should possess strong motivational forces through such special desires as relative freedom from undue restriction and tight supervision; they must also need to excel and to influence others. Emotional maturity is a desirable quality that permits the calling officer to accept criticism, to come back after defeat, to learn from failure, and to avoid blaming others for any mistakes. Being persuasive enables the calling officer to convince prospects, through discussion, to agree or to alter opinions and attitudes. The officer must also be flexible, energetic, acceptable in appearance, and socially skilled. This detailed specification probably explains why there is a shortage of well-qualified calling officers in the banking industry. It also indicates that training is only part of the requirement for an effective personal sales effort.

SALES EFFECTIVENESS. Bank personnel engaged in personal selling can only be as effective as their understanding of what motivates prospects, what products and services are available for sale, and what the competitive situation is in the marketplace. To direct this knowledge in concert, the bank marketing manager must prepare a formal sales plan that outlines the specific action to be taken by sales personnel. Although there appears to be a growing potential for financial services, an effective sales plan requires the specific designation of sales targets. The most attractive targets are always the established customers of the bank, particularly those who are using only a limited number of the bank's products and services. These targets not only are the critical ones for the bank but are often being targeted by competition. Another target with excellent potential is those customers who are experiencing changes in their operation, personnel, or facilities; they often require additional financial services. Banks have the inside track to sell such customers because they are often presold on the bank's capacity to perform, and the selling process is less costly and usually takes less time. A complementary prospect base can also be found among the employees of the bank's established customers, who often turn to the company's bank for individual banking services. Other desirable targets include inactive or previous customers as well as organizations and individuals not being served adequately by competitors.

The bank marketing manager becomes the focal point for coordinating the personal sales effort. The formal sales plan is the key instrument of coordination, and it is responsible for developing sales synergy throughout the bank's delivery system. There are several sections or parts of a formal sales plan that involve great detail. These sections include the following:

1. **Selling situation.** This section of the formal sales plan is devoted to the analysis of the selling opportunities. This is indicated through an identification of the most desirable target markets and their product or service requirements. A thorough review of the competitive situation helps determine ways to offset or neutralize any competitive advantage. This competitive analysis should include an inventory of primary as well as courtesy services provided by competition as well as any organizational or personal features that make them attractive in the marketplace. The situation analysis should also include a review of the bank's delivery system as compared with competition.

2. **Selling proposition.** The attributes of bank products and services must be listed in detail. This should not only include pricing and maturity factors but provide specifics on any strengths or limitations on bank policy and procedure. There are also logistical considerations such as twenty-four-hour availability, one-day loan approvals, network membership, or correspondent relationships that may add to the attractiveness of products and services. The factor of convenience should never be underestimated as a key element in the selling proposition.

3. **Sales objectives.** To provide proper direction for the sales program, a sales forecast must be included in the formal sales plan. This not only is necessary as an integral part of goals and objectives for sales personnel but is needed to justify the marketing expendi-

tures proposed in the total marketing plan. In addition to a detailed sales forecast by product and service, this section of the plan should include both sales and customer contact quotas by territory as well as by individual sales representative. Gross margin targets, goals for expense control, and other quantitative measures of performance should be covered in this section.

4. **Marketing support requirements.** Since support for the sales effort can increase sales effectiveness, a section that provides a review of the sales promotion and mass communication support scheduled for the personal sales effort should be included. In addition to advertising and public relations programs, other essential operations support such as electronic data processing and internal reports affecting customers should also be covered in detail. This section is quite important because it indicates that the total organization supports the efforts of the individual sales representative.

5. **Sales control and coordination.** The methods for reporting and measuring sales performance are outlined specifically in this section. In addition, a detailed operating budget and implementation schedule are provided. Other reports such as market intelligence, economic forecasts, and regulatory bulletins are cited for coordination purposes; sources for obtaining such reports are identified for use by individual calling officers. Finally, sales meetings must be planned and scheduled to conduct sales progress reviews and informal training sessions with appropriate sales personnel. These meetings should be held with sufficient frequency to maintain the desired level of control over the sales effort.

The essential elements to improve sales effectiveness are not limited to the formal sales plan. There are several areas related to the proper orientation and training of the bank personnel responsible for personal sales that require additional attention by the bank marketing manager. These include familiarizing calling officers and other customer contact personnel with the qualitative aspects of the sales function.

1. **General background** to understand and appreciate the bank, its organization, and the opportunity it affords to sell successfully in the marketplace is critical to preparing sales personnel to become effective representatives of the bank. Details to be covered include the bank's philosophy of conducting business, its corporate objectives, its analysis of growth potential, and its marketing policies and procedures for achieving growth and profitability. Each salesperson should also be familiar with the structure and lines of au-

thority of the selling organization, as well as the staff support role of product managers and marketing specialists in advertising and promotion.

2. **Product background** to become well equipped to contact commercial or retail banking prospects, detailed information on new product and service developments, innovative usage by other firms and individuals, and any anticipated changes in application of financial services must be part of each calling officer's base of knowledge. To be a credible source, sales personnel must have a timely and in-depth awareness of the technical aspects of each product relating to its application, quality, customer benefits, fee schedules, and interest rate structures. These micro elements should be combined with macro information of the financial services industry as a whole.

3. **Market background** to become familiar with sources of market information can often provide a service dimension most appreciated by bank customers. This is also useful for the individual calling officer in the necessary function of collecting meaningful data for use in maintaining customer and prospect information files that offer a source of data for use in preparing for sales calls. The current state of the market should be reviewed frequently so that each sales representative can appreciate the strengths and identify any weaknesses of the bank versus competition. If changes in the market can be identified in advance of competition, the opportunity for sales can be enhanced.

4. **Sales methods** enable salespeople to plan productive sales activities to understand the importance of market coverage and calling frequency. This requires an understanding of the elements in the advance preparation of a sales call, the effective use of customer information files (CIFs), and situations necessitating calling on the bank staff for technical support. Sales personnel should also be aware of the factors determining prospect potential and techniques for identifying accounts worthy of additional sales contact and cultivation.

5. **Staff promotional support** making individual sales representatives aware of bank advertising and promotion campaigns in advance allows them to coordinate their sales effort to extend the effectiveness of the promotional activity. This not only requires familiarity with the promotion tools and sales aids available, but an understanding of ways they can best be applied in a specific selling situation. These aids can include simple pieces of product literature or elaborate desk-top presentations of complex banking services such as automatic payroll and cash management. In addition, any

effects of competitive advertising and promotion on present customers should also be discovered and reported by sales personnel.

6. **Reports and correspondence** constituting the required reports for sales administration are often viewed by salespeople as chores taking time away from customer contact. Unfortunately, reports and formal correspondence are a vital part of the selling function. The procedures that make this chore more acceptable are those that encourage concise and informative reports and correspondence. The processing of reports for control purposes and the flow of correspondence should be as expeditious as possible. Procedures should also be understood by both line and staff personnel to prevent unnecessary delay in the distribution and action requirements for the various call reports, customer correspondence, monthly summaries, and so on.

7. **Computer support** is highly cost-effective in respect to time and expense for sales personnel. This type of information is usually the most concise, time-effective way of controlling sales representatives in the details affecting the sales effort. The list of possible applications for computer support in sales is extensive and includes the following:

    Analysis of bank sales by product or industry
    Analysis of competitive sales
    Analysis of individual sales production
    Sales forecasting
    Development and monitoring of sales budgets
    Establishment of sales performance ratios by individuals
    Management of sales inquiries and leads
    Maintenance of customer information files (CIFs)
    Maintenance of competitive information data base
    Development of competitive performance parameters
    Computation and measurement of return on calling time invested
    Development of market penetration ratios
    Monitoring of sales call costs
    Maintenance of customer mailing lists
    Maintenance of file of standard business reply letters
    Generation and storage of sales call reports
    Maintenance of log of sales personnel calling schedules
    Maintenance of customer credit files

8. **Qualitative ratios** improve calling efficiency of sales personnel in the prospect qualification process. These ratios are primarily appli-

cable to commercial loan prospects and are particularly useful to calling officers in the commercial product selling process. These ratios include the following:

Net cash flow ratios to sales, total assets, net worth, and total debt

Net income ratios to sales, total assets, net worth, and total debt

Debt to total asset ratios to current liabilities, long-term liabilities, total debt, and total debt plus preferred stock

Liquid asset to total asset ratios to cash, quick assets, current assets, and working capital

Liquid asset to current debt ratio of current liabilities to cash, quick assets, and current assets

Turnover ratios of sales to cash, accounts receivable, inventory, quick assets, current assets, net worth, and total assets

---

SALES ADMINISTRATION. An effective coordination and control system is absolutely essential as the bank marketing manager assumes the responsibility for managing a complex selling effort for the bank. These administrative responsibilities are extensive and require a careful consideration of the overall activities related to the sales management function. The areas of responsibility assigned to a sales manager include the following:

Selecting sales targets and cultivating customers
Encouraging unscheduled calls of opportunity
Establishing sources of qualified sales leads
Determining high potential product sales mixes
Translating product and sales policy information
Facilitating information exchanges from senior management
Conducting productive sales meetings
Developing and training a dynamic sales team
Evaluating sales performance
Maintaining realistic credit requirements
Monitoring marginal credits for workout action
Supervising loan workout activities
Controlling sales budgets
Representing the sales function in bank management
Establishing efficient administrative procedures

To accept and discharge these responsibilities, bank sales managers are concerned with several key functions that involve the calling officers and other customer contact personnel. For example, a central record of information on customers and prospects is needed to determine specific calling targets. For present customers, most of the essential information is maintained in the standard credit files. Additional background information should include not only the company name, address, and phone number, but other essential data such as the SIC code, annual sales volume currently and historically, number of employees, location of branch plants and offices, and key officials with a special note designating additional information about the chief financial officer. Other information of value concerns which competitive banks provide the products and services used by the customer at present.

Supervision of the sales effort involves the assignment of accounts as well as specific territories or industry classifications. A system of controls based on sales call reports permits the sales manager to monitor the calling effort. Care should be taken to define what qualifies as a legitimate sales call, particularly if the bank sales motivation program or individual performance measurement is based on the quantitative aspects of customer calling. Efforts should be made to assess the qualitative dimensions by determining whether the sales call actually improved the relationship between the bank and the prospect or customer. The sales call report form used by bank calling officers is an essential document for the control and coordination of the calling effort. Although a daily review of each call report may be helpful, it may not be practical in those banks with an extensive calling effort, in which it may be more logical for the bank marketing manager, the sales manager, and the appropriate product manager to review a monthly call report summary or a progress report on the business development effort. Samples of a monthly call summary form (Table 10-1) and a business development progress report form (Table 10-2) are provided as guides for such a review of the calling activity.

One of the essential and most crucial activities for controlling and coordinating the sales effort is the evaluation of individual calling officers or other customer contact personnel. Unfortunately, many of these personal sales representatives are not under the direct supervision of the bank marketing manager, the sales manager, or a product manager. This organizational situation requires that some practical procedure be established for a consistent evaluation of the sales performance of each individual regardless of organizational assignment. This necessitates a set of specific performance standards, both qualitative and quantitative, for administering on a consistent basis at all supervisory levels. For example, some record must be maintained to permit the setting of sales objectives by calling officers assigned to the various departments. These individual goals become the basis for performance measurement. For coordination purposes, the individual officers' recommendations in the form of sales objectives also include the number and timing of sales calls. This permits a practical calling schedule to be prepared in advance. Individual schedules and specific goals not only are an excellent planning tool but allow sales management to establish a benchmark from which to compare planned performance with actual accomplishment.

Once the essential qualitative and quantitative information on the calling effort has been collected, it must be analyzed. The quantitative measurement is relatively simple and can be facilitated by computer-generated data. The calling schedule planned can be input and stored in the computer and used each week to remind calling officers of the planned schedule for sales calls. By an input of the actual calls made, the computer can print the comparative results for use in an analysis. The quality of a sales effort can be evaluated by comparing the dollar totals or account goals by product and service. If the results obtained are not satisfactory, the sales manager must determine whether the goals were realistically matched to the abilities of the calling officer. Consistent short-falls may indicate an inadequate selling proposition, a faulty goal-setting process, a need for additional training, or a change in the method of motivation. Another dimension of quality can be measured by an analysis of the results as compared with the total costs of the calling effort. Senior bank management is always concerned with whether the total bank commitment and investment of its resources are justified by the sales results. They are usually less concerned with individual performance than with the total results of the calling program.

In other pertinent analyses, the bank marketing manager should compare the relationships between specific sales efforts and results with respect to the bank's total marketing plan. Results of the calling effort should be compared not only by each major product or service group, but by organization units as well. It is also helpful to analyze sales according to industry groups, using the SIC code to assess the nature of market penetration. This analysis can be enhanced by determining whether some calling officers appear to be more proficient in the development of business through existing customers than through prospects. Sales can also be analyzed by zip code to determine whether certain geographic areas are more productive than others. For retail banking, zip codes or census tracts provide an excellent basis for setting sales goals. In matters involving trust or brokerage services, referral sources provide another helpful area of analysis.

Although the data for sales analysis must be collected from the summaries of the calling effort, one outstanding source of performance evaluation is the nature and extent of the sales goals and objectives that are established by each calling officer on an individual basis. These objectives are essential, not only in that they must correlate with the total sales forecast of

Table 10-1. Monthly Call Summary

Calling officer. _____ **Date.** _____

Office/dept. _____

Scheduled customer calls made.   _____   Number of first calls made.
Scheduled prospect calls made.   _____   Customers added to call schedule.
Unscheduled customer calls made.   _____   Customers deleted from call schedule.
Unscheduled prospect calls made.   _____   Prospects added to call schedule.
                                                   Prospects deleted from call schedule.
Total calls made.   _____
Total time on calls (hours).   _____   **Net added or deleted.**
Mileage.   _____   Code: C = Customer
Expenses.   P = Prospect
                                                      R = Referral source
                                                      S = Scheduled.
                                                      U = Unscheduled.

Date	Customer/prospect name	C, P, or R	S or U	Length of call (hrs)	Result of call and remarks

Table 10–2. Business Development Progress Report

Officer. _____   Month. _____

Dept./office. _____

Deposits
Demand deposits. _____
Regular time deposits. _____
Money market accounts. _____
Certificates of deposit. _____

Credit instruments
Commercial lines of credit. _____
Commitments. _____
Corporate credit cards. _____
Letters of credit. _____

Loans
Commercial loans. _____
Commercial finance. _____
Export finance. _____
Commercial RE loans. _____
Interim construction loans. _____
Vehicle loans. _____

Type of customer
1 = New business (new customer)
2 = New business (present customer)
3 = Renewal (present customer)

Services
Cash management accounts. _____
Funds collection. _____
Automatic payroll accounts. _____
International banking. _____
Corporate insurance. _____
Corporate trust. _____
Investment banking. _____
Tax accounts. _____
IRA/Keogh/401(K)
  accounts. _____
Equipment leasing. _____
Auto leasing. _____
Courier. _____

Name of customer	Type	Demand deposits			Time deposits		Loans and lines			Remarks
		Opening balance	Expected balance	Acct. no.	Opening balance	Expected balance	Approved	Type	Declined	

Table 10-3. Individual Sales Objectives

Calling officer. _____

Dept./office. _____

	First Qtr	Actual	Second Qtr	Actual	Third Qtr	Actual	Fourth Qtr	Actual	Total Year	Actual
Deposits										
Demand deposits										
Regular time deposits										
Money market accounts										
Certificates of deposit										
Loans										
Commercial loans										
Commercial finance										
Export finance										
Commercial real estate loans										
Interim construction loans										
Vehicle loans										
Personal loans										
Home improvement loans										
Residential real estate loans										
Credit instruments										
Commercial lines of credit										
Commitments										
Personal lines of credit										
Credit cards										
Debit cards										
Credit reserve accounts										
Letters of credit										

Services								
Cash management accounts								
Funds collection								
Automatic payroll accounts								
International banking								
Corporate insurance								
Corporate trust								
Investment banking								
Tax accounts								
IRA accounts								
KEOGH accounts								
401(K) accounts								
Equipment leasing								
Auto leasing								
Courier								
Discount brokerage								
Automatic bill payment								
Personal insurance								
Administration								
Number of customer calls								
Number of prospect calls								
Corporate banking referrals								
Personal banking referrals								
Trust referrals								

the bank, but because they provide a basis for self-motivation by the calling officer and indicate the expectation for sales performance. A suggested individual sales objectives form is provided in Table 10-3 for use by calling officers or other appropriate customer contact personnel.

The final area of sales administration of concern to the bank marketing manager and the sales manager is sales compensation. Most banks compensate calling officers with a salary and bonus plan. However, some banks are now acknowledging the relative importance of personal selling, to the degree that commissions that are based on profitability and sales volume are being paid. This new development notwithstanding, the salary method continues to possess several advantages, the most important probably being the security offered by a guaranteed income. The psychological profile of those attracted to finance often suggests that they are not undue risk takers. This applies to their personal lives as well. From an administrative standpoint, a salary structure is easy to compute and fosters loyalty through its consistency. It also has the advantage of being recognized as a fixed cost. This permits bank marketing managers to prepare a sales budget with greater ease and accuracy. Unfortunately, salaries are seldom tied directly to performance, and it cannot serve as an effective motivator beyond a certain level of accomplishment. Thus, the fixed costs of a salaried sales force often increase the costs of sales because there is little correlation between straight salary and sales volume.

On the other hand, a commission system is the ultimate in pure compensation since performance and pay are tied in directly with each other. Although commissions may be the most productive sales motivator, there is little or no reason for commission salespeople to provide an effective after-sale service since this does not provide a basis for paying commission on sales. Since banks can only thrive and grow on continuing service, sales alone are not sufficient for success. Although selling costs are variable when based on commission, calling officers also have a degree of variability. For example, not only may the loyalty of calling officers vary with the ebb and flow of the commissions earned, but they may develop more loyalty to key customers responsible for their sales than to the bank providing the commissions. Another disadvantage is that the commission structure makes calling officers subject to unstable earnings. At a certain point they may seek the security of a salary elsewhere, particularly during times of reduced sales volume. This insecurity affects the customers through service continuity and the bank through costly attrition.

The issue of compensation is obviously a critical one in sales. However, neither pure salary nor exclusive commission appears to be the solution for bank sales personnel. A combination salary and bonus system, with the later based on volume as in a commission system, offers the most practical means of motivating and retaining those with selling responsibilities.

In addition to such a system, sales efforts can be heightened during specific periods or for individual products by the use of sales incentive programs. This indirect method of compensation is particularly effective on the branch office level with customer contact personnel. Suggested sales incentive programs will be explored in detail in Chapter 11. Whatever the method selected, bank compensation will be affected by the nonbank entrants into the financial services marketplace. Pay is an important criterion, and it requires close monitoring by the bank marketing manager. It is crucial to make certain that the personal sales effort is implemented, not only by adequately compensated calling officers but by well-trained, highly qualified, strongly motivated, and unusually productive bank support personnel. This is necessary in every phase of customer contact where personal selling can become a decisive factor.

11

BANK SALES PROMOTION

The promotional activities which can be implemented by the bank marketing manager include not only the personal sales effort of calling officers and customer contact personnel, but the mass communication programs involving advertising and public relations. The specialized activity of sales promotion consists of those additional marketing functions that banks use to stimulate customer awareness and to heighten their interest in financial services. It offers a direct and immediate reminder to both bank customers and bank personnel and attempts to move the product and service toward the customer at the point of sales contact as opposed to advertising, which moves the customer to the point of contact, where the products and services then become more available through sales promotion. When applied effectively, sales promotion can move bank customers beyond the awareness and comprehension stage into the conviction and bank relationship stage. It can increase the effectiveness of the personal sales and advertising efforts by extending the bank's promotional activity where the customer is most receptive—at the point of sales contact and at the point of service delivery.

One highly specialized sales promotion activity that has widespread application in retail banking is identified as merchandising. This activity has been developed into an essential and distinct art by the most successful mass retailers of merchandise, supermarkets and department stores. The specialized promotional techniques at the branch level of banks require a particular set of materials and activities that are designed to exploit and to appeal to the individual behavior of retail banking customers. Most of the principles governing the retail merchandising by banks have been adapted from other mass retailers. For example, selling the bank products and services at the retail level closely parallels that of mass merchandisers such as Sears and K-Mart. The major difference is that the bank's products and services are equated solely to money, whether they are in the form of interest earned, loans advanced, or checks cleared. In this context, all retailers must provide a wide variety of consumer products and services at a single point of sale in order to attract consumers in sufficient numbers to justify an extensive merchandising effort. The only major differences from a pure merchandising point of view is in the nature of the retail products involved. With the financial services market entry of Sears, J. C. Penney, and others, the differences are narrowing.

Looking at retailing as a whole, most of the products sold are categorized as tangibles. They can be seen, touched, smelled, tasted, sampled, tried on, demonstrated, and so forth. Any differences in style, attributes, features, color, weight, size, or design may be compared with other products without leaving the point of sale. One obvious difference at the bank point of sale is that most financial services involve abstract products, or intangibles. Unlike the products in a superdrug or supermarket, bank products have no physical substance other than the secondary representation of money by a check, deposit slip, or loan agreement. Bank products must be merchandised in such a way that prospects can imagine how their financial needs or material interests can best be served by money in its intangible form. To merchandise money effectively, it must be taken out of the vault, figuratively, and brought out into the open where bank customers can relate to it in a manner similar to that for products in other retail stores.

Many branch lobbies have the look of elegance or efficiency rather than a typical retail merchandising environment. Because of the growing use of self-service in banking, most bankers should place more emphasis on financial services merchandising. As banks rely less on sales personnel, the use of descriptive literature and exciting floor and counter displays is necessary to stimulate retail banking customers. Since the primary responsibility of a delivery system is to serve and to cross-sell customers, in-branch merchandising should accomplish the following:

1. **Stimulate customer interest** to promote the displayed product and related services by increasing customer awareness and providing a brief explanation of features and benefits.
2. **Select appropriate product and service mix** to feature products that have widespread customer appeal and also deliver attractive profit margins with high volume potential.
3. **Build lobby traffic** to attract the attention of customers both outside and inside the branch and to encourage personal visits.
4. **Complement the lobby environment** to make the merchandising materials or promotion program compatible with the general character of the branch, its decor, and its geographic location.
5. **Extend the bank-wide promotion effort** by coordinating the sales promotion to reinforce the advertising approach being used by the bank throughout the market, with particular care not to offer a conflicting program.
6. **Select timely themes;** it is more effective to relate the branch promotion activity to seasonal events, such as April tax time, fall re-

turn to school, summer vacations, or new car introductions, that receive heavy attention by other retailers in the communication media to promote high consumer awareness.

Branch operations people expect merchandising material to be simple to set up, to be durable, and not to hinder movement of the teller lines or access to the platform officers. If the material is so elaborate or complicated that it requires considerable time and effort to install or service, merchandising personnel from a central source rather than the branch operations personnel should be used for that purpose. Merchandising specialists, patterned after the highly successful detailmen used by Procter and Gamble, can be trained to set up lobby displays, to replenish literature stocks in the lobby racks, and to replace damaged point-of-purchase materials. They can operate from a central point and help relieve the branch manager or operations supervisors from the responsibility for organizing sales promotion materials.

Bank marketing managers or sales promotion managers should exercise care in the selection of materials since branches often use only a small percentage of what they receive from the marketing department. From the customer's point of view, materials should appeal to the expected behavior of retail banking customers who can be motivated on occasion by impulse or a speedy decision. It is surprising to many marketing professionals how many cross-selling opportunities in banks are originated through merchandising that encourages consumer consideration on the spur of the moment. A large percentage of unplanned customer relationships involving some of the secondary products or services occur because literature from a display rack near the teller line or an attractive lobby display has appealed to a bank customer waiting in line to be served.

SALES PROMOTION PLANNING PROCESS. The planning function for the sales promotion effort has now assumed greater importance in the activity of the bank marketing staff. The nature of retail competition and the increased number of calling officers from the thrift institutions and other competitors have made it advisable to increase the bank's sales promotion effort. Therefore, it must be incorporated into the regular marketing planning process. Banks have become aware that sales promotion activities may contribute more than an institutional advertising campaign to support a delivery system. This activity has grown along with the dramatic increase of new commercial banks and the threat of nonbank banks. The majority of new banks are limited in their use of high-cost mass advertising media; they must rely more on the use of sales promotion techniques to help them establish a market position. As the number of retail competitors increases, there will be heavier emphasis on sales promotion and the need for advance planning will become equally critical.

A sales promotion plan, like any planning document, must be based on objectives that point the direction or strategy the activity must follow. There are several sales promotion objectives that are appropriate for commercial banks, and they include some of the following:

> To attract new bank customers
> To encourage more frequent use of bank products and services
> To cross-sell additional products and services
> To introduce new products and services
> To merchandise attractive consumer premiums
> To counteract competitive activity
> To build lobby and ATM traffic
> To emphasize features of the bank's selling proposition
> To capitalize on seasonal events and trends
> To stimulate and motivate bank personnel

By the same token, there are objectives that are not appropriate for bank sales promotion. For example, sales promotion is complementary to and not a substitute for mass communication such as advertising and public relations. It cannot overcome an inadequate delivery system, nor can it reverse a continuing downturn in sales by its own efforts. Sales promotion is no substitute for mediocre personnel who are poorly trained or not properly motivated.

The responsibility for the preparation of the sales promotion effort is usually delegated by the bank marketing manager to a sales promotion or merchandising manager. In some banking organizations, the single title of advertising and sales promotion manager is still prevalent, although the actual function may be divided, with an advertising agency handling the advertising effort and the advertising and sales promotion manager concentrating on the planning and implementing of the sales promotion effort in house. The several elements in a bank sales promotion program require a separate plan since various personnel within the bank may be responsible for portions of the implementation. The sales promotion plan is a component of the total marketing plan and, as such, becomes a detailed plan within a master plan. A suggested format for a formal sales promotion plan is as follows:

> I. Sales promotion situation
>   A. Review of previous bank programs
>   1. Bank sales promotion objectives and goals

    2. Bank sales promotion targets
    3. Promotion theme and creative approach
    4. Mix of sales promotion techniques and tools
    5. Sales promotion budget summary
    6. Previous performance results
  B. Current sales promotion situation
    1. Bank product or service emphasis
    2. Nature of bank delivery system
    3. Characteristics of lobbies and point-of-sale areas
    4. Competitive sales promotion activity
    5. Promotional culture of bank personnel
II. Sales promotion strategy
  A. Marketing problem identification and analysis
  B. Marketing opportunity identification and analysis
  C. Bank sales promotion targets
    1. Present retail customers
    2. New retail customers
    3. Present commercial customers
    4. New commercial customers
    5. Bank personnel
  D. Bank sales promotion goals
    1. Information and persuasion
    2. Institutional recognition and acceptance
    3. Bank product or service differentiation
    4. Immediate decision making
    5. Competitive counteraction
    6. New product or service introduction
    7. Build lobby or ATM traffic
    8. Merchandise consumer premiums
    9. Stimulate and motivate bank personnel
III. Bank sales promotion programs
  A. Bank selling proposition
    1. Product and service benefits
    2. Product and service characteristics
    3. Product and service pricing
    4. Product and service convenience and availability
  B. Promotion theme and creative approach
    1. Copy theme
    2. Art and graphics
  C. Promotion techniques and tools
    1. Literature
    2. Signs and displays (Interior)
    3. Signs and Displays (Exterior)

    4. Contact personnel sales aids
    5. Consumer premiums
    6. Consumer contests and sweepstakes
    7. Advertising specialities
    8. Trade shows and seminars
    9. Sales incentives for bank personnel
    10. Pricing concessions
    11. Tie-in sales
    12. Catalogs and guide books
IV. Bank sales promotion management
    A. Organization of the sales promotion effort
    B. Coordination of the sales promotion effort
       1. Production schedule
       2. Implementation schedule
    C. Control of the sales promotion effort
       1. Detailed budget
       2. Performance measurement
       3. Contingency programs
    D. Program approval requirements
    E. Organization communication
       1. Program announcement to bank personnel
       2. Training requirements
       3. Promotion progress report requirements

SALES PROMOTION PROGRAM DEVELOPMENT. As can be seen from the preceding planning format, the task of developing a new sales promotion campaign is very detailed. There are many specific targets among bank customers and bank employees that must be identified and selected. In addition, the degree of acceptance of the promotion programs by the various targets is also a critical consideration. For example, enthusiasm for a new bank product or service must be generated among the customer contact personnel as well as among the bank's customers. If the bank personnel are not supportive initially, they may require special incentives before they commit their time and effort in support of a promotion program. This is particularly true if they are bank operations people with less concern for sales. If they are calling officers or customer service representatives who are reasonably content and comfortable with current products, they may be reluctant to endorse new products with the required enthusiasm and dedication needed for an effective promotion.

    The actual implementation is often the key to sales promotion effectiveness. As important as the formal plan may be, a mediocre sales promotion plan, well implemented, is usually more effective than an outstanding plan, poorly executed. The major responsibility of the bank marketing manager is to develop the theme or creative approach, select the most appropriate techniques and materials, and prepare a well-coordinated promotion program. Once conceived, it must be communicated to bank personnel in a highly persuasive manner that convinces branch personnel and those in contact with customers that the program can benefit each individual as well as the bank as a whole. The assignment of responsibilities for the preparation of the program elements as well as the actual implementation is necessary and requires the use of a wide variety of materials and numerous promotion activities to assure a successful effort.

These promotional activities fall into three main categories. Promotion techniques and materials are either discount or price-driven, information-driven, or public service–driven. Premiums for opening deposit accounts fall into the discount or price-driven category, and literature or financial services seminars are considered information-driven materials or activities. Price-driven promotions are usually based on offering the customer a lower price or a tie-in sale, which is a form of discounting. Price-driven promotions allow banks to differentiate products and services on the basis of price. However, as frequently as price-driven promotions are used, they are considered nonexclusive since competitors can offset any competitive advantage by meeting or cutting prices even further. In a situation in which all competitors are using price-driven promotions as occurred in the airline industry, the competitive advantage is realized by the bank with the lowest price, largest discount, or the greatest value of its giveaway premiums.

Information-driven sales promotion activities are less spectacular but can be equally productive as price-driven promotions because of the absence of competitive retaliation. These promotional efforts are usually ongoing as provided by such necessary tools as product literature, supplies of income tax forms, brochures on financial matters, self-service loan application forms, and notices of community events. Related to these promotions are seasonal seminars conducted on economic forecasts, investment, trust, tax, and other financial topics of interest to customers and prospects. The third type of promotion used by many banks is the public service–driven promotion. This consists of any activity that involves community organizations and includes such activities as United Way drives, student car washes in the parking lot, or the sale of baked goods or handcrafted items in bank lobbies by charity groups. The promotional value of these activities can be justified not only because they are excellent lobby traffic builders but because they can be used to demonstrate the community involvement of the bank.

Bank marketing managers need to determine the proper mix of the two principal categories, price-driven or information-driven promotions. Each has its advantages in certain promotion situations. To assess the proper application, there are certain basics that should be considered:

1. **The role of sales promotion.** The total promotion effort of the bank can be accomplished by the appropriate mix of personal sales, advertising, public relations, and sales promotion. In some marketing situations where the delivery system has exceptional diversity, a promotion mix dominated by mass advertising with heavy sales promotion support may be the most desirable approach. If the bank's delivery system is relatively sparse, a heavy personal sales effort supported by product and service promotional materials may be the most efficient mix. With a delivery system that provides dense coverage of the target market, an aggressive and well-coordinated sales promotion effort may be needed in each branch with mass advertising delegated to a strong supportive role in spite of the economies available through mass media coverage. A need for employee motivation that complements the regular compensation policy will also require a heavy mix of sales promotion in the form of employee incentives. This is particularly applicable during periods when it is necessary to sustain present levels of sales and service.

2. **The nature of the product or service.** Because of the characteristics of the specific product or service requiring promotional emphasis, a different promotion support mix may be appropriate for each major product line. For example, because of its technical nature, automatic payroll services require a heavier personal selling emphasis than a mass consumer product such as credit cards. The promotion mix of personal checking or money market accounts might consist of a sizable expenditure on mass advertising supported by in-branch sales promotion; less personal, one-on-one selling is needed for these products and the sale is actually closed by the one who assists the customer in filling out the application. For corporate banking products and services, personal selling by individual calling officers is essential, whereas the use of mass advertising media may not be cost-effective because of the waste circulation. When bank products and services are innovative and being introduced for the first time, consumer interest and awareness are critical to its success. This situation requires a strong advertising and sales promotion effort in concert to secure customer recognition and to inform interested prospects. However, this recognition can be extended and reinforced at the point of sale with appropriate product promotion techniques and materials.

3. **The state of the marketplace.** Each bank has a specific market presence that may be based on geographical, demographical or SIC coverage. Thus, different promotion mixes are necessary. Corporate customers do not necessarily have geographic commonality but may share the same industry similarities. They require customized attention from an industry specialist that is only available by means of a strong personal sales effort. However, this effort can be made more effective by providing the calling officer or customer service representative with supportive sales promotion tools. Bank products and services targeted toward the upscale segment of the demographic spectrum for such products as Keogh accounts or IRAs may require information-driven promotions rather than those based purely on price. This is particularly true for those accounts which have the self-directed option. For routine bank products such as personal checking and passbook savings, the consumers are normally prospects who are in a decision-making mode, sitting on the edge of change because of service dissatisfaction, or those seeking greater location convenience. For these types of products and market segments, advertising in mass media, strongly supported by sales promotion premiums or pricing concessions, offer the most productive promotion mix.

Once the proper mix has been determined, the production of these diverse promotion elements must be coordinated so that the most timely and appropriate schedule can be established. The more comprehensive the sales promotion program is planned to be, the greater the number and variety of the elements in the promotion mix. To assist the bank marketing manager or sales promotion manager in coordinating the myriad of production and implementation details, several planning techniques such as time line, chronological task, or program evaluation and review technique (PERT) allow all of the many activities to be scheduled in a logical order or succession. These essential systems for coordination and control of the sales promotion effort are covered in Chapter 15 devoted to the marketing management effort.

TECHNIQUES AND TOOLS. The bank sales promotion program requires many unrelated activities and a variety of promotion techniques and materials. Some of these tools of promotion are designed for bank customers; others are used to stimulate and reinforce the sales efforts of bank customer contact personnel. Those activities directed primarily at current bank customers include the information-driven materials such as literature and point-of-purchase displays or price-driven tools such as contests, premiums, and advertising specialties. The internal bank organization can be supported by information-driven activities such as trade shows and seminars. They can also be motivated by price-driven techniques such as employee referral contests and sales incentive programs.

Literature. Literature is a type of information-driven promotion tool that is almost an indispensable product or service support item for the consumer to use in the decision-making process. General banking services brochures provide a master list of products and services offered by the bank, the locations of its delivery system, hours of business, and a list of key bank officers. The products and services are described briefly and the brochures serve as an overview of the bank, its products, and its convenience. Specific product and service folders are used to promote individual or related products with details on customer benefits, costs, and availability. These folders also include some of the required legal disclaimers and regulations. For continuity and reinforcement of image, the literature usually bears a family resemblance in size, shape, graphics, and color. These folders extend the selling effort by enabling customers and prospects to do comparative shopping off bank premises. They also serve as reminders when they are given to prospects at the conclusion of a sales presentation.

Another form of literature is categorized as announcement fliers. This literature is used to communicate changes quickly and at a reduced cost. They are effective to announce changes in interest rates, changes in bank hours, new branch openings, local contests and drawings, and other bank activities of more than a routine interest. The statement stuffer is a condensed promotional piece or announcement that contains a brief sales message and an urge to action in the form of an abbreviated loan application or temporary account signature card as part of an off-premises product or service promotion. Goodwill folders have seasonal applications for anniversaries, holiday greetings, service or loan maturity reminders, or other expressions of appreciation by calling officers and customer service representatives for new or existing business.

The First Bank System in Minnesota uses several effective information-driven promotion tools. They publish a quarterly personal finance magazine called *Your Money*. It is distributed to over forty thousand selected bank customers to provide pertinent information on personal finances. They also have another effective set of information-driven tools that are *Blue Book* pamphlets covering in detail many important financial subjects such as retirement considerations, discount brokerage usage, and a review of the various investment products available. These pamphlets are distributed directly to interested customers and provide an excellent way to qualify prospects for a personal sales follow-up call.

Literature of an informative nature can be distributed in several ways to reach interested customers and prospects. The most practical method is to provide easily accessible literature racks in high traffic areas in branches or adjacent to ATMs or in-store POS terminals. The statement stuffer can be distributed as part of a direct mail campaign to accompany a sales letter, or it can be enclosed with monthly checking or savings account statements. The literature that is used as a sales reminder when it is left behind with prospects after a personal sales call can also be used as an enclosure in a follow-up sales letter after the call. The particular use planned for the literature will often determine the form it should take. The content of the printed piece should feature information that is stated in the self-interest of the consumer and is presented in an easy-to-comprehend manner. Benefits must be emphasized and detail on how the product or service can be obtained is essential; once interested, prospects expect to be told where the product or service is available. These information-driven tools serve not only as sources of details regarding bank products but make excellent, passive sales representatives in the absence of bank sales personnel.

Point-of-Purchase Materials. Banks use display-type materials in bank lobbies to attract the attention of customers, to communicate the availability of additional bank products and services, and to stimulate their purchase or use. These materials also remind bank personnel of the inventory and options available for sale to customers. In some cases, they serve as extensions of the sales and product training received by branch personnel.

Specifically, point-of-purchase promotion activity involves the use of display materials such as posters, easled counter cards, literature racks with displayed message reminders, interior and exterior signs, motion displays, audio recordings, banners, and price or interest rate cards. Banks have been extremely reluctant to take advantage of this relatively low-cost promotion medium even though a 1985 study by the Stanford Research Institute concluded that point-of-purchase advertising for retail establishments had exceptional customer reliance and acceptance. In spite of this evidence, the image of bank safety might conceivably be tarnished if such point-of-purchase promotion methods used are too garish or aggressive. Notwithstanding this factor, there is a middle ground that can be attained since most bank lobbies and platforms are relatively sterile as far as point-of-purchase material is concerned. To those banks with a strong retail presence, there are several rules for guidance as well as beneficial characteristics which bank marketing managers or sales promotion managers can consider in the preparation of an acceptable and contributory point-of-purchase effort:

Sales messages must be concise with one, strong, persuasive argument featured on the material.

Customers waiting in line are usually not pre-occupied with other matters and are receptive to promotional messages.

Customers in a bank have a limited attention span if the branch servicing is speedy and efficient.

If the servicing is delayed unduly, customers are less receptive to promotional messages.

The most effective areas for merchandising bank products are those near teller lines, drive-up windows, or ATM facilities.

Remote areas of bank lobbies are not recommended for point-of-purchase materials since they have less customer visibility.

Point-of-purchase materials must be removed once they become frayed, damaged, or soiled.

Any materials displayed must be consistent with and complementary to the basic bank lobby decor.

Messages should feature benefits to the customer rather than those in the self-interest of the bank.

Point-of-purchase messages require repetition and should be limited in length but not in their appearance on various display media at the same time.

Any permanent display racks or fixtures should be flexible and mobile to permit occasional rearrangement in the lobby or removal to other branches.

Encourage customer involvement and an immediate decision for action by providing timely instructions and directions.

One particularly appropriate use of point-of-purchase materials is to make announcements to bank customers that are sufficiently timely that the normal production of announcement advertising or detailed literature is not possible. Simple lobby posters can be designed, produced, and distributed in a relatively short time for announcing such overnight events as deposit and prime rate changes or consumer loan rate reductions.

As banks begin to emulate the most effective and less garish point-of-purchase practices of mass retailers, there are new developments which the bank marketing manager should recognize and consider for adoption in the most appropriate form. The merchandising managers of many consumer products companies have determined through experience that two-thirds of the buying decisions are made at the point of sale. As a result, such successful merchandisers as Pepsi-cola and H. J. Heintz have now increased their in-store promotion efforts. New methods that include video display screens and commercials over the public address system are evolving. Although such techniques may not be compatible with the environment of bank lobbies, they can be adapted for use with freestanding ATM installations or in small minibranches that emphasize self-service.

Consumer Premiums. Consumer premiums as a technique of financial services promotion are among the most popular, particularly among thrift institutions. Premiums are articles of merchandise that have widespread acceptance and use by bank customers. They are offered free or at reduced prices, depending upon any legal limitation placed on the value of the premium, particularly as applied to deposit-related accounts. These premiums are offered as desirable incentives that may encourage the use or purchase of specific bank products and services. Although the basic objective or goal of any sales promotion campaign using consumer premiums is to help increase sales at the point of sale, there are other more specific reasons for bank premium promotions:

> To offset the impact and negative effects of a new competitive product or service
> To maximize any competitive advantage in a current selling proposition or market situation
> To attract new customers from competitive financial institutions who are receptive to a second banking source
> To build bank customer loyalty and to facilitate the cross-selling effort by bank sales personnel
> To offset any seasonal deposit or loan run-off
> To stimulate customer impulse buying behavior through the offering of a benefit for immediate action
> To provide an easily recognizable differentiation when there are great similarities in bank products

Obviously there are almost unlimited numbers of premiums but only two basic types. Direct premiums are given to the customer immediately upon opening the account, adding a deposit, or other specific qualification. It is difficult, however, to limit the offer to new customers only. Present customers can circumvent the rules with a simultaneous closing and opening of accounts. Therefore, it is best to devise premium promotions that include present as well as new customers; good customer relations dictate such a promotion policy. Direct premiums are limited only by the imagination of the sales promotion specialist, although some courage is often needed by management to accept some of the recommended premiums. In the face of public acceptance and the competitive environment, management of many banks are becoming more courageous. For example, First City Bank in Houston has offered Arabian foals to $100,000 depositors as a way to increase long-term deposits with five-year CDs. For the $500,000 depositor over the same period, customers earned a Steinway piano, personally autographed by the current Steinway family head. A small $30,000 five-year CD qualified for a Rolex watch or a forty-five-inch, wide-screen RCA television set. For a few jumbo depositors, a $1 million CD for five years earned a new Porsche or a Cessna airplane. After only the first few days, over $14 million of long-term deposits were generated as a result of this direct premium promotion. Needless to say, to exercise good judgment and to remain within the regulatory guidelines, these premiums were provided in lieu of interest earned with the certificates of deposit.

The second type, self-liquidating premiums, require the bank customer to make a payment for the premium being offered after opening an account or other qualifier. The required payment generally equals the cost of the premium to the bank plus in some cases, the cost of the promotional support provided by the advertising and the distribution of the premium. This technique is particularly attractive to a bank since it can offer a desirable article or merchandise at little or no cost to the bank. These kinds of premiums can include a variety of items such as sets of steak knives, jewelry, glassware, portable TV sets, china place settings, silverware, and other personal merchandise. These premiums attract customers because the cost of the merchandise is usually considerably lower than the regular retail price. Research indicates that customers respond most favorably when the cost of the premium is no more than 50 percent of the perceived retail value. Since the sources of the merchandise realize profits through higher volume purchases and also receive free exposure through bank advertising and promotion support, they are able to offer premium merchandise at attractive discounts to the bank. Eastman Kodak has a special camera premium line using the brand name Hawkeye, which is provided for premium promotions at extremely attractive prices below the cost of comparable Kodak cameras sold in retail stores.

One version of the self-liquidating premium type that has particular application for building lobby traffic and encouraging repeat visits to the point of sale is continuity premiums. These premiums are offered on the basis of repeat purchases or account usage such as credit card transactions. They are also an excellent way to promote a continuous increase in savings account deposits. This practice develops continuity by using premiums that require several items to make a set. For example, table place settings can be offered as a premium on a monthly basis. By requiring a series of deposits or other continuing product use over a period of time the bank allows customers to accumulate a complete set of the particular premium offered. Unfortunately, administration of continuity premiums is complicated. Although they are targeted to the same customers during each promotion period, they can cause confusion and disappointment if the premium offer is withdrawn before a full set is accumulated by the customer. There are several other concerns in the implementation of such a program:

> To set up an efficient selection, buying, and branch inventory system requires an expertise normally outside of the province of bank personnel.
>
> To select appropriate and desirable premiums is difficult as well as critical since any mistake in consumer acceptance may be costly in both money and reputation.
>
> To provide the necessary promotion support requires the commitment of resources that might be devoted to institutional advertising or other needed activities.
>
> To commit itself to a continuity premium program the bank must ensure that the premium offer is almost open-ended to prevent customer dissatisfaction.

The selection of premiums is most critical to the success of a consumer premium promotion. It is difficult at best and bank marketing managers or sales promotion managers should use professional premium consultants or recognized premium suppliers. The actual selection of premiums should fall within the following criteria:

> The premium selected should have an easily recognizable value that is perceived to be worth more than the price asked or the extent of the qualification requirement.
>
> In the minds of the consumers, the premium should be of more than passing use, and have a personal, prestigious, or practical appeal.
>
> One unique feature that can make the premium more attractive is some exclusivity by its not being readily available in local retail stores.
>
> Although not absolutely essential, the premium selected should have some relation to banking and reinforce the customer relationship.

Contests and Sweepstakes. Promotion involving contests and sweepstakes not only establishes an aura of excitement to sales promotion programs but has a greater consumer acceptance now that there is such an increased interest in state-run lotteries. The lure of monumental prizes helps make the appeal universal. The two versions of this promotion, contests and sweepstakes, have important differences. Contests require that participants apply some degree of skill that can be judged against other contest entrants. Entries are evaluated and prizes awarded on the basis of independent judgment. Sweepstakes are games of chance that do not require any demonstration of skill or knowledge. Winners are selected at random through a drawing so that all entrants have an equal opportunity of winning. Most bank promotions are based on random drawings with lobby registration and are actually sweepstakes rather than skill-related contests. Many of the prizes are in the form of large appliances, automobiles, or travel trips. The objective of bank contests and sweepstakes is to encourage product usage by present customers or to build branch traffic at openings or other special events. Generally, this type of promotion is a well-publicized effort of wide appeal. It requires heavy advertising and promotion support if product usage and lobby traffic are desired.

Sales Incentive Programs. Sales incentive programs are a form of promotion that is part premium and part sweepstake. It is used for promoting within the bank's internal organization as a way to motivate sales and branch operations personnel. The same logic with respect to customer contests and premiums applies to sales incentive programs. These programs are based on improving sales over a previous period's performance; goal attainment drives this type of promotion. There are several guidelines for sales incentive programs:

> Establish realistic, attainable sales goals.
>
> Set sales or other contact quotas that permit some degree of participation by all bank personnel.
>
> Select time limits that do not extend over periods so lengthy that employee enthusiasm diminishes.
>
> Build the sales incentive program around a clever, but highly emotional, theme for employee actualization.
>
> Issue frequent incentive program progress reports that publish the relative standings of all participants.
>
> Award prizes as soon as they are earned and make the awarding ceremony very visible.
>
> Build and maintain enthusiasm with promotion materials, staff meetings, publicity in employee publications, and correspondence to the homes of participants.

Advertising Specialties. Advertising specialties are giveaway premiums of less value, which often bear the donor's name and a promotional message. They are particularly popular in the insurance industry. In banks, they are given without cost by calling officers, loan officers, branch managers, and other customer contact personnel. Typical advertising specialties include ballpoint pens, calendars, key chains, checkbook covers, etc. This promotion tool has many applications in bank sales promotion activities, including branch openings, initial sales calls by account officers, introduction of new products and services, or opening of new loan or deposit accounts. A major benefit, in addition to goodwill, is that the bank's name and message receive repeated exposure since the most effective advertising specialties are those that can be used over extended periods. Unfortunately, one disadvantage is the widespread use of similar specialties; most consumers have desk drawers filled with the ballpoint pens of retail and service organizations as well as those of competing banks and thrift institutions. Bank employees also have a tendency to take these specialties for personal use.

Trade Shows and Seminars. There are a growing acceptance and participation by banks in trade shows and exhibits. These well-attended shows include not only those featuring capital equipment for manufacturers, but for a wide variety of consumer goods such as boats, automobiles, appliances, home furnishings, and mobile homes. These trade, boat, auto, and home shows provide banks with an opportunity for promoting consumer loans, capital equipment leasing, and other applicable financial services. Trade shows play a dominant role in industrial markets that offer opportunities in commercial lending. They are now well attended by consumers seeking high-ticket personal and household items.

Seminars are also increasing as a promotional technique to attract customers. Insurance and investment competitors use them to prospect for new customers. They can be particularly applicable to banking in the form of information sessions that feature a variety of topics. These include trust and investment services, tax law changes, economic forecasts, and other relevant subjects. Guest lecturers of local or national prominence as well as in-bank experts can be used to attract attendance. Well-known personalities can be used for promotional purposes as well. Participation in either of these forms of promotion activity is costly. There are two accepted measurements for use of the bank marketing manager to evaluate the value of both of these promotion techniques—a verifiable count of attendance, and a well-defined audience profile that matches the selected targets of the bank.

As stated earlier, the number of sales promotion techniques and tools for use in developing a successful program is only limited by the imagination of the bank marketing manager or the sales promotion manager. Of all point-of-sale merchandising activity, personal salesmanship continues to be the most effective means for closing the sale of bank products and services.

All loan applications and account signature cards are sales promotion tools in a sense, as are the other administrative forms such as monthly account statements. Although they are used primarily for operations control, they are distributed directly to the customers and, therefore, offer an opportunity for sales action during the time of customer contact. Most customer forms can be used as catalysts for the one-on-one sales communication process between bank personnel and the customer. Sales promotion can become the marketing activity that sets the buying process into motion or provides the final motivation needed for favorable customer action. Sales promotion is not only equally effective, but most essential for both bank customers and bank personnel.

12

BANK ADVERTISING

The last of the three essential promotional activities is mass communication. It is sufficiently complex that it is divided into two major areas—advertising and public relations. Because of the functional differences of each, they are best considered separately. Therefore, public relations will be covered in Chapter 13. As for advertising, it is often the most visible of the several bank promotion activities. It consists of the various types of informative and persuasive messages about the bank and its products and services that are delivered through mass communication media. Since all advertising cannot be of interest to all audiences, the bank's advertising program must be as selective as possible while taking advantage of the cost efficiencies available through mass communication media that reach large bodies of bank customers and prospects at one time.

Any marketing strategy requires effective communication since the sale of bank products and services is dependent upon a continuous exchange of information during the selling process. For the calling officers and customer service representatives, personal, one-on-one communication is required; however, a foundation of knowledge or familiarity by the customer or prospect in advance of the personal sales contact can improve the communication effectiveness. The communication process in both instances is uncomplicated in concept and is structured around five elements that react in an ordinal sequence. The process has been described in the most simple terms as who says what, in what way, to whom, and with what effect. In terms of communication theory, the elements are identified as the sender, the message, the channel or medium, the receiver, and the feedback. To explain more theory, the sender, or the bank in its role as an advertiser, must prepare a message; encode it for sound and sight; and transmit it over an appropriate communication medium, where it can be decoded by the receiver or audience who represent the target market of the bank. The verification of reception and the decoding can be determined through appropriate feedback indicators such as telephone inquiries, lobby traffic, or actual sales.

Communication theorists explain that the most common reason for miscommunication is the variation or misunderstanding that may occur between the encoding and the decoding. In addition to the failure of the targeted audience to understand or appreciate the message, the media operate in an extremely competitive environment where many advertisers vie for the eyes and ears of the consumers. Thus, the advertising message noise level is very high. There are other key considerations in communication theory that bank marketing managers must be aware of when preparing the message for mass communication programs:

1. **Message decoding.** All communication is perceived and evaluated by consumers in terms of their own needs, personality, and field of experience. The message must be encoded in the self-interest of the target audience if it is to be received and accepted in the way the bank intended.
2. **Message appreciation.** A receiver will review a message in terms of past experience and criteria although the situation or circumstances may be completely new. New information must be presented in a form that is more meaningful and more significant than previous evaluation criteria.
3. **Communication blocks.** The failure to communicate is a misnomer since any verbal or nonverbal action over a channel may communicate something, although it may not be the precise message the bank planned to transmit. Breakdowns in encoding and decoding result from the differences in the fields of experience and the frames of reference of the bank versus its target market.

Advertising and its true value have often been challenged by bankers. However, an increasing number of businesses are turning to advertising as a cost-effective way to reach customers. Research reported in *Advertising Age* indicates that dollar sales increase 20 percent when the prospect is exposed to advertising before a personal sales call. In spite of this finding, many banks continue to regard advertising as a cost and believe that the money could be better spent on other bank activities. There are parts of communication theory that indicate ways in which advertising works well. These are represented by certain concepts, and many successful advertising programs have been implemented by banks who understand some of the following:

Bank advertising can help promote sales by generating personal demand through direct advertising exposure.

Responses to bank advertising vary from no change to a heightened demand for products and services.

The message content directly affects the extent of demand generated, and many of the unidentified variables such as experience and perception play important roles in the ultimate response.

The target audience as a group may differ in its banking preferences, and advertising can activate an individual to assert personal demand that does not necessarily follow peer norms.

Current bank advertising may be reinforced by the effect of previous advertising and may also enhance the demand to be created by future advertising.

Personal demand, once altered through advertising, tends subsequently to revert to its level of demand prior to the bank advertising exposure.

When personal demand for bank products and services is at a high level, it generally decays less rapidly and is less vulnerable to competition than when at a lower level of demand.

Bank advertising, in addition to its effect on personal demand, may affect availability, price, and other elements in the bank's selling proposition favorably as an essential supporting activity.

ADVERTISING PLANNING. Effective communication by the bank in its mass advertising effort requires that the bank marketing manager, the advertising manager, or the advertising agency develop, coordinate, and integrate a series of messages that are of interest to targeted audiences by using appropriate advertising media. There are several key components in an advertising program that require planning before they are assembled into the advertising section of the formal marketing plan. The advertising manager or the advertising agency usually prepares the advertising plan, which should include some provision for the following activities:

1. **Creative strategy.** This is the basic approach of copy and art to inform and persuade bank customers and prospects about the selling proposition
2. **Media strategy.** The establishing of communication objectives and the selection of communication channels for delivery of the messages, including the reach, frequency, size, and timing
3. **Advertising production.** The conception and preparation of message content including the form of the encoding instrument
4. **Advertising control.** The monitoring of feedback, measurement of results, and administration of the budgets
5. **Advertising research.** The collection and evaluation of qualitative and quantitative data on creative and media variables as they affect consumer comprehension and buying behavior relative to bank products and services

Rather than consider advertising as a pure cost, the concept that advertising by banks is an investment should be a prerequisite of any bank advertising program. The decision of senior bank management is to determine how much to invest in future growth. However, this decision can not be made until specific advertising objectives are established and costs for accomplishment have been estimated. Vague objectives and goals such as increasing sales or consumer awareness, although well intended, are not sufficiently precise to permit proper advertising planning. Although it is difficult to isolate the results of a total bank marketing effort by awarding credit to the efforts of a single component—sales versus advertising, for example—separate objectives and goals for each component are necessary for both planning and control purposes. Several specific objectives can be established for the bank advertising effort, including the following:

1. **Attracting new customers.** This objective requires convincing customers who have not used a bank product or service to do so, or to persuade consumers to switch from competitive financial institutions. The first objective is appropriate when introducing new products or services; the latter requires a unique strategy to attract customers from competitors.

2. **Expanding customer relationships.** This objective involves encouraging present customers to use additional products and services and is part of a synergistic cross-selling effort by bank customer contact personnel.

3. **Obtaining qualified sales leads.** Good prospects for contact by calling officers and customer sales representatives can be uncovered by the use of responsive advertising that includes prospect qualifiers as part of the advertising message.

4. **Increasing account size.** Because of the favorable effect of economies of scale, increases in deposit totals and loan outstandings on an average-per-customer basis generate additional bank revenue if appropriate spreads are maintained.

5. **Encouraging delivery system usage.** If the servicing costs of branches and ATMs can be spread over a larger volume of customers, they will result in a lower cost per transaction. Since most of the delivery system costs are fixed, this will improve operating efficiency and provide a cost advantage for the bank.

6. **Improving bank recognition.** The target market of customers and prospects can be convinced to use bank products and services by establishing a favorable image of safety, convenience, price, or service through the promotion of the bank as an outstanding source for each of these attributes.

7. **Neutralizing competitive advantages.** When it is necessary to refute or match competitive claims, a defensive type of advertising message may be required. This can be used to obtain the time needed for an aggressive type response with a new or revised bank product or service.

Whether it is a single advertisement or a complete campaign, the advertising program must have specific short-term goals that help achieve long-term objectives. Goals should help build immediate bank awareness since customers seldom do business with a relatively unknown bank without a strong inducement. Customers are also reluctant to use products or services that they fail to understand or if they lack conviction regarding personal or company benefit. All consumers, bank or otherwise, seek the immediate assurance that their decision to buy was a sound one. Consistent with these advertising requirements over the short term are some of the following appropriate goals:

To inform and persuade bank customers about product and service benefits

To invite further investigation by consumers with a personal visit to a branch or contact with a calling officer

To encourage greater product and service usage

To foster the trial and use of additional bank products in support of the bank's cross-selling effort

To support the bank's delivery system by helping to build lobby traffic and ATM usage

To establish the recognition and acceptance of the bank as a safe, convenient financial institution

To obtain and qualify sales leads for calling officers and customer contact representatives in the branches

To counteract the claims and favorable marketing actions of competitive financial institutions

To support the bank's sales promotion effort with appropriate mass communication

To augment the bank's public relations effort by communicating to those publics not covered adequately

The basic section on the advertising portion of the complete bank marketing plan is used to provide guidance for the advertising manager or the advertising agency to prepare a detailed advertising plan. Adequate guidance consists of specifications concerning the product features to be emphasized, the important customer benefits, the identification of targets, and specific advertising objectives and goals. A suggested format for the advertising plan is outlined next and is usually prepared as a separate document that is incorporated in the bank marketing plan appendix.

I. Advertising situation
   A. Review of the previous advertising program
      1. Bank advertising goals
      2. Bank advertising target audience
      3. Creative approach used
      4. Media mix used
      5. Advertising expenditures
      6. Summary of performance results
   B. Current bank advertising situation
      1. Bank product or service to be emphasized
      2. State of the market
      3. Nature of the bank delivery system
      4. Evaluation of competitive advertising
      5. Regulatory restrictions
      6. Bank organization requests and suggestions
      7. Limitations specified by senior management
II. Bank advertising strategy
   A. Identification and analysis of advertising problems
   B. Identification and analysis of advertising opportunities
   C. Advertising target audience
      1. Bank customers
      2. Bank prospects
      3. Bank correspondents
      4. Bank regulators
      5. Bank employees
      6. Local community leaders
      7. Financial analysts
      8. Suppliers
   D. Bank advertising goals
      1. Information and persuasion
      2. Confirmation and reinforcement
      3. Image and reputation
      4. Recognition and acceptance
      5. Sales prospecting
      6. Traffic building
III. Bank advertising programs (Campaigns)
   A. Product and service positioning
      1. Benefits and appeals

       2. Features and characteristics
       3. Pricing and qualifications
       4. Availability and restrictions
    B. Creative approach
       1. Copy theme
       2. Art and graphics
    C. Media plan (to be provided in detail as addendum)
    D. Advertising research
       1. Copy and art testing
       2. Advertising media research
       3. Performance feedback and analysis
IV. Bank advertising management
    A. Organization of the bank advertising function
    B. Coordination of the bank advertising effort
       1. Advertising production schedule
       2. Verification of advertising media insertions
    C. Control of the advertising program
       1. Bank advertising budget
          a. Advertising production
          b. Advertising media
          c. Advertising research
          d. Department administration
       2. Performance feedback
          a. Sales growth
          b. Bank prospect contacts
          c. Increase in bank acceptance and recognition
          d. Improvement in bank image and reputation
       3. Corrective advertising action
          a. Procedures for determination
          b. Contingency advertising programs
    D. Advertising program approval requirements
          a. Senior management
          b. Marketing management

    The preparation and implementation of the advertising plan require a detailed budget, not only for the control by the bank marketing manager, but to satisfy corporate controls on bank expenditures. In advertising, the expenditures required are substantial and the determination of how much is the proper amount is a question that bank marketing managers must be prepared to discuss with senior management. The response that is most likely is that the advertising budget must be large enough to accomplish the desired goals and objectives. Several factors affect the establishing of an advertising budget as well as the total bank marketing budget. These include bank affordability, competitive action, and anticipated return on the bank's investment in advertising. Because of the importance of budgeting and the particularly secular interest of bank management in all matters financial, budgeting will be covered in detail in Chapter 15.

While considering goals and objectives, the bank marketing manager and the advertising manager should also be familiar with some of the specific approaches or activities in bank advertising planning which may enhance the outcome. These planning guidelines include the following:

1. **Plan a total program.** All aspects of the program should be considered including a specific time period, a central theme, and supporting promotions. Preparing one advertisement at a time or any single advertising activity by itself without considering the synergistic effect of personal sales and sales promotion will lessen the effectiveness of the advertising program.

2. **Set long-term objectives.** Although some flexibility is desirable, a statement of continuing purpose or identifying a permanent strategy or direction is necessary for the establishing of short term goals that contribute to accomplishing crucial objectives over the long term.

3. **Consider advertising as an investment.** The accounting principles used by the bank may treat advertising as an expense item; however, the budget should only include those activities designed to increase the net income of the bank over the long term. This requires accepting the concept of investment rather than considering advertising as an immediate expense.

4. **Avoid herd advertising.** Rather than emulate competitive advertising, develop innovative approaches and techniques for delivering advertising messages to target audiences. It may be less risky to follow the success of competition, but there is less chance that the communication will be as cost-effective when it echoes the bank's leading competitors.

5. **Use appropriate media.** In spite of the claims of specific media regarding market coverage or audience delivery, some advertising media provide a more compatible bank message environment. There are qualitative as well as quantitative factors to consider when selecting a message channel.

6. **Resist corporate stardom.** Although some executives of the bank may be well qualified to represent the bank personally in business or social functions, none of them are professional models or actors. Rather than create believability through the use of actual bank per-

sonnel, advertising of this kind is often amateurish and reflects poorly on the professionalism of the institution, its people, and its products.

7. **Consider message length.** Some advertising messages need to be short, and others require length. A complicated bank product needs a complete explanation, whereas a simple statement of rate can be communicated directly. Rather than consider that all advertising space or time must be filled to the utmost, let the amount of the explanation be governed by audience comprehension instead of the media cost or the time and space that are available.

8. **Rely on advertising continuity.** Some advertising is designed to achieve immediate results; others build message comprehension and acceptance over time. However, some advertisements or programs may outlive their effectiveness even though they continue to be favored internally. Some advertising has a lag effect; other types need a build-up period of repetition of the message. The bank should allow the advertising program the time needed for success but it should not be continued once the feedback indicates that the results are less than those achieved initially.

ADVERTISING EFFECTIVENESS. Most members of senior bank management need reassurance concerning the effectiveness of bank advertising. E. B. White once wrote that if man were a predictable being, if he were selfless, humorless, saintly, and unacquisitive, advertising might be unnecessary. There is another saying that 50 percent of the advertising is wasted but that no one knows which 50 percent! This latter cliché may still be in the minds of many bankers. However, because of the importance of advertising in the bank marketing effort as well as the size of most bank advertising budgets, it is essential that the effectiveness of advertising be evaluated. In most banks, doubts notwithstanding, very little of the advertising budget is allocated to research and feedback analysis that is necessary to measure the effectiveness of advertising. This is in spite of strong evidence that senior management appears to be more receptive to proof than staff or agency reassurance.

Unfortunately, measuring the effectiveness of advertising is one of the least developed areas of marketing research. There are monumental problems involving the methodology required to isolate or identify the specific contribution of a single advertisement or an entire advertising program. The one exception may be the response to a direct mail campaign, which can be tallied upon receipt. The measurement of other types of advertising is difficult because so many variables affect a productive marketing effort.

For example, a new product may be successful because of its benefits, its features, the convenience of the delivery system, the rate, the selling ability of the customer contact people, the cumulative effect of previous advertising, or the current advertising effort. What is not known is the precise contribution of each.

The basic goal of a single advertising program does not have the primary aim of an immediate sale, even if such a sale was possible. Most marketing managers agree that it is almost impossible, except in the case of mail order marketing, for an advertisement to close a sale on its own. Bank customers, in particular, are sold as a result of a decision-making process that relies on informative and persuasive messages from the bank during the stage of decision consideration. Many advertising messages announce new branch openings, ATM locations, new banking hours, rate structures, and altered bank policies. This information is stored by the prospect or bank customer until the time of decision making. Measuring how much each of these advertisements contributed to a favorable decision would be next to impossible because of the time lag between the consideration and the decision for most bank products not open to impulse buying. Institutional advertising, which is designed to create a favorable image, build goodwill, or influence consumer attitudes is even more difficult to measure the contribution.

Professional advertising people are usually quick to voice opinions to bank marketing managers regarding the effectiveness of advertising, particularly if they are the source of origination. The area of conflict is obvious since they may be overly influenced by the technical aspects of a particular advertisement or campaign rather than by any reaction from the target audience verified by empirical evidence. Although it may be an added cost, the bank marketing manager should use an accepted research technique to sample consumer reaction. The effectiveness of an advertisement may be pretested or posttested. The most direct test after the fact is to measure the sales results, remembering that other variables made an undetermined contribution. As a consequence, most tests are indirect measurements and are primarily concerned with the communication effect as measured in terms of audience knowledge, feelings, and convictions. Most marketing research experts believe that the cause and effect correlation between sales and advertising is too complicated and long-term to allow for direct measurement. Their conclusion is often a simplistic quantitative one—the greater the number who see, read, and remember a bank advertisement, the greater the number who will do what the advertisement suggests.

For those banks who wish to make an effort at measurement, there are several ways to pretest or posttest the effectiveness of a single advertisement or a complete campaign. Opinion research uses data from potential bank customers who provide personal reactions to a given bank advertisement. This technique does not measure the attention-getting ability of the advertisement or the period it is remembered. Recognition tests can be used for message copy testing by having a respondent peruse a medium and note the advertisements that are recalled from a previous experience. In a recall test, the consumer is not shown any advertisements but is asked to remember and identify any advertising noticed recently. The recall can be aided if the bank is identified first or unaided if no identity is offered. These methods have achieved some degree of success, but it is extremely difficult to provide specific verification of the direct contribution of advertising to the total marketing effort of the bank.

ADVERTISING AGENCY SELECTION. Most banks must rely on the expertise of advertising agencies to prepare advertising campaigns. These professionals develop creative ideas and compose effective messages in a setting of art, film, and music that provide the most favorable means for decoding by the target audience. They can also conduct a specialized form of marketing research dealing solely with advertising. Advertising research that they initiate is concerned with the study of audience characteristics, media demographics, editorial environment, and message reception as well as many of the advertising measurement techniques discussed above. The selection of an advertising agency is very critical, but not all banks may require the in-depth services of a fully staffed agency. To determine whether or not to seek the services of an advertising agency, the following should be determined by the bank marketing manager:

Does the bank have the expertise in house to create and produce effective advertising?

Does the bank require the counsel of outside advertising specialists to reinforce internal expertise?

Does the bank require specialists in sources of advertising research and the essential promotion components related to mass communication?

Does the bank depend upon external sources to augment an internal staff that is limited in size and capability?

The evaluation process in the selection of the proper advertising agency is a time-consuming and extremely subjective exercise that the bank marketing manager must labor over as part of the advertising responsibilities. It is unfortunate that advertising agencies can not be compared on an objective basis. However, as with the principal variable, creative excellence, it is a matter of personal taste that makes the comparison of the capabilities of advertising agencies to be primarily one of subjective judgment. The impression created by a "dog and pony" show to demonstrate creativity and advertising philosophy is usually less than adequate to judge accurately the ability of the advertising agency to provide the expertise the bank requires. Although it is difficult to establish definitive criteria for advertising agency selection, some means of qualification and elimination should be used by the bank marketing manager before selecting finalists for an in-depth analysis of capability and compatibility with the advertising requirements of the bank. As an aid to the initial screening process, an advertising agency selection worksheet (Table 12-1) is provided for use by the bank marketing manager or the advertising manager.

COMPUTER USE IN ADVERTISING. There are very few industries who have a more accessible computer support capability than banks. The computer was incorporated into bank operations as a substitute for paper processing and record keeping; its true potential for use in marketing is still being realized only in a superficial way. The fundamental problem in the use of the computer in advertising as well as marketing has been the slow development of software to support the requirements of advertising data processing. The most promising areas are those in data collection and storage for the results of a specific creative approach involving message content—price appeals versus fear versus snobbery versus greed, for example, Much has been done, however, in the area of advertising media planning, execution, and control to the extent that much of the media selection and purchase has been programmed for computer processing. They are limited to the very large advertisers, however. One well known, large-scale media model has been developed under the COMPASS project through the joint effort of several national advertising agencies.

Advertising research analysis is concerned with the determination of the relationship of advertising variables in order to understand the communication process and to predict the outcome or benefits of an advertising program. Many of the statistical techniques used to analyze data have been used for many years in the social sciences but have only been adapted recently in marketing and, somewhat, in its component, advertising. There are four basic techniques for computer-based analysis:

1. **Factor analysis.** This is a technique to reduce redundancy in data. The computer program identifies those advertising variables that are associated with each other and reduces the number of factors to only the most significant ones.
2. **Chi-square analysis.** This quantitative technique determines

Table 12-1. Advertising Agency Selection Worksheet

	Agency A	Agency B	Agency C	Agency D
General background				
Agency time in business (years)				
Number of consumer accounts				
Number of industrial accounts				
Billings at present				
Billings in previous year				
Dominance of any account				
Have bank client at present				
Had bank client previously				
Local or national agency				
Member of AAAA				
Good business reputation				
Good credit references				
Organization				
Excellent facilities				
Sufficient staff support				
Experienced account head				
Staff available to work on account				
Compatible account people				
Office in close proximity				
Experience				
Any banking experience				
Good analytical skills				
Good samples of work				
Emphasis on creativity				
Emphasis on marketing				
Planning capability				
Media expertise				
Production expertise				
Research capability				
Sales promotion capability				
Public relations capability				
Financial				
Monthly service fee				
Commission structure				
Creative services rate (hour)				
Terms of payment				
Contract period				
Cancellation notice period				

whether the differences observed in sample advertising data from the theoretical expectations are true or whether it is likely that the differences are due purely to chance.

3. **Regression and correlation.** These measure the association of advertising variables and are widely used in other marketing components. These techniques determine whether or not a relationship exists between changes in advertising variables and changes in sales. Regression techniques are also used in forecasting and predicting quantitative outcomes.

4. **Analysis of variance.** This statistical technique is used in experimental research to analyze the contribution of the different advertising variables to the experimental result.

ADVERTISING MESSAGE. The message to be encoded for transmission through a communication channel should be one which relays the features or attributes of the bank products and services in terms of customer needs and desires. Communication theory explains that message comprehension is the result of a common understanding between the bank and its target audience. Before an advertising message can be decoded, it must attract the attention of the audience and hold their attention for a sufficient length of time to permit decoding, assimilation, understanding, and appreciation. Thus, gaining audience attention is an essential requisite for an advertising message.

Banks and other advertisers use a variety of approaches to gain attention such as the use of humor, sex, nostalgia, fear, snobbery, or greed. Since money is involved in the exchange of any product or service, emotion plays an important role in the mood of any audience for the reception of the advertising message. Few purchases of consumer products are made for entirely rational reasons. For example, most detergents are bought for the satisfaction of seeing children in bright, clean clothing, and to eliminate any guilt of being an inadequate parent or poor provider. Beer is a product that appeals to the feeling of masculinity and permits flights of fancy into the role playing of a professional athlete or other celebrity. The emotional quality represented by fashion, regardless of the discomfort or cost, is the feeling of stylishness and the boost of morale through an improved self-image. New cars are seldom purchased because of the mechanical failure of the previous car; many $10,000 cars are sold for the rationale that $250 worth of tires was needed on the old car. There is a pride and snob appeal of new car ownership that is even reinforced by the odor of the interior, which provides a pleasant sense of smell. In banking, the emotional influence of money is without parallel. Fear and greed play important roles in the selection of a safe, convenient, income-earning harbor for deposits.

There are some basic factors to be considered in the content of the bank advertising message. Basic rules for an effective message include unquestioned credibility, an attention-getting device, appropriate words to increase desire, and a direction for the audience to follow for the recommended resolution. There are several approaches to the proper message presentation:

1. **Informative approach.** The target audience receives an objective statement based on fact or strong evidence, and no evaluative statements that color the facts are included. It is successful if the audience is actively seeking financial information such as interest rates or loan availabilities from banks. This approach assumes that an audience will seek out the advertisement, decode the information, and make immediate judgment.

2. **The persuasive approach.** This creative approach not only uses facts but also judges and evaluates them. Instead of relying on facts alone, the audience is taken through a structural process of identifying and explaining the benefits of the features of the bank products or service. This approach is used in situations where high involvement decisions are appropriate, such as in refinancing or a second mortgage. The advertisement attempts to guide the customer's evaluation with strong rationales.

3. **The emotional approach.** By depending upon a pure emotional appeal, the message places its primary emphasis on the mood of the art, music, or the situation of the setting of the advertisement; product attributes receive secondary consideration only. This approach assumes that an emotional appeal will be more effective than an objective, rational treatment of product or service features. For banking, there are two strong appeals—fear and greed; humor is also used frequently. Banks use the first two appeals as a rationale for deposit safety; humor is used when products have little differentiation and the message relies on entertainment for attention and comprehension.

4. **The repetitive approach.** This is used with simple, uncomplicated advertising messages. This approach features one idea or premise that is stated continually in words, art, and sound. This simple, repeated message is used by banks when the frequency of the idea is more effective than the total substance of the selling proposition. Banks usually use this approach in relatively low audience involvement situations such as branch openings or the seating of a image-supportive slogan.

5. **The command approach.** In situations in which familiar products and services of the bank are being promoted, a more directed consumer behavior may be advisable. This approach states in a positive manner the course of action that the audience is expected to follow. It is often associated with such bank slogans or headlines as "Save now with safety," "Don't miss our extra interest," or "You need our bank—let us show you why."

6. **The emulation approach.** The message is encoded on the assumption that the bank customer will be motivated by the desire for association with a particular type of person or social or business group. This approach features endorsements or testimonials from presumably admirable individuals. The late John Wayne was used in television commercials with great success by Western Savings in California and the deposits increased dramatically as a result.

7. **The symbolic approach.** In this approach, symbols are used to establish a favorable association between the message and the bank. The symbol should appear as a key word or short phrase, a brief slogan, a recurring illustration or trademark, or a musical theme that can be easily recognized and remembered. Banks use this approach for the reminder advertising necessary for low customer involvement products when easy recall is important for the sale of such perennial products as IRAs, education loans, and Christmas Club accounts.

The advertising message must be encoded into some appropriate form for transmission to the target audience. The individual elements of the advertisement should be combined to create a total impression consistent with the content of the message. Since the message must be transmitted through a channel or medium, the final form of the advertising must be adaptable to the particular medium selected. For the purpose of characteristics and creative limitations, advertising channels or media can be segregated into four major categories—broadcast, print, outdoor, and transit.

Broadcast Commercials. The use of radio or television by banks is prevalent in every market of appropriate size. Unlike for other advertising media, the audience usually considers radio to be a source of background sounds or oral chatter rather than a medium with a particular editorial position or as a source of elaborate programming. A radio commercial may even be ignored unless it can overcome the limitation of being exclusively audio. The opening sounds of a radio commercial must command immediate attention by being dramatic and provocative in order to intrude into the listener's mind momentarily without being annoying. The product benefits must be stated in terms that are easy to understand. The name of the bank and the product or service must be repeated for memorability since most of the audience may require breaking through their current state of concentration. The message must be kept simple but it should make certain that the basic selling proposition is stated.

The television commercial offers an opportunity for the use of both audio and visual message techniques. The message must be encoded clearly since it has little sustained life and the audience may exhibit apathy during the decoding process because of the number of commercials that appear during each break in television. The bank commercial must attract attention immediately as well as sustain viewer interest against the distractions of home, family, or other competing elements in the viewing environment. If this is not accomplished during the first three to five seconds, the remaining time of the commercial will not be decoded satisfactorily. Since most bank products featured on television may be categorized as those with low customer involvement, it may be necessary to rely on some elements of entertainment. The video portion can be used to present the message humorously or dramatically by changing scenes as well as controlling the message sequence for the most effective story development. The visual techniques that can be used include personal endorsement; portrayal of a real-life situation at home, at work, or at the bank; a demonstration of the product being used to solve a financial problem; a customer's testimonial; pure humor; product or rate comparisons; and animation. The latter is usually the most expensive to produce. The audio portion is an essential and integral part of the message that works in concert with the video elements. The spoken word, music, and sound effects help to develop the thought behind the visual picture. The audio portion continues to have some communication value even when the audience loses eye contact with the commercial.

Print Advertisements. There are three essential elements in print media that make the encoding and decoding process effective. They comprise the headline, the words or copy that provide the details, and the illustration, picture, or style of graphics. The headline is used to attract the attention of the reader and must appeal immediately to the self-interest of the bank customer or prospect. The headline that promises benefits is more likely to attract reader interest than the one that highlights the past accomplishments of the bank. Headline words with a strong benefit appeal are *free* and *new.* A newsworthy element such as *now, at last,* or *for a limited time* is also effective. Because of the nature of bank products, words with an emotional impact such as *money, love, security, family, baby,* or *safety* have high attention-getting value. Research verifies the importance of the headline in print advertising by indicating that five times as many people read the headlines as the detailed copy in the body of the advertisement.

Notwithstanding the reduction in readers, the body copy or detailed explanation is an essential element for those who survive the headline attention and interest qualification. Copy should be succinct, direct, enthusiastic, and written with expressions that are easily decoded by the reader. Humorous copy is the most difficult to write since it requires that helpful information be combined with entertainment without having the bank or its products lose credibility. Positive appeals are more effective than those that are negative in their approach. Directly attacking competitors is not only dangerous, but with the correspondent and loan syndication possibilities, the bank may be burning its bridges for little gain in communication effectiveness. Body copy for bank products should be specific without being tiresome; the laws require that advertising copy be factual in most instances; exceptions are permitted in situations that are obviously fantasies. The copy should avoid superlatives, generalizations, and platitudes; readers usually discount them, and they make impressions that are not favorable over time. Another word of caution: avoid leisurely essays by getting to the point quickly and emphatically.

The art dimension of a print advertisement is also a key element whose importance may be overlooked by the nonprofessional. The illustration should have story appeal that indicates a real-life, believable situation. Because money is involved, bank situations should attempt to portray some reward in the form of interest, material possession, safety, or convenience. To attract women readers, use babies or women in the illustration; to attract men, show other men, particularly successful businessmen, community leaders, or celebrities of high repute. Most historical illustrations should be avoided since they usually require some explanation as to why they are being used in a selling situation. This may detract from or water down the copy devoted to information that the audience may desire for use in the decision-making process.

The use of color in print usually results in greater recall of the advertisement. From a psychological standpoint, certain colors can be used to create appropriate moods for the printed message. For example, red expresses anger, excitement, action and danger, making it rather inappropriate for banking messages. On the other hand, green, the color of money, denotes freshness, youth, nature, serenity, and safety. White is used to portray purity and cleanliness; black suggests mystery, death, and mourning. Sorrow, truth, or coolness can be represented by blue, and yellow and orange may indicate either fall or spring seasonal activities as well as heat, fire, or caution. The last dimension of art is identified as graphics. This represents the style of typeface used for the printing or the layout, the way the advertisement is organized. Script typeface is considered feminine, while bold black letters masculine. This element of the printed message requires highly professional advice from the bank's advertising agency or art service.

Outdoor and Transit Showings. The messages transmitted over these media must be relatively short and to the point. It has been estimated by media experts that any message more than ten words in length will be lost because of vehicle or passenger mobility. Viewers are subject to many distractions that make the art or illustration less likely to create an impression unless it is kept simple and large in size. Many banks use these media to establish concepts or slogans since the message over these channels usually remains over a thirty-day period. This provides continuity and a degree of message permanence. The key to an effective message is the succinct wordage and the attractive use of color illustrations.

MESSAGE EFFECTIVENESS. There has been extensive advertising research regarding the various message techniques used to increase reception and decoding accuracy. In television, the most effective techniques are those that deliver a message in a problem-solving situation or that feature conditions in which the resolution is one that converts a doubter into a believer. Using relevant and familiar characterizations can help in bank and product association. News in the form of new products, new uses, new information, or new ideas gets viewer attention immediately. Candid testimonials with credible subjects and demonstrations of product in use or customers being served are also extremely effective. Less effective techniques are those with messages built around celebrities whose high repute is not accepted automatically; controversial personalities tend to draw the bank into the controversy. Adults are not as susceptible to animation or cartoons as children appear to be. Very short scenes and many situation changes do not permit the viewer to concentrate on a recurring theme or rationale. If the opening scene of the television commercial has a key idea or concept that does not seem to have relevance that is easily recognized, it becomes more difficult for the viewer to decode the message accurately. For example, an opening fire scene can be used for information on fire extinguishers or insurance but does not set the scene properly for checking accounts or IRAs.

The most effective techniques for print advertisements are those that use messages with some elements of news value. Story appeal should be a part of the illustration, and those situations that have a "before" and "after" dimension are also very effective. In banking, the product or service should be demonstrated in use before a description of the result of using it is portrayed. Also for banking, long headlines may be more productive than short ones because of the impact of emotion in money matters and the need for a fairly complete explanation at the attention and interest stage. In printed messages, some of the techniques that are less effective for television are also applicable in the print media. Illustrations using celebrities as bank spokespersons require using those individuals with excellent reputations. Cartoons do not portray the image of stability and safety that the banks need to be associated with—Smokey the bear notwithstanding. Key concepts or ideas that are pertinent must also be used in print media illustrations to reinforce the body copy.

BANK ADVERTISING MEDIA. The channels used by the bank to deliver the advertising message normally represents the largest expenditure in the bank's advertising budget, so the selection of the most effective channels is critical to the communication effort. No one medium is likely to reach the total target market of the bank. To select the most appropriate media, both the qualitative and quantitative factors must be considered. There are four quantitative criteria used for the evaluation of advertising channels: reach, frequency, gross rating points, and cost per thousand persons in the audience.

Reach is the ability of the medium to deliver messages to readers, listeners, viewers, or riders. It consists of the number of people who are contacted by the medium during a stated period. Reach is expressed in terms of circulation for print media, or listeners and viewers as audiences for broadcast media. Outdoor or transit circulation readers are described as riders. Frequency is the number of times that an advertisement appears during the specified time period in the medium used. Each insertion of an advertisement or commercial can also be used to indicate frequency. The frequency quantitative element is significant because it can be used to indicate the amount of message repetition that is required to obtain sufficient message exposure. Gross rating points is a summary measure of reach and frequency, with reach expressed as a percentage of the total audience and with frequency indicating the number of times the advertisement appears. The gross rating points (GRPs) only reflect the magnitude of the media effort since the effectiveness of the media plan is highly dependent upon the specific way the GRP is delivered. The cost per thousand element evaluates the efficiency of the amount of media used on the basis of its cost relative to the audience reached. To use this quantitative measurement, the same size space or time units between media must be used for comparison.

The qualitative considerations of message channels can be used to augment the objective measures obtained from the quantitative factors. One quality involves waste circulation, or a share of the audience that is not in the bank's target audience but cannot be excluded from the coverage. This wasted portion must be paid for as part of the total even though the message may not be pertinent or of any interest to that segment of the audience. Banks must also be concerned with the appropriateness of the medium selected. Some of the determinants of this qualitative dimension are the editorial climate, as represented by the kind of audience it appeals to, and the nature of the bank product being advertised: messages about trust services would be wasted on a radio station playing rock music. An additional factor is the technical characteristics of the medium. For example, television is most appropriate for messages requiring visual effects, and technical publications have a very selective readership that is susceptible to information that is presented in depth. Newspapers provide for parochial interests with special sections devoted to business, sports, local news, and so on.

The relative exposure capability is another qualitative measurement. Some media are more likely than others to provide message exposure: television may suffer from scheduled absences during commercial breaks. Page or section positions in print media vary in the amount and type of readership delivered. The chances of getting reader or viewer attention should also be estimated; at certain times, radio may only serve as background music for someone busy with other activities. Newspaper readers may pass over or only notice advertisements as they search for the continuation of a news article. The matter of repeated exposure can also be qualitative because there can be a favorable cumulative effect among an audience with strong media loyalties.

From a bank's perspective, there are differences in message channels or advertising media that the bank marketing manager must recognize before the preparation of the media plan within the advertising plan. Each medium has its own strengths and weaknesses, and they usually differ in three respects—the costs for delivering the advertising message; the type of reader, viewer, listener, or rider who uses the medium for information or entertainment; and the technical characteristics or capabilities that affect the way the message can be delivered.

Television Media. Television is a message channel that combines sight, sound, and motion and is unique among all advertising media. It appeals to the senses of an individual while providing mass audience coverage. It is a dynamic attention getter, but it attracts a mass horizontal audience rather than one that is more secular or vertical. The television audience is less selective, and the impressions it makes are fleeting and require costly repetition for a lasting impression. The short life of commercials make them expensive for banks in spite of the relatively low cost per thousand rate. Household television usage has been estimated to be almost seven hours daily, reaching 60 percent of the households at a given time. Unfortunately for banks, the target audience for bank products and services can best be reached during the prime time of the evening hours when the commercial time costs are highest. Few banks can justify the wide audience of television, although, under certain circumstances when information must be communicated to a mass audience very quickly, television offers the necessary reach and dynamism for bank usage.

Radio Media. The use of an audio channel is second only to that of newspapers by the banking industry. The major advantages of radio are its reach and audience selectivity at a relatively low cost. Radio caters to an audience that is out of the home during the day since the evening hours require competition with television. Because of its technical structure, radio has geographic flexibility that permits vertical audience coverage that can be coordinated with the bank's branch office locations. Production costs, particularly when compared to those for television, are modest and with the nature of the medium being audio only, the message can be imaginative, using low-cost sound effects to create situations and locations without an actual presence. However, radio has some disadvantages since it requires a minimum of audience emotional participation or involvement. Although the audience of a television channel must watch the programs actively, or readers of magazines or newspapers must make a conscious effort to digest their contents, playing the radio is not usually the primary focus of the listener's attention; the radio audience reads, drives, works, or studies with the radio turned on while concentrating on other activities.

Newspaper Media. The newspaper is the principal channel used for the advertising messages of banks because this medium provides excellent coverage of the local market. A Simmons readership study indicated that over 75 percent of all households read a newspaper daily and that over a one-week period, almost 90 percent of all adults have read at least one newspaper. People read newspapers for the information that is conveyed on local as well as national events. Other media studies reveal that the printed word is usually more credible than the spoken word. This credibility offers a media advantage to bank products and services. By association with a reliable source of news, bank messages may also attain some measure of news value and an urgency to act. Newspapers are also more unique than broadcast media since the advertising is considered an attribute; people often buy a

Sunday newspaper for its advertising. One technical advantage is the short lead time required for the production and insertion of a newspaper advertisement. Banks can take advantage of recent events that may increase the attractiveness of the bank's selling proposition. Of particular interest to banks is the capability of a newspaper advertisement to accommodate the long, detailed message necessary for a complicated product or service such as cash management or personal trust accounts. Its disadvantages as a message channel are its short life, its poor reproduction quality, its lack of arresting colors other than black and white, and the clutter of competing retail advertisements.

Magazine Media. Magazines provide banks with a more vertical or precise audience selection option. They feature the relatively high demographic and psychographic selectivity that most bank products and services require. The editorial content associated with magazines can be used to complement the bank and its selling proposition. The types of magazines—consumer, business, farm, hobby, or technical—can be matched with the message. Unlike newspapers, magazines have a relatively long life. They are reread, retained, and passed along to nonsubscribers for additional coverage. The message is enhanced with high-quality reproduction and the widespread use of color. The geographical limitations that work to the disadvantage of local banks are mitigated somewhat by local and regional editions of national publications. The major disadvantages are the lengthy lead time required, the clutter of the many and varied advertisements, and the relatively high cost of production of the advertisement.

Outdoor and Transit Media. Outdoor and transit media have many similarities that can be considered together when making an analysis of message channels. In many smaller communities, transit media are not available. Except in those areas where local legislation prohibits it, outdoor or billboard advertising is almost universally available. The principal advantage of each of these media is the reach obtained with excellent geographic selectivity. Shopping areas or transit routes in proximity to the bank's delivery system can be selected for outdoor or bus card locations for advertising. The audience is out-of-home, and, because of consumer driving or public transit patterns, repeated exposure to the message is possible. Both of these channels have a low cost per thousand rate and can provide excellent visual impact. The audience is large for each medium, but the attention level is low because of viewer distractions and the clutter of competing signs. Space in transit advertising is often limited, and the primary factor in its audience characteristics is geographic rather than demographic or psychographic.

Direct Mail Media. Direct mail can serve as either an advertising medium or as a sales promotion technique. If offers the most audience selectivity of any message channel and the advertising can be personalized with exceptional flexibility in the format and design of the message. Personalization is achieved by the use of mailing lists of business firms and individuals which have been prequalified according to certain specifications. Obviously, the particular characteristics are those that indicate excellent banking potential. The advertising schedules are also flexible and can be controlled by the bank. The quality of personalization is achieved through expense; this medium has the highest cost per thousand rate, although its use on a fewer number of people may net out to be a smaller total expenditure. There is some consumer resistance to direct mail media, which has been categorized as "junk mail." However, the use of first-class postage or a bulk mail rate, provided that the bank is clearly identified on a business-type envelope, helps assure that the letter will be opened rather than discarded immediately.

Videotex Media. Videotex is a relatively new channel that can serve as an advertising medium or become the key element in providing a home banking service. A more detailed explanation of this channel is provided since it offers excellent potential for bank usage. *Videotex* refers to computer services that display textual and graphic information on remotely located video screens such as personal computers or specially adapted television sets. These terminals are linked to a central host computer through the telephone. Another method of receiving videotex is by cable. It can also be transmitted over optical fiber or by satellite. Because this medium allows the consumer to receive from and send information to the central host computer, videotex is not only an advertising medium, but a two-way, interactive communication system. The value to a bank is that it can provide home banking services through a new geographic reach. Citibank's HomServe offers account information, bill paying, and cash through pre-signed travelers checks. Chemical Bank's Pronto also offers account information and a bill-paying service. Both systems have the capability to provide information on products and services with effective advertising messages.

Programs, Catalogs, and Directories. Directories, catalogs, and programs have a particularly important role in providing basic information for banks. These channels include such essential consumer directories as the yellow and white pages of the telephone companies, as well as the R. L. Polk directories that report bank financial statements, officer listings, and transit numbers. Many organizations, from the chamber of commerce to service and social clubs, provide a variety of communication vehicles. Bank marketing managers should be very selective since some of these are marginal in value and would be more appropriate if carried in the budget of the bank's contribution committee instead of being charged to the advertising budget. These media may affect customer relations by situations that may require advertising in certain fund-raising programs. Although they usually have little advertising value, if their use is necessary, an effort should be made to deliver a message of some substance.

MEDIA PLANNING. The communication process of encoding a message will not reach the target audience unless the most effective communication channel is used. The numerous options in the selection of bank advertising media, as indicated by the many types described here, must be analyzed as part of an overall media strategy. The appropriate selection and scheduling of channel delivery is necessary if the message is to be decoded by the target audience at the most opportune time in a message environment that is favorable. The bank media strategy is determined by identifying and selecting communication objectives once the target market has been specified. The media strategy is also affected by the type of advertising message planned because the various channels have individual characteristics that enhance or lessen the impact of the message. One final consideration in the strategy is the competition that exists in the marketplace to reserve or monopolize the most efficient and productive channels. The best times or the most desirable space in key media are usually at a premium so plans must be made well in advance to obtain the most favorable channel positions.

The media plan includes the type of information necessary for sound recommendations. The media plan is supplementary to the advertising plan, which, in turn, is an integral part of the complete bank marketing plan. The following outline can be used by the bank marketing manager or the advertising manager in making the media recommendations necessary for the bank advertising program:

    I. Media objectives
       A. Target audience
       B. Geographic area
          1. Nationally
          2. Regionally
          3. Statewide
          4. Locally
       C. Period of time

       D. Product image requirement
       E. Product information requirement
   II. Media strategy
       A. Technical specifications
          1. Reach and frequency requirements
          2. Media dominance by competitors
          3. GRP requirements by product and service
       B. Selection of media
          1. Specific types of media available
          2. Efficiency standards (cost per thousand)
          3. Scheduling limitations
  III. Media action plan
       A. Identification of primary media to be used
          1. Name and location
          2. Space and time units to be used
          3. Duration of schedule
       B. Quantitative analysis
          1. Reach
          2. Frequency
          3. Gross rating points
       C. Qualitative analysis
          1. Waste coverage
          2. Editorial climate
       D. Competitive considerations
          1. Media dominance
          2. Media void
       E. Provisions for flexibility
          1. Lead time for production of advertisements
          2. Schedule cancellation provisions
       F. Media schedule
          1. Detailed schedule of dates and times
          2. Coordination requirements
          3. Verification of appearance of advertising
       G. Media budget
          1. Expenditures by product and service
          2. Cost allocation per medium
          3. Cost of advertising production
          4. Administrative cost
          5. Reserve for media price increases
 IV. Media performance feedback
       A. Comparative ratings of media
          1. Reach

2. Cost per thousand
B. Reader–viewer response to advertising
C. Contingency media plan

The advertising management of the bank is concerned with the three essential activities that contribute to an effective communication effort to bank customers and prospects. These activities include the message, the channel, and the reception by a targeted audience. Basic decisions must be made regarding communication objectives, media strategy, and message approach. The results, as indicated by feedback, must be monitored to permit revision or adjustments. Major changes may require the implementation of a contingency media plan. The importance of the mass communication effort is such that it may be essential to enlist the professional expertise of an experienced advertising agency in the process of program development as well as for the continuous implementation of the bank advertising effort.

13

BANK PUBLIC RELATIONS

The second major area of mass communication is concerned with situations that affect banks because they operate in a human environment that is fueled by personal opinions and attitudes. Perceptions have become more significant than fact. To counteract negatives and to reinforce positions, bank public relations attempts to establish and enhance a favorable image of the bank as a whole among its various publics. To the extent that the human environment is less than favorable, the marketing effort of the bank will be less effective, relationships with regulators or other banks may suffer, or customers will express their negative opinions by moving to another financial institution. In its most academic form, public relations includes all activities and attitudes of the bank and its people to respond to or to influence the opinions of individuals or groups of persons in the secular interest of the bank. This aspect of mass communication attempts to persuade the various publics that the bank is a responsible member of the local community and an excellent organization to patronize in the conduct of their banking requirements.

The role of public relations differs from that of the other promotional components, personal sales, sales promotion, and advertising. These components seek to establish and enhance a positive bank product or service image through informative and persuasive techniques as a prelude to sales. Public relations attempts to win the esteem of the bank's publics by its corporate conduct in order to earn and deserve that respect. This is accomplished by the bank's communication activities to establish and maintain their regard. Carefully planned and managed communication and special event programs are designed to improve the opinions and attitudes of the appropriate publics. Since there is a close link between the image of the bank and its reflection on bank products and services, the two must be consistent and reinforcing. Therefore, public relations has an important role in an effective, synergistic bank marketing effort. The importance of public relations is growing, not only because of the heightened sensitivity about bank safety, but because of the proliferating of mass media and the fragmenting of audiences into special interest groups. Less traditional bank marketing communication techniques such as public relations are becoming increasingly efficient and productive in relation to mass advertising

PUBLIC RELATIONS VERSUS ADVERTISING. Although advertising may play a supporting role to public relations in some communication situations, and contrary to the belief of some bankers, advertising and public relations are not synonymous. The old explanation that advertising is paid for and that public relations is free is not only an oversimplification but incorrect. There are three dimensions to corporate communication as it relates to the degree of control that can be exercised by the encoder of the message—the content, the channel, and the timing. All three may be controlled by the bank if advertising is the form of mass communication used since it is contracted and paid for. With public relations, none of the three dimensions can be controlled completely. The message is subject to editing by the media, the decision to transmit the message in part or not at all rests with the media, and the time and place of transmission are also determined solely by the media involved. Incidentally, public relations is never free because the preparation and implementation have variable costs, as does any bank promotional activity.

Public relations pertains to the bank as a whole and not solely to the building of demand for specific bank products and services. The difficulty in integrating public relations into the overall bank promotional effort is that the public relations program is directed toward many important audiences other than to bank customers and prospects exclusively. Its activity is oriented toward image building with such pertinent publics in addition to bank customers as the investment community, bank regulators, materials suppliers, community leaders, and the bank's own employees. As a result, a public relations specialist in the bank may have neither the expertise for product and service marketing nor the time and attention to devote to it. Because of government involvement, the legal complications, and the high emotional considerations that the public associates with banking, the public relations function is not always a normal part of the marketing organization. Under certain conditions, it can report directly to senior management or, if through the bank marketing manager, with frequent bypassing of the normal bank reporting structure. In spite of the organizational exceptions and the broad nature of the public relations function, it can still play an essential role in the bank's promotional effort by the use of supportive product and service publicity in mass communication media.

Many banks have some confusion regarding the differences between public relations and publicity, a form of public relations that is more akin to advertising. *Public relations* is the macro term used to describe a philosophy of total bank behavior relative to a wide variety of publics. *Publicity* is a micro activity that is a specialized technique used in the promotion of the bank and its products and services as part of the total marketing program. The direct responsibility for publicity is often assigned to the marketing department, whereas the overall public relations effort is closely monitored by the executive office of the bank. Public relations has certain characteristics making it not only unique but essential in banking. Although not free of cost, it can often reach a target audience with a more credible message at much less cost than a comparable advertising effort. It is possible to target the particular interests and attitudes of small, yet important, market segments. This is in contrast to advertising, in which high media and production costs can only be justified with mass audience coverage. Since most public relations activities are not based on an obvious commercial message, audiences tend to attach the credibility of the communication medium directly to the message. The quality or the newsworthiness of the message will help the bank compete with other financial institutions seeking media exposure. Editors are seldom interested in stories that lack human interest or novel information; most try not to be influenced by the amount of advertising expenditures committed by the bank in their medium, but the realities of business make editorial integrity difficult to maintain.

THE BANK PUBLICS. As the era of deregulation continues, all financial institutions must cope with the growing number of customers or other influential publics whose first concern is institutional quality and reliability. Performance is subjective, and it is measured or judged through both personal experience and unfounded rumor. Opinions and attitudes of noncustomers as well as those of customers have tremendous influence over a bank's image and reputation. All competitors in the marketplace must constantly offer proof of performance with candid words, completed deeds, and corporate behavior which matches or exceeds the public's expectations if the bank wishes to operate successfully. In an effort to establish and maintain an acceptable bank image, the public relations effort must be directed toward a wide range of audiences. The present customers are at one end of the spectrum, and government regulators are at the other. In between, there are shareholders, employees, and suppliers, to name a few of the major publics.

Bank Customers and Prospects. The public most sensitive to the image of the bank consists of present and future customers. This is the public segment that is not only the most responsible for bank revenue, but the one in which the crucial opinions and attitudes originate. These perceptions are based on the corporate communications as well as user experience. The way the bank performs its banking functions is a prime factor because customers equate the bank's image with the nature of its services and the way they are performed. The types of business or customers the bank seeks also tend to differentiate it in the public mind. From an image perspective, in most markets there are "the biggest bank," with the greatest number of branches or assets, or "the businessman's bank," which appears to be most interested in commercial accounts; "the upscale bank," which attracts customers of more affluence by specializing in customized, more costly, personal services; and "the price bank," which pays the highest interest for deposits but does not offer the lowest cost for other types of service. These are images that banks can assume and that customers as well as prospects recognize because many of the overt activities of the bank reinforce them.

There was a time when the bank's image was based on the single premise of providing money when the customer needed it—immediate access to the customer's own deposits or the availability of bank money whenever the customer requested it. Deposit and loan relationships are still fundamental to this important public but more is expected now. This public expects more efficient service, greater convenience, genuine employee concern, and unquestioned safety. Although the customer public may display some lack of concern, they often demonstrate dissatisfaction after the fact by leaving the bank for a competitor. To prevent this ultimate reaction, the maintaining of good customer relations with this public is an activity that is one of the most essential in the public relations program. This activity recognizes the importance of the customer public to the bank and numerous techniques are used. New branches or renovated facilities can attract new customers. New products or services create new banking relationships and strengthen present ones. Marginal courtesies such as making tax and license forms available or offering free notary service build goodwill with the customer public. A courteous, well-trained staff gives the impression of professionalism which will reflect a favorable image. Delivery system hours and locations suited to the accepted requirements of the consumer public for convenience are also necessary to foster good customer relationships. Present customers are also the most productive source for new customer referrals.

Business and Professional Community. The image and reputation of the bank among the local, regional, or national business firms is an important relationship factor for corporate banking. This public includes such corporate entities as large national corporations and their local offices or plants, middle-market firms, and small neighborhood businesses. The many professionals consist of medical doctors, dentists, engineers, technicians, lawyers, accountants, and educators. In most instances, these publics are opinion leaders in the community, and the bank needs to establish a reputation among them as an innovator in bank technology through the development of new products and services as well as a more efficient delivery system. These business influentials will be impressed with the bank's size and its earnings record; they will also require more personalized service by bank officers who are experts in financial matters. These individuals usually occupy positions of importance and serve as referral sources as well as individual customers. This public also expects bank awareness of social issues and active participation in community projects. It requires an especially effective public relations effort to cultivate these influentials successfully.

Government Officials. The government is very important to banks because of the regulatory issue. Representatives of the federal as well as state bank regulatory agencies are particularly sensitive to situations or issues involving the bank that reflect adversely on the financial institution, its employees, or its customer relationships. The laws and regulations that govern the banking industry can be influenced to some extent by the nature of the relationship developed with those legislators who make the laws and those bureaucrats who regulate banks by enforcing the laws. Their regulatory province ranges from local traffic and zoning ordinances that affect the physical operations of the bank to the federal regulation of credit and deposit products and services. State and local governments can also be important customers for the bank because they are often a source of large deposit balances and are users of many bank services. One problem area involving this public concerns the ease with which local and national politicians make the banking industry a scapegoat. The mysteries and misunderstandings about finance among both the electorate and their elected or appointed officials permit the negative impressions of a mortgage foreclser, a usury interest charger, an international cartelist, or a deliberately slow check clearer to be associated with all banks. Although some of these generalizations are a problem for all banks, it can be countered individually be recognizing both the power and the lack of banking knowledge of most public officials not directly engaged in bank regulation.

Financial Community. There are several segments of the financial community public that affect the bank. Other commercial banks are an important public, not only as ethical competitors, but as possible correspondents or loan syndication participants. Many times, a competitive bank may serve as a referral for business that cannot be serviced profitability because of lack of expertise or because of loan portfolio limitations that inhibit its capability. In addition to direct competitors, others in the financial community such as investment bankers, stockbrokers, financial counselors, accountants, security analysts, and investors are not only sources of business but also business advisors and opinion leaders. These publics can be prospective sources of capital, deposits, loans, or users of fee-based services. From a public relations perspective, these publics look for a healthy pattern of growth in bank earnings as well as a strong balance sheet. They welcome and expect quarterly statements of condition, bank presentations to meetings of security analysts, and interviews with the editors of financial publications and business sections of the local newspapers. They are also interested in branch expansion plans, earnings projections, asset and liability management perspectives, and economic forecasts for the primary markets served by the bank.

Shareholders. The banks can no longer assume that shareholders will agree to whatever management suggests. The typical bank shareholder is no longer a passive, silent investor who appears to be indifferent to the policies of management. Few banks really know the characteristics and attitudes of their shareholders unless the bank stock is closely held and not traded. A knowledge of shareholder motivations, opinions, and investment philosophies is necessary to understand their bank information requirements. One segment of this public, whose characteristics are probably well-known, is the board of directors who represent other shareholders. Although the board is ultimately responsible for the operation of the bank, they also represent the key public between the bank employees and the investors. They are also very susceptible to rumors and negative opinions concerning the bank which are voiced by their business and community associates. They can serve as a public relations advocate or channel in addition to their role as a sensitive public that merits special public relations emphasis.

Bank Employees. Another public are the bank's operations, technical, contact, and supervisory personnel who are involved with credit denial, check cashing, customer complaints, and many of the sensitive areas of customer relations that can be a source of public relations problems. These employees are crucial in customer contact and require an excellent state of satisfaction and understanding that can only result from an atmosphere of good employee relations. This is accomplished by providing adequate compensation, satisfactory working conditions, acceptable terms of employment, opportunity for advancement, enlightened supervision, and respected leadership. The way that branch managers and department heads respond to individual personnel problems and employee needs, as well as to legitimate questions or concerns about bank policies and procedures, also affects employee relations.

Bank Suppliers. Bank suppliers constitute a public that is often overlooked as a source of endorsement or negative opinion. Suppliers are a knowledgeable and highly visible resource that provides essential materials and services to the bank. They are not only privy to many of the bank's internal problems through direct contact with bank employees, but they can help ensure continuity of supply, fair prices, and responsive service if good relations are maintained. By keeping them current on the business needs and the financial condition of the bank, they can often make practical suggestions for cost savings, recommend substitute materials, and provide technical and administrative support in their areas of expertise as well as referrals in the local business community.

Society-at-Large. The general public, in its role as members of society rather than as individuals, is a large, heterogeneous group that can be contacted effectively with a public relations program. This public includes the people in the communities and neighborhoods served by the bank and its delivery system. Some of the important issues of interest to this public include the stability of the bank, its employment policies and opportunities, and the community support it provides. The latter includes participation in the local charitable, cultural, and recreational programs. Society-at-large has a strong interest in having the bank be a member of the community as an important resource, and by sharing in many of the community's responsibilities. This includes all forms of participation from little league teams, to United Way drives, to symphony sponsorship.

Once the key publics have been identified, it is necessary for the bank marketing manager or the bank's public relations specialist to analyze these publics to determine how they view the bank as an institution, its people, and its products and services. This is the initial step in the public analysis process. When the public attitudes and opinions have been determined, it is necessary to list some of the actions appropriate for the bank's institutional behavior to bring about a change or to neutralize those public opinions or attitudes which are less than favorable. Once these requirements have been determined, the formal planning of the public relations program can be initiated.

BANK PUBLIC RELATIONS PROGRAM PLANNING. To develop an effective program, it is necessary for the bank marketing manager or the public relations specialist to plan in terms of cohesive programs rather than a series of separate events. It is very possible, particularly if the bank does not have a public relations specialist on staff, to seek the expertise of a public relations agency. Unless uniquely qualified, most advertising agencies are not well equipped to provide public relations services; advertising expertise is not comparable. Those who develop public relations programs should provide messages whose content is not exaggerated. If the information is credible, and the program helpful, favorable media coverage and effective public relations will be forthcoming. Selection of any program should be based in part on the particular needs and culture of the local community. Overly ambitious programs should be avoided; they should be funded and managed within the resource limitations of the bank. It must be remembered that there is a primary business function for the bank. However, the bank should always be aware that economic gain can not be the sole purpose of a public relations program. Unless there is an obvious commitment to involve the bank in some way with a community event or problem, the public may consider the effort to be profit oriented rather than for the betterment of the community.

Each bank has a unique approach to public relations, however, most have many similarities in the functions performed. The following are some of the public relations activities directed toward the most important publics of the bank.

Customer Relations. Customer relations require that the bank train its employees, particularly the customer contact personnel, to conduct business transactions in a professional manner. The bank products and services are the basis for contact so that the nature of most customer relationships is determined by the satisfaction the customer receives. Commercial banks are often confused with thrifts, mutuals, and other financial institutions by the average customer; therefore, literature, feature articles in print media, special subject coverage over broadcast channels, and other informative techniques are needed to explain the differences and the limitations of nonbank institutions. Bank personnel must perform personal services for customers willingly, handle the smallest checking accounts with careful attention, and treat installment loans as one of the most essential products. If this is done with courtesy, understanding, and with an obvious intent to serve customers well, the relationship will become closer and bank patronage will grow.

Government Relations. To determine the need for public relations activities involving the government the bank must maintain dependable sources for intelligence concerning government policies and proposals. This will require effective and productive contacts with appropriate elected and appointed city, state, and federal officials. Public relations support can be provided in the preparation of letter responses, formal briefings, agency or legislative testimony, or other techniques to communicate the bank's or the industry position to key government officials. Banks should also participate in legitimate lobbying efforts.

Shareholder Relations. Shareholders are most concerned with the financial condition of the bank. Such information can be presented by preparing and distributing quarterly statements of condition and annual reports directly to shareholders. Annual meetings are required by law, but they are also essential. These, and occasional letters to shareholders from the CEO, provide a valuable communication vehicle to keep shareholders informed. Letters of welcome to new shareholders and rapid response to any letters of inquiry from shareholders will also foster better relationships. Because of their influence on potential investors as well as current shareholders, security analysts should be contacted with some regularity by the bank's chief financial officer.

Employee Relations. In addition to the basic requirements of adequate compensation and good working conditions that are necessary to establish a positive internal relationship, employees need to have more information about the bank, its plans, and its progress. House organs and newsletters, employee recognition programs, the staff or department meetings with two-way discussion, and bankwide social gatherings are some of the techniques that can be used. Occasional employee surveys and a complaint procedure or suggestion system will help provide leading indicators of possible problems affecting morale, operations procedures, bank policies, or employee attitudes.

Community Relations. Community relations should include not only the location of the bank's headquarters, but the communities and neighborhoods where branches are located or planned. Programs and techniques to foster good community relations include the involvement and support of local philanthropic, youth, and cultural organizations, for example. To maintain contact with local press and broadcast representatives is extremely important; some may even become good customers of the bank. Media contact can be enhanced by establishing a speakers' bureau and having key bank people, with appropriate skills, accessible to the press and also available for community forums. In this regard, public relations is the function responsible for interpreting the bank's policies, actions, and positions on public affairs to the press and other mass media. This will require press conferences, detailed briefings, and personal interviews. Press statements, news releases, news pictures, feature stories, broadcast tapes, and other appropriate communication tools are all used.

Education Relations. Relations with the academic community are a growing area of concern to banks because of the liberal bias of some educators, which may result in misinformation about banking functions and banks as institutions serving the public. To counteract any bias, banks must become more visible on campus and continue their longstanding support of education through financial contributions. Educational materials and guest speakers should be provided as well as bank tours for students and teachers. Effective relationships should be maintained with key educators and membership on the bank's board of directors may provide an excellent means for bank involvement with these influential individuals. One key technique is to participate in a summer hiring program for teachers as well as students.

Before preparing a formal plan for a bank public relations program, the bank marketing manager should conduct an audit of the various elements which must be considered. Such an audit can help determine the state of the public relations effort in the bank. It can also assess the adequacy of the basic bank policies and procedures as related to the various bank publics and their requirements for improved relations. The important variables for analysis are included in the following outline:

    I. Internal considerations
       A. Bank policy
          1. Understand and support a public relations program
          2. Initiate an aggressive marketing program
          3. Cooperate with industry public relations efforts
          4. Enlist strong director and shareholder support
       B. Bank facilities
          1. Condition of building exteriors
          2. Appeal and attractiveness of lobbies
          3. Facilities available for customer convenience
          4. Accessibility of officers and staff
       C. Bank products and services
          1. Appropriateness to target market
          2. Competitive position of deposit interest rates
          3. Competitive position of loan interest rates
          4. Viability of lending policies
          5. Competitive position of bank fee structure
          6. Product and service innovations
          7. Strengths and weaknesses in availability

II. Key public considerations
  A. Customer relations
    1. Staff conduct in customer contacts
    2. Staff training in customer relations
    3. Staff communication skill level
    4. Officer calling program requirements
    5. Nature of customer complaints
    6. Reasons for customer defections
  B. Community relations
    1. Participation in community programs
    2. Personnel participation in clubs and social groups
    3. Financial contributions
    4. Participation in charity activities
    5. Initiation of programs for community betterment
    6. Civic committee or association memberships
    7. Conducting financial forums
  C. Government relations
    1. Results of recent bank regulator visit
    2. Activity in state or national banking associations
    3. Participation in industry lobbying
    4. Sources for legislative intelligence
    5. Personal visits with government officials
    6. Nature of any agency or legislative testimony
  D. Education relations
    1. Involvement in local school issues
    2. Financial contributions
    3. Summer work policies for students and teachers
    4. Availability of educational materials
    5. Bank officer campus visits
    6. Bank tours for students
    7. Special school savings program
  E. Employee relations
    1. Opportunities for education and training
    2. Bank-sponsored social activities
    3. Fringe benefit package
    4. Grievance procedure
    5. Employee suggestion system
    6. Internal communication vehicles
    7. Accessibility of senior management
    8. Employee family involvement
  F. Press relations
    1. Relationship with local media representatives
    2. Accessibility of bank officers to press

3. Designation of official bank spokesperson
4. Relative editorial integrity of media
5. Fairness of media in their treatment of banks

With the completion of the audit, it is necessary for the bank marketing manager or the public relations specialist to establish the most advantageous direction for the bank's public relations effort. This can be done by
selecting both the long-term objectives and the short-term goals that are
needed for an effective program. Possible public relations objectives include
the following:

To be known as an innovator of bank products and services, including
not only deposit and loan products but fee-based services as well
To be recognized as an institution of high quality as measured by the
efficiency of its delivery system, the expertise of its personnel, and
the nature of its facilities
To be accepted as an organization whose management is responsive
to customer concerns and societal issues as well as providing an
excellent working environment
To be respected for its corporate citizenship by its participation in
community programs, personally and financially, in a leading role
for community improvement
To be identified as an outstanding member of the business as well as
banking community on the basis of operational excellence as indicated by growth and profitability
To be considered by the press to be a source of candid, truthful information about financial and societal matters affecting the bank and
the community

Since it is a highly specialized activity within the mass communication
province, planning a public relations program varies within banks. In some
banks, this effort is controlled at the executive office level; in others, it is
an integral part of the marketing function. The precise nature of the public
relations requirements must be the determining factor for the level of supervision. In some cases, the responsibility for both the function and the
planning may be divided. Separating the various public relations activities
within the larger banks may result in costly duplication of contacts or damaging omissions in communication. Notwithstanding, because of the realities of regulation and public sensitivity, it is recommended that the bank
public relations effort in such specialized activities as relations with government agencies, shareholders, security analysts, and employees be guided
from the executive office. It should be closely integrated with the public

relations efforts to such broad publics as customers, suppliers, and the local communities.

There are several steps to be followed in the public relations planning process. These steps will help plan an extended program rather than a series of relatively unrelated activities. Public relations activity in banks has a tendency to be defensive or reactive so that it goes in many directions without a central thrust. In some instances, public relations suffers from too many ideas and not enough planned consideration. The program should cover periods of one year in duration to coincide with the same period covered by the bank marketing plan. The suggested planning process for public relations includes the following actions:

Collect background information on the bank, including copies of press clippings, annual reports, newsletters, advertisement, and literature of previous years as well as those being used currently.

Meet and talk with key customers of the bank as well as with some average customers of the branches, representatives of the public at large, security analysts, editors, and other members of the press.

Prepare a series of bank position statements that senior management will accept as an expression of the bank's corporate objectives, its philosophy of banking, and the attitudes it wants specific publics to develop toward the bank; these must be translated into bank public relations objectives.

Establish a communication theme that will serve as a catalyst or umbrella for the various public relations activities so that the program achieves a cumulate effect.

Prepare a list of possible activities by identifying specific projects that will not only elicit maximum public exposure but generate the interest and enthusiasm of bank customers as well as personnel: the most promising and exciting projects should be identified and incorporated into the final plan.

Prepare the formal public relations plan by stating the situation and the objectives and describing the various activities to be implemented, including the procedures for control and coordination.

Present the recommendations as indicated in the formal plan to senior bank management so that they can participate actively, issue the necessary approvals, and make any personal commitments necessary for its successful completion.

Review the progress of the implementation of the public relations plan by collecting evidence of media coverage, consumer attitude change, and other indicators of results for dissemination to management through periodic progress reports and an annual audit.

The responsibility for the preparation of the public relations plan should be delegated to the bank's public relations specialist and, if the requirements warrant it, to a well-qualified public relations agency. It is usually more effective to separate the bank advertising and public relations assignments by using separate agencies. Like the bank advertising plan, the public relations plan is a component of mass communication, which is an integral part of the complete bank marketing plan. A suggested format for the bank public relations plan follows; it may be issued separately, become part of a mass communication plan when combined with the advertising plan, or be included as a document as part of the appendix in the bank marketing plan:

I. Public relations situation
   A. Review of the previous public relations program
      1. Bank public relations goals
      2. Bank public relations target publics
      3. Public relations theme used
      4. Media used
      5. Public relations expenditures
      6. Summary of performance results
   B. Current bank public relations situation
      1. Bank activity to be emphasized
      2. Bank product or service to be supported
      3. Critical attitudes or opinions in the market
      4. Sensitive areas of influence
      5. Opinion levels of supportive publics
      6. Bank regulatory situation
      7. Limitations specified by senior management
II. Bank public relations strategy
   A. Identify and analyze public relations problems
   B. Identify and analyze public relations opportunities
   C. Public relations target publics
      1. Bank customers and prospects
      2. Business and professional community
      3. Government officials
      4. Financial community
      5. Shareholders and directors
      6. Bank employees
      7. Bank suppliers
      8. Society-at-large
   D. Public relations goals
      1. Bank image and reputation

      2. Bank product and service information
      3. Bank personnel recognition
      4. Government influence
      5. Financial endorsement

III. Bank public relations programs
    A. Bank corporate charter
      1. Banking business philosophy
      2. Bank operating policies
      3. Bank societal responsibilities
      4. Bank employee commitments
    B. Public relations activities
      1. Management publicity
      2. Product or service publicity
      3. Institutional advertising support
      4. Staged events and activities
      5. Financial relations
      6. Shareholder relations
      7. Customer relations
      8. Public affairs and government lobbying
      9. Press relations
     10. Employee relations
     11. Supplier relations
     12. Internal publications
    C. Media plan
      1. Primary media for maximum coverage
      2. Selected media for special influence

IV. Bank public relations management
    A. Organization of the bank public relations function
    B. Coordination of the bank public relations effort
    C. Control of the public relations program
      1. Bank public relations budget
        a. Production of materials
        b. Media entertainment
        c. Opinion and attitude research
        d. Institutional advertising
        e. Department administration
      2. Performance measurement
        a. Image and reputation improvement
        b. Increase in acceptance and recognition
        c. Government influence
        d. Financial endorsement
    D. Public relations program approval requirements

BANK PUBLIC RELATIONS TECHNIQUES. The various methods for implementing a public relations plan require different techniques and a variety of tools since the communication serves multiple purposes to reach many divergent publics. The list of possibilities can be extensive since the range of techniques and tools is only limited by the imagination and creativity of the public relations specialists. In an effort to provide a comprehensive list of the possible activities and techniques, detailed guidance is provided for the use of the bank marketing manager. The detailed public relations activity checklist in Table 13-1 can be used to indicate both previous and current activities by the bank as well as those that are planned in the program being developed. This checklist also provides space to indicate the extent of the public relations activities of major competitors.

PUBLIC RELATIONS PROGRAM IMPLEMENTATION. The execution of the program requires central control because of the relatively high sensitivity of the various publics to any public relations activities of a financial institution. The bank should speak with the voice of consistency through every bank communicator, official or ad hoc. An official bank spokesperson should be designated as the main point of contact for representatives of the press. This person should develop close rapport between the bank and the press, civic leaders, government officials, and others who have the greatest influence

Table 13-1. Public Relations Activity Checklist

	Bank's prior activity	Bank's current activity	Bank's planned activity	Bank A	Bank B	Thrift A
Community activities						
Participation in charity drives						
Leadership in civic improvement						
Activity in public functions						
Support of public services						
Support of better housing/zoning						
Historical observances						
Nonprofit organization board membership						
Service and social club participation						
Support farm improvement programs						
Industrial development activity						
Conduct financial forums						
Finance community improvement projects						

Table 13-1 (continued)

	Bank's prior activity	Bank's current activity	Bank's planned activity	Bank A	Bank B	Thrift A
Exhibits and displays in bank						
Advocacy advertising participant						
Public meeting facilities available						
Youth activities						
Scouting programs						
4-H Club and FFA projects						
Junior achievement						
Scholarship and prize awards						
Bank tours by students/teachers						
School visits and talks						
School savings program						
Athletic league sponsorship						
Employee activities						
Social and athletic events						
Anniversaries of service						
Hobby pursuits						
Profit sharing and bonus plans						
Achievement awards						
Retirement activities						
Organization changes						
Training completion						
Bank policy changes						
New advertising campaigns						
Employee suggestion program						
Employee clubs and organizations						
Promotion opportunities						
Publicity opportunities						
New product announcements						
Employee promotions						
New personnel						
Community service by employees						
Bank statement of condition						
Dividend announcements						
Annual reports						
Director appointments						
Changes in bank rates/charges						
Public appearances and officer speeches						
Bank honors and awards						
Civic appointments of officers						
New branch or office openings						
Office remodeling progress						
New drive-up or parking facilities						
Special depositories						
Bank safety features						
Robbery recoveries/convictions						
Human interest events						
Important bank visitors						
Press relations						

over public opinion and attitudes affecting the bank. Others in the bank may serve as communicators, but subjects of controversy or intense public interest should be reserved for the official spokesperson. Efficient coordination of the release of information or responses to public or press queries are not only essential, but failure to act accordingly may result in negative reactions and unfavorable publicity. Since the bank serves a variety of publics, the precise information needs of each to satisfy their special interests must be recognized and considered. One word of caution: appropriate bank personnel should be briefed in advance about any important issues which may be raised in public. Invariably, and regardless of the control imposed, these employees may become informal sources for information. To prevent misstatements or incorrect responses, the most effective internal bank control is to make appropriate employees aware of the facts and the bank's official position.

Proper organization and an understanding of the bank public relations function require the use of well-trained specialists and a department with an appropriate support capability. Some banks create a separate department; others believe that the public relations function should be more limited in scope. Some banks view public relations as only a form of marketing communication that uses particular techniques to exert influence over customers and prospects in an effort to sell bank products and services. The most common organization structure places the responsibility for product and service publicity directly under the control of the bank marketing manager. The other aspects and activities involving community and government officials are usually designated as the function of a specialized area, public affairs. This specialized activity is usually under the close supervision of the executive office and sometimes requires the involvement of the legal department. Regardless of the way that the public relations function is organized, there must be a strong link with the marketing function. Public relations remains a component of mass communication and as such is a key activity in support of a successful bank marketing effort.

V

BANK MARKETING MANAGEMENT

14

BANK MARKETING PLANNING

Few banks have embraced the marketing concept in total. The degree of marketing orientation of a particular bank is relative, which means that each organization approaches bank marketing from a different point of origin. The resources of banks vary as much as the philosophies of bank management. However, regardless of these differences and the approaches used, it is essential that the resources of a bank be committed in the most effective and efficient way. To accomplish this, a systemic approach is necessary. By integrating the bank marketing plan into a corporate planning system, the various elements of a marketing planning sequence can be properly related to environmental variables before a course of marketing action is finalized. This places the formal marketing plan in its proper tactical position in relation to the bank strategic plan as part of the corporate planning process. Together, they become inseparable components of a bank management system.

Some note should be taken of one important aspect of systemic procedures as applied to the bank planning process. Any system, judicial, monetary, political, or even betting in Las Vegas, is dependent upon the actions of the various participants in the process. Therefore, those responsible for the implementation determine how well any system performs. Corporate planners must be marketing-oriented, know their bank and its functions well, and be able to identify problems as well as recognize opportunities. In short, they must do their homework diligently as they perform the corporate planning function.

The macro contribution of corporate planning is that it offers a procedure for analyzing the economic, regulatory, and competitive prospects for a bank to succeed by helping to chart a continuing course of action. The total planning function is a basic responsibility of every level of bank management. The staff support role of the bank marketing manager is to prepare the master plan for marketing that can serve as the catalyst for change, but not to take the place of the tactical planning requirements of each of the line units of the bank. In the past, many banks have used overly quantitative techniques for the macro strategic planning effort, producing micro tactical plans based on growth in market share rather than on actions designed to increase customer penetration, to develop innovative products and services, to reduce costs of operations support, or to improve delivery system convenience.

The state of the financial services industry is one of revolutionary change. Regulators cannot agree on which changes in the laws are necessary, customers have grown in sophistication and require new or revised products and services, and competition is increasing as both nonbanks and banks rush to satisfy customer need by exploiting inconsistencies in current banking regulations. This situation makes the marketing planning function crucial for banks. However, there are also other compelling reasons for banks to initiate a formal marketing planning effort.

Reviewing the current and anticipated marketing situation can help identify which environmental factors are within the control of the bank, which can be neutralized, and which are uncontrollable.

The formal plan requires that bank management establish a positive direction for the bank by setting specific objectives and goals for accomplishment within a prescribed time period.

Bank personnel can become familiar with their specific roles in the marketing effort as well as the responsibilities for interaction between bank units.

The control procedures in the formal plan can provide a basis for feedback and the measurement of performance to permit appropriate changes in bank strategy and tactics.

The coordination requirements can be specified for the most effective implementation by the efficient commitment of financial and human resources.

There are differences in the planning province that are necessary because of the use of both macro and micro approaches. Strategic planning is focused on the macro view, and it seeks to clarify the purpose and direction of the bank to assure growth and profitability over the long term. Tactical planning is short-term, usually one year to correspond with the budget year of the bank. The management instrument associated with tactical planning is the formal business plan of the bank, which reflects the immediate application of the principles covered in the strategic plan. The business plan provides additional detail on the tactical effort with its four key components— the financial plan, the operations plan, the human resources plan, and the marketing plan.

BANK CORPORATE PLANNING. Bank corporate planning is usually initiated at the senior management level of the bank; however, because it has an essential role in the bank marketing manager's planning responsibility, it should be reviewed. Corporate planning is not just an exercise in futurism to predict the prime rate, to forecast the state of the economy, or to identify consumer behavior trends. Strategic planning is the major vehicle of the corporate planning effort and is the outcome of a process to determine how the bank can operate more profitably, what its strengths and weaknesses appear to be, the gap or performance improvement requirement between the current position of the bank and the one desired. As a result of the corporate planning deliberations, the senior management can identify the problems and opportunities which aid or constrain the future success of the bank to reach its desired position in the marketplace. The expectations of senior management for accomplishment not only require understanding the present state of the bank and the external business environment, but reconciling the standards for bank performance to achieve the necessary objectives and goals. The following are some of the important factors in the corporate planning deliberations and analysis by the senior management of the bank.

    I. State of the bank
       A. Present bank strategy
          1. Product and service orientation
          2. Market segmentation philosophy
          3. Growth emphasis
          4. Profit objectives
       B. Financial condition
          1. Historical review of statements of condition
          2. Performance analysis with peer group
          3. Asset portfolio analysis
          4. Liability portfolio analysis
       C. Human resource situation
          1. Compensation comparison with competition
          2. Depth of management
          3. Level of technical skills
          4. Training requirements
          5. Review of key employee performance
          6. State of employee morale
       D. Philosophy of management
          1. Style of management
          2. Corporate charter
          3. Corporate culture considerations
   II. Bank external environment
       A. Opinions and attitudes of corporate publics
          1. Customers

2. Community leaders
3. Government officials
4. Shareholders
5. Financial community
6. Creditors and suppliers
7. Society-at-large
B. Competition
1. Volume leader
2. Price leader
3. Quality leader
4. Distribution leader
C. Economic and regulatory situation
1. State of the economy
2. Economic forecasts
3. Legal and regulatory restrictions
4. Future legal and regulatory climate
D. Banking industry dynamics
1. Growth projections
2. Technical developments
3. Marketing innovations

Once the corporate analysis is completed, the formal strategic plan is prepared which should provide the guidance necessary from senior management for the staff and unit managers to begin the process of tactical planning. The strategic plan should consist of a series of directives that indicate the strategic objectives of the bank and an identification of the business segments that appear to offer the greatest potential and any new activities of a general nature that may be required to exploit this potential. New delivery system possibilities or changes in the present system, customer convenience requirements, and any revisions in loan policies and pricing structures should also be covered in the strategic plan. Suggestions for the application of cost savings, new human or technological resources to be made available, and general guidelines on business risk philosophy, capital availability, and those areas of business or internal activity that are no longer appropriate should also be included in the strategic planning document.

There is no single, accepted format for the bank strategic plan. It can be limited to a few pages and be in memo form, or it can be a voluminous document prepared by an outside consultant such as Management Analysis Center, McKinsey, or other recognized sources. Whether by memo or an extensive project, the strategic plan should seek line and staff participation in the planning process. This can be encouraged by leaving much of the detail to staff and line discretion in the tactical planning phase, when policies and activities can be proposed in a complete business plan with its four major components. Once these four tactical plans, finance, operations, human resources, and marketing, have been prepared, the senior management must complete a reconciliation process comparing the strategic plan with the business plan. Any discrepancies are resolved by senior management before the final approval of the business plan and its four key elements. Resolution can be achieved by altering the strategic plan, revising the business plan, or parts of each. The complete corporate planning process is diagrammed in the model in Figure 14-1. The model indicates the need for a marketing feasibility study prior to the preparation of the four key tactical plans in the business plan. This relatively recent addition to the tactical planning process is the result of the growing cost of market entry or new product introduction and the increasing statistical likelihood of failure. When translated into its effect on bank earnings, there is less risk by determining the possible success of entry or introduction by the completion of a marketing feasibility study in advance. This particular marketing planning activity will be reviewed in detail later in this chapter.

MARKETING PLANNING MODEL. The preparation of the formal marketing plan requires a system so that the various plan components can be considered in sequence. This systemic approach attempts to apply the bank resources in a given marketing environment to elicit favorable customer response. The planning system deals with the marketing situation, bank marketing strategies, marketing programs or courses of action, marketing management, and internal bank support. The critical path through the sequences of the system may vary with each marketing situation since it is affected by people, product and service, timing, unusual circumstances, and numerous bank marketing variables that interact in the environment. Some of these affect the marketing planning effort favorably, and others are unfavorable or neutral. In the course of interaction, these bank marketing variables alter their relationships or effects with little or no warning given to the bank marketing manager. This nonprogrammable and unpredictable interaction results in a smorgasbord of cause and effect, action and reaction, dominance and dependency that leads to marketing success or failure.

To make the bank marketing manager's planning responsibilities less enjoyable, many environmental variables cannot be controlled. Those that offer some modicum of control are always vulnerable to the effects of the numerous uncontrollables. By identifying all variables readily apparent and cataloging them into similar effects to be anticipated, the bank marketing manager can attempt to counteract, exploit, or neutralize them. It is the nature of any system to be designed to satisfy a specific set of requirements. The requirements identifying the task of the bank marketing manager in a

Figure 14-1. Bank Corporate Planning Process

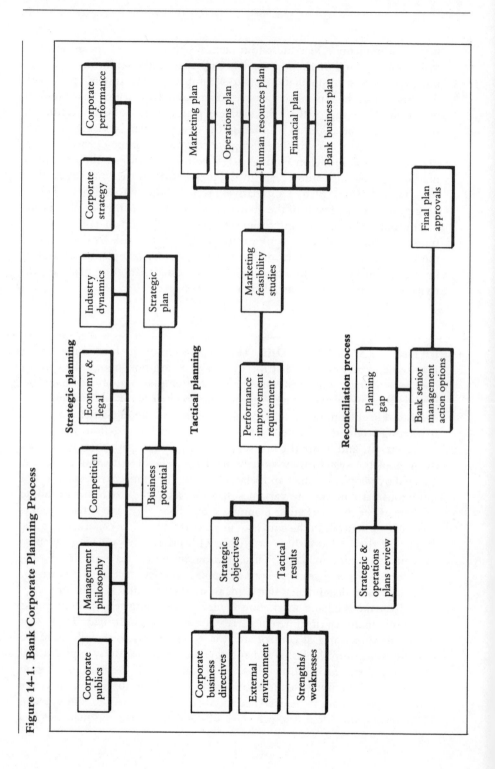

particular marketing situation can be stated systemically as the marketing strategy, which is concluded with an explicit set of bank marketing objectives and goals. As stated previously, strategy is sometimes confused with the programs or course of action devised to cope with the bank marketing situation. As a reminder, keep those planning system components separate entities by considering the marketing strategy as the direction or destination of the bank marketing plan and the programs or courses of action as the vehicles for getting there.

Every system should proceed to a logical conclusion and, therefore, the marketing planning system requires a loop to close the circuits. The desired conclusion in a marketing planning system is favorable customer response. Provisions for information gathering and feedback between each planning sequence provide an information loop not only at the end of the process but in the middle stations as well. Thus, the collection flow and the exchange of data between system components becomes omnidirectional. The bank marketing planning model in Figure 14-2 provides an overview of the complete bank marketing planning system.

MARKETING PLANNING PROCESS. When using the bank marketing planning system, one must differentiate between the formal bank marketing plan and the planning process; they are not synonymous. The marketing planning effort is a systemic process embracing many marketing-related functions such as the collection and analysis of data, the assessment of market risk, the identification of problems and opportunities, and the evaluation of bank resources. The formal marketing plan, on the other hand, is a written document that details and recommends marketing courses of action for the bank that are directed toward the accomplishment of specific marketing objectives and goals within the limitations imposed by an identified bank marketing situation. The formal marketing plan is used as an action tool of management that states in advance the way the bank intends to exploit a specific number of marketing opportunities. Putting such intentions to work usually involves the coordinated effort of many individuals, functions, and resources. This, in turn, requires a control mechanism, best represented by a tool for constant referral that makes action or performance variance apparent to the bank marketing manager. To be precise, the bank marketing plan is a valuable management tool oriented to specific results and may be considered the result of the bank marketing planning process.

The marketing planning process is a detailed and complicated procedure which deals with facts, assumptions, and opinions. Unfortunately, some bank marketing managers have difficulty differentiating between them. Fact is something known with certainty, usually objectively verified.

Figure 14–2. Bank Marketing Planning Model

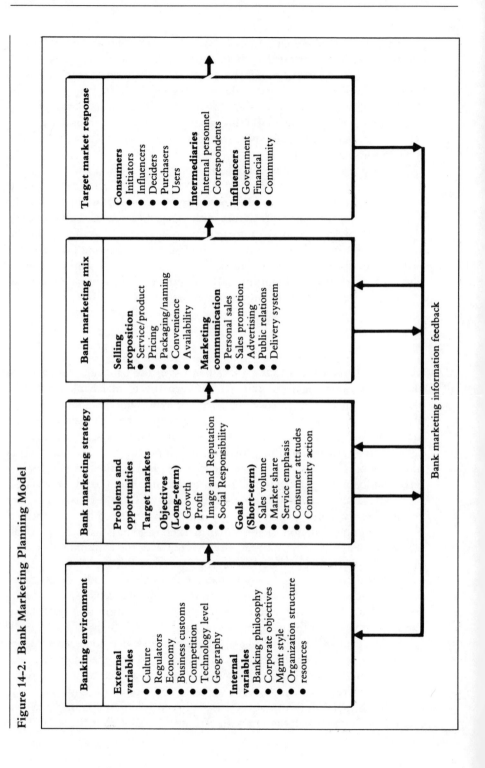

In the case of bank marketing, a fact must have real, demonstrable existence supplemented with pertinent studies, reports, and charts. All planners must rely on many assumptions. They are merely suppositions that have been accepted or supposed true without proof or demonstration. As individuals, bank marketing managers have certain underlying banking beliefs, premises, notions, rationales, generalizations, and principles. Most are not substantiated by reality. Thus, many assumptions are false or may only be opinions. To add to the risk marketing planners assume when relying on opinions is the fact that many bank marketing managers are totally unaware that they are planning with fallacious notions. However, all of the facts needed for planning are seldom available. Thus, bank marketing managers must make assumptions when estimating future bank operating conditions, competitive developments, and the interaction of other significant bank marketing variables.

It is essential that any assumptions used in the marketing planning process be identified as such. This is extremely important in the establishment of a bank marketing strategy because it identifies some key factors that are relatively unpredictable and usually uncontrollable. Assumptions differ from opinions. An opinion is an evaluation or judgment based on special knowledge provided by a qualified individual or source and is accepted or rejected on the basis of their credibility as experts. Assumptions are usually made after collecting and evaluating the opinions from several sources to arrive at a logical conclusion. Depending upon the source, every opinion can be held with confidence, but they are never substantiated by positive knowledge or proof at the time they are expressed. In some instances, opinions of the bank marketing managers are the only immediate means for justifying a recommended course of action.

There is a special sequence for the bank marketing planning process that should be followed in the course of preparation of the bank marketing plan. The detailed marketing planning process consists of numerous steps and assumes that a marketing feasibility study has been completed for a new bank product or service introduction or for an entry into a new market.

1. **Initial preparation for planning.** To set the stage requires that secondary research channels, planning personnel, and internal bank marketing information system components be alerted to the planning effort and the schedule for its completion.
2. **Determine the marketing situation.** Both the external and internal environment must be investigated in order to establish the current and future situation in the marketplace.
3. **Select a bank marketing strategy.** Once the marketing situation has been analyzed, the task of determining the marketing strategy by identifying marketing problems and opportunities,

designating target markets, and establishing bank objectives and goals must be completed.

4. **Review the selling proposition.** This will help establish the criteria for the development of new products as well as the improvement of existing products and services.

5. **Correlate bank products with target markets.** The bank product and service opportunity and vulnerability are analyzed in relation to consumer demand by reviewing market size and trends, market investment requirements, the nature of the operations support, human resources available, and the delivery system established.

6. **Conduct a target market analysis.** Delineate target market characteristics and opportunities including determining the degree of market saturation, present bank satisfaction and loyalty, competitive sales trends, and relative share of the market.

7. **Develop bank product and service concepts.** This should be based on marketing research to define the customer demand level for products based on quality, price, convenience, susceptability to promotion, and availability.

8. **Test bank product and service strategies.** Determine which will generate the strongest customer demand including the testing of alternatives and variations in bank positioning and product emphasis.

9. **Analyze the operations support capability.** This requires examining the data processing programs and the technical level of expertise as well as costs by product and service groups.

10. **Determine resource requirements.** This is an evaluation of the investment requirements in financial and human resources and an analysis of the return on investment as compared with the risks entailed.

11. **Assess profit opportunities.** Evaluate the profit potential from the basis of return on assets as well as the return on investment.

12. **Review course of action options.** The various programs in the marketing mix should be considered including the possibilities for mass advertising, sales promotion, pricing, distribution, and the personal calling effort.

13. **Conduct formal test marketing.** This activity should include the pretesting of products, advertising creative approaches, promotional programs, pricing alternatives, and methods of distribution through various delivery systems.

Once the bank marketing planning sequence reaches this point, there is sufficient information to base a marketing decision. If the data indicate that the proposed marketing program may not be successful, or if sufficient possibility of failure exists, the bank marketing manager must alter the proposed strategies and programs or develop a new approach. If the strategies and programs have favorable test results, the following sequence can be followed for the implementation of the marketing plan:

1. **Update previous information.** During the time of plan preparation and implementation, the changes in the marketing situation should be identified and the plan should be revised accordingly.
2. **Reinforce the consumer franchise.** The customer loyalty of the bank can be determined by the number of bank products and services used per capita by the target market and every effort should be made to increase this penetration.
3. **Implement the selected course of action.** The precise marketing mix should be selected and committed to support the product strategy and the positioning of the bank and to secure a competitive advantage wherever possible.
4. **Measure program results.** The results of the marketing effort should be evaluated continuously, not only for control purposes, but for making improvements as the marketing situation changes during the program period.
5. **Marketing plan revision.** When new directions are necessary, there is a tendency to alter the objectives rather than to replan, revise or strengthen existing marketing programs to attain original objectives that remain valid.

In spite of the general agreement among professional planners that the process outcome should be a written document, many banks rely on a series of memos or comprehensive financial budgets from the various line and staff units which outline the general course of marketing action. However, there is no substitute for the formal plan if a comprehensive proposal is desired. The written plan must be substantiated by an appropriate mixture of fact, assumption, and opinion. It should follow a format that makes it easy for bank personnel who have not participated directly in its preparation to understand and accept the logic of the contemplated action. It should also be readily apparent to those receiving copies of the plan of what is expected of them in the implementation of the bank marketing plan. These requirements make it necessary that the format for any marketing planning document be followed so that each marketing component is identified and covered in a logical sequence to provide the details and rationales for the recommended course of action. Formats are always subjective and can be developed by each bank marketing manager to suit the particular needs of the bank. However, the proposed formats that follow have been used by banks as well as in other industries and have been very helpful.

MARKETING FEASIBILITY STUDY FORMAT. The bank marketing planning process provides for systemic consideration by the bank's senior management prior to a decision to commit bank resources in a new product introduction or a new marketing program in support of entry into a new market. The essential planning document for this purpose is the marketing feasibility study. To conduct such a study, portions of the bank marketing planning system model are followed to develop an appropriate format. Obviously, since the decision for new product introduction or new market entry depends upon a detailed analysis of the bank marketing situation and an estimate or marketing potential, consideration of the marketing environment and the marketing strategy are critical elements for entry decision making.

The marketing feasibility study must be prepared as part of the decision making process of bank management. It helps establish the parameters of entry feasibility through the use of the scenario technique which indicates the extremes of success or failure as well as the most likely expectation of bank marketing results. The study not only considers such essentials as compatibility with the corporate strategy, but provides for the systematic collection of related information upon which to base a logical management decision for market entry or new product introduction. The following format has been suggested for the formal marketing feasibility study:

I. Senior management summary
II. Bank marketing situation
   A. External environment
      1. Economic outlook
      2. Legal and regulatory climate
      3. Cultural considerations
      4. Competition
      5. Technology level
      6. Local banking customs and practices
      7. Geographical considerations
   B. Internal bank environment
      1. Banking business philosophy
         a. Corporate charter
         b. Corporate policies
         c. Corporate procedures
      2. Corporate objectives

        3. Style of management
        4. Bank organization structure
        5. Corporate resources
           a. Financial strength
           b. Human resources
           c. Bank facilities and equipment
III. Bank marketing potential
    A. Identify and analyze potential problems
    B. Identify and analyze potential opportunities
    C. Potential target markets
        1. New customers
        2. Present customers
        3. Special market segments and niches
        4. Internal bank organization
        5. Financial community
        6. Government regulators
        7. Other influence centers
IV. Bank marketing feasibility
    A. Three separate scenarios
        1. Optimistic
        2. Pessimistic
        3. Realistic
    B. Content of each scenario
        1. State of the bank market
           a. Economy
           b. Legal and regulatory climate
           c. Competition
        2. Bank marketing strategy
           a. Bank marketing problems
           b. Bank marketing opportunities
           c. Bank target markets
        3. Selling proposition
           a. Customer acceptance
           b. Product and service benefits
           c. Competitor positioning
        4. Bank delivery system
           a. Distribution channels
           b. Operations support
        5. Communication channels
           a. External media support
           b. Internal bank media support
        6. Bank target market potential

a. Annual sales forecasts (five years)
b. Annual income projections (five years)
c. Competitive counteraction anticipated

C. Feasibility study recommendations
1. Corporate support requirements
a. Annual operating budget (first year)
b. Operations/computer support
c. Human resources
d. Capital commitment
2. Specific bank management recommendations
a. Market entry without qualification
b. Market entry with qualification
c. Market entry later (estimated date)
d. Market entry not recommended

PREPARATION OF THE BANK MARKETING PLAN. If the marketing planning process is followed faithfully by the bank marketing manager, the preparation of the formal bank marketing plan is relatively routine. In some banks, however, the emphasis has been to produce a written plan while omitting some of the steps in the planning process. The planning document, regardless of format, should begin with some review of the current marketing situation. From a practical view, this should be a summary of many of the items covered in the strategic planning document issued by senior management. It may need to be revised slightly to be brought current to account for any new developments since the preparation of the strategic plan. Once the external and internal environmental variables that comprise the marketing situation have been identified and described, the marketing strategy is established and described in the formal plan. The bank marketing strategy is more than a simple statement of an increase in revenue or share of market. It must analyze the marketing problems and opportunities which the bank can expect, it must identify the specific market targets, and then it must include the bank objectives and goals to be accomplished.

BANK OBJECTIVES AND GOALS. This portion of the marketing strategy section is the natural extension of the marketing problems and opportunities as well as the bank targets that have ben identified through the information provided by research. Bank objectives and goals constitute a statement of purpose for the marketing strategy once they have been established. The long-term results which a bank marketing manager establishes are defined as the corporate objectives in the marketing function. The period of time associated with each bank objective is usually more than one year because most long-term results require the completion of several intermediate goals. Bank objectives can be qualitative, quantitative, or a combination of both. Usually, objectives are established on the basis of an actual result to be achieved within a specified period of time. They can be related to bank growth or profit, deposit and loan volume, earnings, improvement of the bank's image or reputation, or satisfaction of the social responsibilities of the bank. Objectives are the essence of the bank marketing plan because everything in the plan format that has preceded has been documented to establish bank objectives and all the sections that follow are devoted to the methods for achieving these objectives. Bank objectives and goals were discussed in detail in terms of bank marketing strategy in Chapter 5.

BANK MARKETING PLAN FORMAT. It is obvious that the marketing plan which proposes a comprehensive course of marketing action by the bank should follow a prescribed format. This makes it easy for the various individuals in the bank to understand and accept the plan even though they may not participate directly in its preparation. The formal document also makes it apparent to each of the plan participants what is expected of them in the implementation of the plan.

    I. Bank marketing situation
       A. External environment
          1. Economic outlook
             a. GNP and industrial production
             b. Business sector
                (1) Capital spending
                (2) Inventories
                (3) Corporate profits
             c. Consumer sector
                (1) Retail sales
                (2) Housing starts
             d. Inflation rate
             e. International
                (1) Balance of payments
                (2) Foreign exchange rates
          2. Legal and regulatory climate
                (1) Regulatory restraints
                (2) Regulatory assistance
                (3) Pending legislation

        3. Financial climate
            a. Monetary and fiscal policies
            b. Interest rates
        4. Competition
            a. Commercial banks
            b. Thrift institutions
            c. Nonbank banks
        5. Local banking customs and practices
        6. State of banking and computer technology
        7. Social or cultural considerations
        8. Geographical factors
    B. Internal environment
        1. Corporate philosophy of banking
            a. Corporate charter
            b. Corporate policies affecting marketing
            c. Corporate procedures affecting marketing
        2. Corporate objectives (strategic)
        3. Style of management
        4. Bank organization
            a. Line structure
            b. Staff functions
        5. Corporate resources
            a. Financial strength
            b. Human resources
            c. Bank facilities and equipment
II. Bank marketing strategy
    A. Bank marketing problems
        1. Identification
        2. Analysis
    B. Bank marketing opportunities
        1. Identification
        2. Analysis
    C. Bank target markets
        1. Customers and prospects
            a. Commercial
            b. Retail
            c. Trust
            d. Agribusiness
            e. Investment
            f. Advisory
            g. Computer support
            h. International

      2. Organization (internal)
        a. Line units
        b. Staff departments
        c. Directors
      3. Regulatory bodies
      4. Financial community
      5. Community influence centers
  D. Bank marketing objectives
      1. Volume or growth
      2. Profit or earnings
      3. Image and reputation
      4. Social responsibility
  E. Bank marketing goals
      1. Volume or growth
      2. Profit or earnings
      3. Image and reputation
      4. Social responsibility
  F. Sales forecast
      1. Asset-based products
      2. Liability-based products
      3. Fee-based services
III. Bank marketing programs (courses of action)
  A. Selling proposition
      1. Product or service emphasis
      2. Customer benefits (by product and service)
        a. Commercial
        b. Retail
        c. Trust
        d. Agribusiness
        e. Investment
        f. Advisory
        g. Computer
        h. International
      3. Pricing decisions (by product and service)
        a. Pricing objectives
        b. Pricing philosophy
        c. Pricing strategy
        d. Pricing policy
        e. Pricing structure
          (1) Commercial
          (2) Retail
          (3) Wholesale

        4. Availability of bank support services
B. Personal sales program
    1. Bank calling officers
    2. Branch contact personnel
    3. Line and staff personnel
    4. Directors and senior management
    5. Detailed budget
    6. Program coordination schedule
C. Sales promotion program
    1. Sales aids
        a. Bank calling officers
        b. Branch contact personnel
    2. Point-of-purchase effort
        a. Literature
        b. Signs and displays
    3. Account premiums and sales incentives
        a. Customers
        b. Bank personnel
            (1) Bank calling officers
            (2) Branch personnel
            (3) Staff personnel
    4. Shows and exhibits
    5. Catalogs and directories
    6. Detailed budget
    7. Program coordination schedule
D. Mass communication program
    1. Advertising
        a. Communication message
        b. Communication channels
            (1) Mass media
            (2) Trade media
            (3) Internal media
    2. Public relations
        a. Communication message
        b. Communication channels
            (1) Mass media
            (2) Trade media
            (3) Personal contact
            (4) Internal media
    3. Detailed budget
    4. Program coordination schedule
E. Marketing research program

    1. Consumer opinion and attitude studies
    2. Market studies
    3. Bank product and service testing
    4. Sales and calling effort analysis
    5. Professional shopping surveys
    6. Communication effectiveness measurement
    7. Detailed budget
    8. Program coordination schedule
  F. Distribution expansion program
    1. Current delivery system
      a. Commercial coverage
      b. Retail density
      c. Network membership
      d. Agribusiness coverage
      e. Correspondent relationships
      f. International presence
    2. Expansion priorities
    3. Detailed budget
    4. Program coordination schedule
IV. Bank marketing management
  A. Organization of the bank marketing effort
    1. Changes in marketing organization
      a. Responsibility and authority
      b. Staff functions
      c. Line functions
    2. Personnel requirements
      a. Supervisory
      b. Nonsupervisory
    3. Facility and equipment requirements
  B. Coordination of the bank marketing effort
    1. Consolidated program schedule
      a. PERT or time line chart
    2. Motivation program
      a. Bank calling officers
      b. Branch contact personnel
      c. Staff personnel
  C. Control of the bank marketing effort
    1. Consolidated marketing program budget
      a. Personal sales program
      b. Sales promotion program
      c. Mass communication program
      d. Marketing research program

    e. Distribution expansion program
  2. Performance measurement criteria
    a. Marketing goals (growth)
      (1) Share of deposits
      (2) Loan volume
      (3) Customer base
    b. Marketing goals (profit)
      (1) Earnings per share
      (2) Return on assets
    c. Marketing goals (image and reputation)
      (1) Change in consumer attitudes
      (2) Opinions of selected publics
    d. Marketing goals (social responsibility)
      (1) Government agencies audits
      (2) Community involvement
  3. Marketing performance feedback
    a. Measurement research
    b. Internal meetings and seminars
    c. Internal reports and audits
    d. Industry and government reports
  4. Corrective action
    a. Initiation procedures
    b. Contingency plans
V. Internal staff support requirements
  A. Bank staff departments
    1. Operations
    2. Cashiers
    3. Data processing
    4. Product research and development
    5. Personnel
    6. Finance and accounting
    7. Properties and facilities
    8. Legal
    9. Purchasing
    10. Auditing
  B. Executive office
    1. Bank marketing plan approvals
      a. Marketing programs
      b. Marketing budget
    2. Executive participation
      a. Customer contact
      b. Employee motivation
      c. Public relations activities

The complete marketing plan should be distributed selectively. Staff departments and subordinate line units should only receive those parts of the formal plan that are appropriate to their assigned portions for implementation. To expect a local branch manager or staff to comprehend the total bank plan is not realistic. Rather than attempt to specify the action expected by individual branch offices, a special, local business plan should be prepared by each branch manager for approval by the next supervisory level in the bank. This special branch office business plan should be consistent with the bank marketing plan and serve as an extension of the strategic and tactical objectives. A sample bank branch office business plan format is provided by Figure 14-3. The bank marketing manager should schedule meetings with the branch managers to assist them in the preparation of the branch business plan.

BANK MARKETING PLAN IMPLEMENTATION. The staff services provided by the bank marketing manager are growing in importance and acceptance as a bank management activity. The rising costs of bank marketing along with the increased risks involved in bringing bank products and services to the marketplace emphasize the economic importance of sound bank marketing plans. The plan is a detailed document of marketing situation and counteraction but it should attempt to provide decisive answers to the following basic questions facing bank marketing managers:

1. What is the current marketing situation?
2. Where does the bank want to go?
3. How can the bank get there?
4. Who is responsible for what marketing action?
5. How long will the marketing effort take?
6. How much will it cost?
7. Is the effort worthwhile to the bank?
8. Does the effort contribute to community improvement?
9. Is the public well served by the bank's effort?
10. Is the effort legal and ethical?

Once the bank marketing manager has found the answer to these simple, but essential, questions, the primary instrument of action, the formal bank marketing plan, can be developed, approved, and implemented. Putting the plan to work involves the interaction of many individuals and departments within the bank who are responsible for a wide range of activities within the outside marketing function. Monitoring the progress of these synergistic activities can only be done effectively through constant referral

Figure 14-3. Bank Branch Office Business Plan

Jan–Mar _____
Apr–June _____
July–Sept _____
Oct–Dec _____

Branch office: _____ # _____   Date: _____

Facilities: Drive _____ ATM _____ SDBx _____ IL Rep _____
    CL Rep _____ Trust _____ Ins _____

Local market: Zip _____ Census Tract _____ Population _____ Med Age _____
    Households # _____ Med hhld income $_____ Home ownership _____%
    Urban _____ Suburban _____ Retired _____ Community _____
    Rural _____ In-plant _____

Competition (Within 2-Mile Radius): Bank A _____ B _____ C _____ D _____ E _____
    F _____ G _____
    S&L A _____ B _____ C _____ D _____ E _____ F _____ CU _____ Local finance _____

(Assign code for each local financial institution)

I. Marketing plan

Manager: _____ Asst: _____

Customers: # _____ Income range $_____ to $_____ Avg Dep $_____

Type: Commercial ____% Professional ____% White collar ____% Student ____%
    Retired ____% Government ____% Blue collar ____% Military ____%

Marketing performance:

	As of: _____	Objective as of: _____
Core deposits	$ _____	$ _____
Checking accounts	# _____	# _____
Money market accounts	# _____	# _____
TCD (under 100 mm)	$ _____	$ _____
TCD (over 100 mm)	$ _____	$ _____
Ready credit accts	# _____	# _____
Credit card accts	# _____	# _____
IL outstandings	$ _____	$ _____
IRA deposits	$ _____	$ _____
Personal credit lines	# _____	# _____
Accts over 25 mm (transaction)	# _____	# _____

Outside sales calls:

Local merchants	# _____	# _____
Attorneys	# _____	# _____
MD & DDS	# _____	# _____
Insurance agents	# _____	# _____
Real estate agents	# _____	# _____
Civic officials	# _____	# _____
Service club meetings	# _____	# _____

II. Operations Plan

Operations officer: _____ Sr teller: _____

Last HQ staff visit: _____ Last region visit: _____ Last audit: _____

Literature stock needed: _____

Facility maintenance required: _____

Staff performance:

As of: _____ Objective as of: _____

	As of	Objective as of
Employees (full time)	# _____	# _____
Employees (part time)	# _____	# _____
Transactions (monthly)	# _____	# _____
ATM transactions (monthly)	# _____	# _____
Audit exceptions	# _____	# _____
Teller balancing	_____%	_____%
Employee turnover	_____%	_____%
Staff teller trained	# _____	# _____
Staff operations trained	# _____	# _____
Staff marketing trained	# _____	# _____
Staff AIB enrolled	# _____	# _____

Staff meetings schedule: frequency _____ Time _____

III. Financial plan

Financial performance:

As of: _____ Objective as of: _____

Monthly expenses:

	As of	Objective as of
Salaries	$ _____	$ _____
Utilities	$ _____	$ _____
Telephone	$ _____	$ _____
Supplies	$ _____	$ _____
Travel/entertainment	$ _____	$ _____
Marketing	$ _____	$ _____

Monthly income:

	As of	Objective as of
Deposit credit	$ _____	$ _____
IL earnings	$ _____	$ _____
Fee income	$ _____	$ _____

IV. Remarks _____

_____

_____

Plan submitted by: _____

Plan approved by: _____ Date _____

to the formal marketing plan. In a sense, the implementation of the plan results from the applications of the planning function and how closely it follows the planning process.

Many bank marketing planners are only temporary refugees from their primary responsibilities as the head of the staff marketing function. If the one charged with the responsibility for marketing planning is not the director of marketing for the bank, it is the responsibility of the latter to evaluate the effectiveness of the planner's performance. This performance is usually measured on the basis of the content of the plan that was prepared. The characteristics of a sound bank marketing plan should include the following for performance evaluation:

Consistency with bank capabilities, resources, and objectives
Realistic forecasting based on clearly identified factors
Sound analysis of accurate, complete data
Thorough consideration of major factors and objectives
Recommended courses of action that are practical and realistic
Program lead time sufficient for careful implementation
Flexible plan that permits changes when needed
Appropriate detail without including irrelevant data

Those banks that rely upon complete marketing planning can be identified through their standard operating procedures. For example, major marketing decisions should only be made after the completion of a detailed analysis covered in the formal marketing plan and a review of the recommendations resulting from such an analysis. In banks that are planning oriented, the marketing plan is often used as the basis for budgeting and other corporate control procedures after the provisions of the plan have been approved by senior management. In some cases, individuals in management may have strong reservations about certain aspects of the bank marketing plan. These doubts may be the result of such factors as a lack of understanding because of insufficient study of the complete plan, too little participation in the planning process by those department and branch managers expected to be motivated and guided by the plan, or a failure to provide proper assurance that the various staff departments and line units can support and implement the bank marketing plan adequately.

Obstacles to proper marketing planning with a bank can be encountered through overt or passive resistance by individuals in management, senior as well as middle management. The various dysfunctional actions and activities include such elements as resistance to proposed changes or to new ideas introduced by others, failure to consider measures designed for general bank improvement that require certain department or unit sacrifices, and the unwillingness of department and branch managers to make a

personal commitment to a plan of action which precludes further delibera-
tion once approved. Resistance can also be the result of professional jeal-
ousy, internecine bank warfare, political jockeying, undue preoccupation
with day-to-day operations, or a natural complacency due to past successes
that may have been achieved without the benefit of a formal bank marketing plan. In some severe cases of noncooperation, vital bank marketing information may even be withheld.

Additional elements or conditions that are not conducive to formal
marketing planning include the cost of planning, the executive hours to be
committed, and the time required for data collection and analysis as well as
plan preparation. As a result, some bank marketing plans may become obsolete before completion, others may possess too much useless detail or be
overly complicated, and some may be prepared by individuals whose planning knowledge and skills are less than necessary to prepare the bank marketing plan properly.

Increased reliance is being placed on the use of simulation, model
building, business gaming, role playing and linear programming as aids to
bank marketing problem solving. Because of the universal acceptance of
profitability as the index for business performance, financial accounting remains as one of the most reliable measures for marketing success. Thus, the
marketing planner must become familiar with capital budgets, expense
budgets, the ebb and flow of cash as well as detailed operating statements.
In short, the bank marketing manager must be qualified as a banker as well
as a marketer.

PLANNING PROBLEMS. The use of marketing planning system requires that
the bank marketing manager develop certain procedures that will assist in
the gathering and processing of marketing data as well as identifying problems and opportunities and selecting appropriate courses of marketing action. Problems that bank marketing managers face in the planning function
include the following:

> Understanding the bank marketing planning function, including its
> strengths and limitations
> Recruiting and training a knowledgeable staff and building a practical
> organization structure
> Obtaining the cooperation of other bank staff and line units as well as
> individual managers and supervisors
> Making the planning process work according to a predetermined
> planning system

Obtaining productive primary and secondary sources for reliable bank marketing data

Identifying bank marketing problems and opportunities before they reach the critical stage or mature

Analyzing marketing data to reach logical conclusions based on fact and valid assumptions

Developing bank marketing courses of action that are innovative, practical, and productive

Monitoring the plan implementation process while being prepared to initiate appropriate corrective action

Being amenable to change when justified, regardless of the source of suggestions and ideas

In spite of such a demanding list of particulars, the most severe problems of a bank marketing manager are usually the result of the senior or middle management in initiating the formal marketing planning process for the first time. Such banks are usually characterized by tradition-directed thinking that compounds the difficulties of the tasks facing the bank marketing manager. Banks have survived and even prospered for years without the implied luxury of formal marketing planning. Therefore, some members of senior management may question the need for spending time and money on the formal plan; this sentiment will have its supporters in middle and branch management as well. However, the era of deregulation and the entry of highly professional competitors have turned what was once considered a luxury into a necessity for survival.

In many banks, traditional operating procedures enjoy wide support. Line management is budget-oriented and is accustomed to operational planning coincident with annual budget building from the lower levels of the bank through successive layers to the top. The development of a formal marketing plan is characteristic of a "top-down" or highly centralized approach, which is counter to what the banks units have done in the past. There are also a few old-line branch managers who may consider the formal marketing plan academic nonsense that only adds needlessly to their already heavy administrative workload. In many instances, such attitudes are defensive mechanisms against the improvements in the state of the art or science of bank management that may be beyond their scope of knowledge. For others, such an attitude is merely a screen to hide their reluctance to come to grips with the future—the era of deregulation and marketing unknowns. These individuals are exhibiting the normal human tendency of avoiding the future by adhering to the past.

The ultimate standards to be established for the results expected from the planning function are only a reflection of the bank's philosophy of business as espoused by the CEO and his key subordinates. In one organization, quality of service may reign supreme; in another, corporate growth may be primary. The cornerstone of the philosophy of bank management can usually be identified in the internal environment section of the marketing plan. Thus, the marketing planning effort can often be judged by criteria that are contained in the formal marketing plan itself. The main thrust of the bank marketing planning effort is the result of the desire or motivation of senior management to proceed in a predetermined direction, to solve marketing problems, and to exploit marketing opportunities along the way. Senior bank management must be aware of the bank's objectives and direct strong support to the marketing planning function. Only with strong management support can the function be effective. However, the implementation of the planning function in an effective manner is only half of the marketing battle. The other half must be concerned with the implementation of the completed marketing plan by accomplishing what the bank has set out to do.

15

BANK MARKETING ORGANIZATION, COORDINATION, AND CONTROL

Many banks have a restricted conceptualization of the organizational requirements for the marketing function. The senior management of some banks believe that organizing for the marketing effort can be accomplished by simply establishing a marketing department on the organization chart. This somewhat myopic approach overlooks the importance of cascading the marketing concept throughout the bank. Although the function may require specialists working out of a single, centralized staff unit, it is primarily a line management responsibility that is supported by technical specialists on the staff marketing level. Bank marketing must be part of the daily operating philosophy of senior management that is made readily apparent to the entire bank. Without such visible support, no organization structure or functional assignments can produce an effective bank marketing effort. The mere establishment of a marketing department does not guarantee marketing orientation. Thus, marketing is not only a function or a position on the organization chart, but a philosophy of doing business and a concept for product and service development, sales, and delivery.

One basic organizational concept can not serve the marketing requirements of all banks. Banking is becoming more complex, large nonbank institutions are entering the arena, and the state of the art is improving. Organization structures vary according to the size of the bank, the number of branch offices, the markets served, and the extent and nature of the products and services offered. For a small bank, a single marketing department, staffed with a few marketing generalists, may be sufficient. For those banks serving two distinct markets such as corporate and retail, a central marketing support organization should be provided to serve each area of emphasis. In the large money center banks or multibank holding companies, staff marketing groups may be appropriate as well as separate product managers for specific product or service groups. This latter type of organization is one used by many successful consumer and industrial product companies. Some of the more aggressive banks have adopted this type of organization structure for use on the staff level. Regardless of the type of staff organization, the marketing function must be so oriented as to apply the marketing effort of the bank successfully.

REQUIREMENTS OF THE BANK MARKETING MANAGER. Before selecting a specific organization structure, the bank must establish the requirements for the head of the bank marketing function. A bank marketing manager should be an experienced marketing specialist who accepts the marketing concept in total and considers all areas of marketing activity rather than favoring a single component such as television advertising or literature preparation. The technical aspects of the more complex deposit, loan, investment, and other financial products and services should be understood in depth; to gain the necessary acceptance and respect in the line organization, the bank marketing manager should possess acceptable commercial banking credentials. If this expertise in finance is deficient, time must be spent learning the business as well as maintaining close contact with line personnel and staff department heads. Technical knowledge can be obtained through such contact; by attending A.I.B. courses, various schools of banking summer programs, local seminars and workshops; as well as by membership in or attendance at the meetings of key committees of the bank.

Very few marketing decisions affecting bank policies and procedures are being made by intuition in this era of professional management. Thus, the personal qualifications and abilities of the bank marketing manager become increasingly essential as part of the skills necessary to head the marketing organization. The skills most important include the following:

1. **Analytical skills** to identify, analyze, and recommend solutions for complex bank marketing problems and opportunities that are apparent.
2. **Communication skills** to communicate effectively by informing and persuading appropriate publics inside and outside of the bank.
3. **Finance skills** to be familiar with bank finance and accounting practices and to be proficient in financial analysis.
4. **Business skills** to be knowledgeable about general business and economic principles as well as those applicable to the bank and its commercial customers.
5. **Technical skills** to appreciate and understand technical matters, including familiarity with the important technological advancements within the banking industry.
6. **Sociological skills** to be sympathetic with and understand the sociological and political implications, cultural and legal, that affect the operations of the bank.

It is no longer possible for a bank to take a chance on a bank marketing manager who lacks proper qualifications. Those who are recruited from large, consumer product companies bring an invaluable breadth of experience in retail merchandising which can be applied to retail banking. The adapting of these sound principles to corporate banking and some of the fee-based services, such as cash management, automatic payroll, and asset-based lending, requires time and technical expertise. Although there may be a cross-over between toothpaste and credit cards, the marketing similarities between canned tuna and an IRA are more difficult to appreciate. The best choice between hiring experienced bankers and developing their marketing skills or employing professional marketers who can learn banking cannot be easily determined; both approaches have been used successfully since the outcome is dependent upon the individual involved.

PRODUCT MANAGEMENT. One of the organizational innovations being used by larger banks is the product management concept. Various organization structures such as product committees, product venture teams, and product managers are being assigned the responsibility for bank product and service development. The product or brand manager concept was developed by Procter and Gamble over 50 years ago but is a relatively recent addition to the bank organization structure. In banking, product managers are specialists in a particular product or market such as liability-based products or the corporate banking market. They should also be banking generalists since they will be concerned with all of the components of the marketing mix as well as the financial controls that are relevant to their products or markets. The most successful area for product management is in retail banking; at Citibank and Manufacturers Hanover it has been particularly effective. Product managers are now being used in some banks for both trust and corporate banking as well.

This approach is a variation in the normal system of management in that it is organized by product or the market served rather than by a productwide function such as sales, operations, accounting, or credit analysis. Expenses are allocated by product instead of function so that profitability can be more easily determined. By assigning the responsibility to a product manager, the operation of the branches can be concentrated on the functions of delivery and service rather than on a specific product. This assures that products will have both the technical expertise and tight controls necessary provided by a well-qualified staff specialist. It will also add accountability and vitality to product development by identifying specific products or markets with particular individuals in the bank. The product manager can be a task force coordinator or the individual actually responsible for preparing a tactical or strategic plan for a specific product or market. If serving as a coordinator, the product manager is not only designated as the key product planner, but the controller and sales motivator as well.

The product manager must coordinate new product development, operations support, and sales by the line units. The customer contact units of the bank continue to be responsible for tactical planning, pricing application, product delivery, after-sales service, and training of unit personnel. Bankwide staff support functions such as marketing research, legal, accounting, public relations, and advertising should be the responsibility of the staff departments and used whenever necessary. Some of the primary responsibilities of a product manager include the following:

> To prepare plans for bank products and services that include product definition, operations support standards, marketing strategies, cost controls, and pricing recommendations
>
> To coordinate marketing staff support requirements with advertising, public relations, sales promotion, and sales training specialists
>
> To maintain liaison with the special staff departments in the bank such as accounting, data processing, personnel, and legal that are required to provide support to both line and staff units, including outside suppliers such as advertising agencies
>
> To contact line units regularly and encourage the sales of specific products or services including obtaining appropriate feedback about both customer and competitive reaction
>
> To develop new products and services including general concepts and detailed specifications, test marketing requirements, and the conducting of marketing feasibility studies for growth and profit opportunities

There are cost savings possible with product managers as part of the marketing department. They can be responsible for new product development as well as the ongoing marketing of existing products and services. The new products usually proposed have been an extension of current product lines or a modification of present products and services. Regardless of the specific duties, the job of the product manager is a staff function. The nature of the job is one of coordination since a product manager does not have line authority and must rely on other staff and line units in the conduct of the product management responsibilities. The product manager coordination checklist in Table 15-1 indicates some of the areas of coordination and the units or departments to be used as resources within the bank.

In addition to a product management approach, new product task forces can be organized. The membership of these committees comprises personnel from the different functional areas of the bank. They are used to

Table 15-1. Product Management Coordination

	Corporate units	Retail units	Operations	Accounting	Advertising	Public relations	Sales promotion	Marketing research
Product development								
Product Concept								
Detailed Specifications								
Marketing Feasibility								
Growth Potential								
Profit Potential								
Bank Reaction								
Competitive Products								
Capital Requirements								
Test marketing								
Bank Unit Participants								
Consumer Opinions								
Sales Forecast								
Competitor Reaction								
Product Modifications								

Product planning
Marketing Strategy
Target Market
Delivery System
Pricing Strategy
Cost Controls
Operating Budget
Coordination Schedule
Management Approvals

Staff support
Operations Support
Standards
Mass Communication
Promotional Activity
Training
Cost Analysis
Profit Measurement
Performance Feedback
Trademark Review
Regulatory Clearance
Copyright Provisions

review and evaluate new product suggestions but are not expected to serve as a "brainstorming" group that discovers ideas on its own. The task force should establish standards or criteria for new products and services based on return on investment, minimum revenues, profit margins, payback periods, and corporate compatibility. The venture team is a more sophisticated version of the evaluation task force. It is made up of bank individuals who are selected on the basis of skill or expertise that may be required for a specific bank project. They are responsible for developing and bringing the new product to market until it reaches the point where it is accepted as a permanent addition to the product or service portfolio of the bank. This group requires a degree of specialization or expertise that is usually found in large banks. In the extremely large and well-diversified financial institutions, the venture team can be replaced by a fully staffed department for new product development. This extensive department is responsible for the screening and developing of new ideas and for performing the staff duties necessary for eventual commercialization.

If the new product emphasis is such that product managers of existing product lines cannot devote sufficient time to it, some banks add a manager exclusively for new products who becomes a member of the marketing staff. This individual should be a generalist and not oriented specifically to any of the other regular functions of staff marketing. The strong support of bank management for the individual should be made obvious. The new product manager should possess some entrepreneurial qualities and be one who takes risks instead of avoiding them. However, because of the risk-related responsibilities, the individual should be able to make sound marketing decisions with or without extensive research.

ORGANIZATION STRUCTURE. The relatively simple bank organization structure of the past has been replaced because the many bank products and markets make it less efficient. Single marketing departments are only practical for small, unit banks. As banks increase in size and the number of markets served, the marketing responsibilities should be organized on the basis of customer groups. For example, corporate accounts require different marketing component emphasis and structure than retail banking services; pricing differs between markets, service requirements change, promotion techniques are not the same, message content and advertising media vary widely. Examples of both retail and corporate banking marketing departments are shown on the organization charts in Figures 15-1 and 15-2.

In some banks, the major responsibility for the marketing function is assigned to line units of the bank. The marketing department is a staff unit that provides marketing support to the line. The department develops the

Figure 15-1. Retail Banking Marketing Department

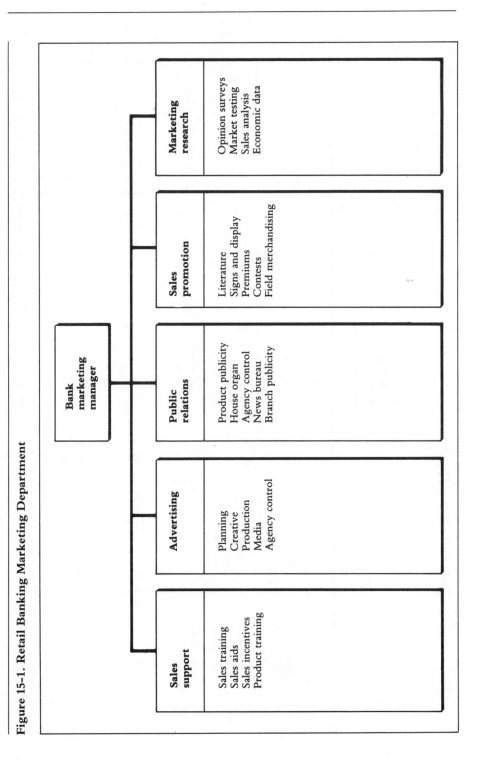

Bank marketing manager

Sales support
Sales training
Sales aids
Sales incentives
Product training

Advertising
Planning
Creative
Production
Media
Agency control

Public relations
Product publicity
House organ
Agency control
News bureau
Branch publicity

Sales promotion
Literature
Signs and display
Premiums
Contests
Field merchandising

Marketing research
Opinion surveys
Market testing
Sales analysis
Economic data

Figure 15–2. Corporate Banking Marketing Department

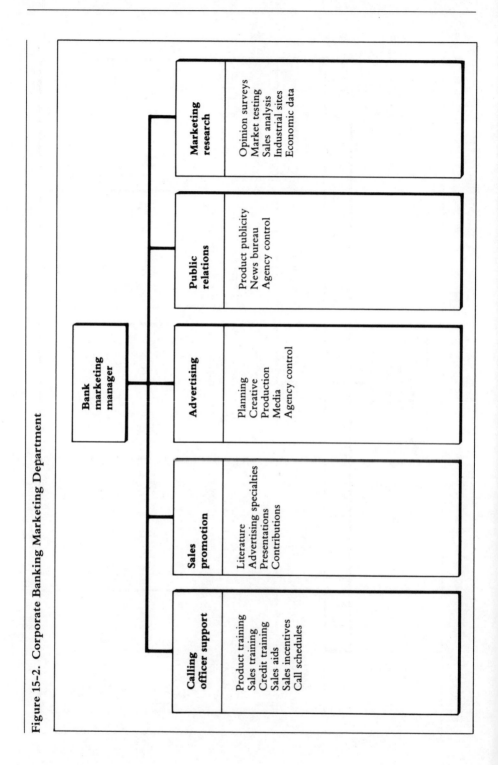

various marketing programs needed for the courses of action specified in the formal bank marketing plan. It also develops procedures and controls to monitor the performance of the line units. The management of the line units depends upon the staff marketing department for guidance and support. This includes assistance in the planning of an effective calling effort including the pricing and potential target markets. This relationship between staff and line is particularly appropriate for a product management organization structure. An organization chart that indicates the bank marketing department with a provision for product management is shown in Figure 15-3.

The larger money center banks and bank holding companies often provide marketing support that is centralized in the corporate headquarters at the banking group level. This permits policy formation and central control to be maintained at the senior staff and management level before it is cascaded to the subordinate banks or the large specialized financial subsidiaries. In these or other corporate situations, the marketing department can also be organized on the basis of its perceived importance in the bank by senior management. There is often an indication of the relative importance of the marketing function by the level of the reporting channel used by the bank marketing manager. Those banks whose marketing head reports directly to the CEO are usually committed heavily to the marketing concept. Depending upon the internal attitude toward marketing and the level of marketing importance in the bank, there are three strata of marketing acceptance that affect the organization structure:

1. **Marketing is essential.** In this organization marketing is considered both essential and fundamental to the business of the bank. Its activities are necessary in the day-to-day management decisions, and the bank marketing manager reports directly to the CEO. This provides the marketing function with a high degree of organizational acceptance, status, and importance.
2. **Marketing is necessary.** In this organizational climate, marketing is considered necessary or highly desirable but not an essential function for the success of the bank. The marketing head reports directly to the CEO but does not have the overt support required for the status and acceptance of the marketing function within the organization.
3. **Marketing is useful.** In such an organization the bank marketing function is acknowledged as making a contribution to the successful operation of the bank but not essential in the conduct of business. The bank marketing manager reports to those on one or two strata below the executive level, and the department is usually vulnerable to budget and staff cutbacks.

Figure 15-3. Marketing Department with Product Management

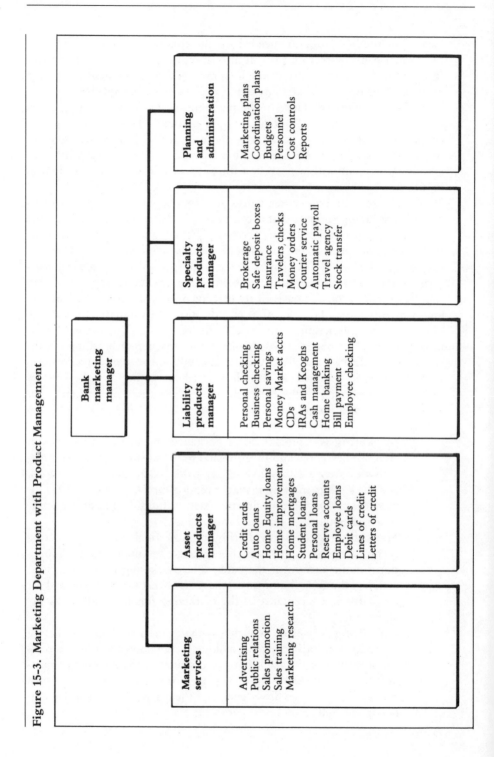

Obviously, there are a number of different organization structures that banks can use to facilitate their operating requirements. The development of the product management concept provides additional options. Although it has been successful for consumer product companies, a banking organization may have difficulty understanding and accepting the role of the product manager since their authority is not always consistent with their responsibilities. For example, they may be responsible for product and service pricing as well as for sales forecasting. Yet, they have no control over operating cost or the sales force. This situation can lead to organizational conflict; however, it can be minimized if proper coordination and control procedures are established in the bank.

MARKETING COORDINATION. The most critical factor in the successful implementation of a bank marketing plan is cooperation within the various line and staff units involved. Once marketing action is planned and the bank is organized properly, close coordination of the effort is essential. The marketing plan must be compatible with all of the other tactical plans—finance, operations, and human resources, as well as with those of the line units of the bank. It is crucial that all interrelated tasks be integrated to reach corporate objectives. This bankwide effort requires close coordination and tight control, which can be facilitated through the preparation of a detailed coordination schedule. This master schedule should include all of the major activities of the marketing effort. There are several methods for coordination of the various marketing programs and activities. One of the most efficient is provided by network modeling. When prepared properly, network models assist the bank marketing manager in establishing completion time limits, to identify interdependencies and problem areas, to reallocate bank marketing resources to the most critical activities, to isolate or eliminate nonessential steps in each project, or to reschedule tasks as simultaneous or parallel instead of sequential. This enables the bank marketing manager to focus attention on the most crucial aspects of the marketing program or activity.

There are several network models for use in bank marketing. These include the critical path method, which is based on the activities required to obtain specific results, or the program evaluation and review technique (PERT), which focuses on events in which a group of activities are completed in the most efficient sequence. Gantt charts also provide the means to organize the marketing activities in sequence so that projects can be completed on time. Each of these three coordination techniques based on networking has software available, permitting them to be performed on personal computers or other compatible hardware. Of the three network models, PERT is particularly adaptable to bank marketing activities.

A typical PERT network for banks can be simple or complex; the technique has the capacity to coordinate thousands of activities and events, far more than a normal bank marketing program. One limitation of network modeling, however, is that it normally only charts time without cost considerations. In PERT, there are two essential conditions in the coordination schedule—the sequential relationships between the various program elements must be specified and the time to complete each of the activities must be estimated as accurately as possible. Both of these, the sequential order and the time, must be used as input for the computer program. There is a particular advantage of a PERT network model. PERT is programmed to accept and calculate three different time estimates. It is assumed that the most accurate estimate will be somewhere between the two extremes of the three estimates. The three time estimates used in a PERT program include the following:

1. **Pessimistic time estimate.** This is the longest period that the bank marketing manager estimates for the completion of each activity in the specific marketing program and it allows for the numerous difficulties that may cause disruptive delays.
2. **Optimistic time estimate.** To establish the other extreme in time, this is the shortest estimate, and it assumes that the marketing activity or event will be completed relatively free of problems or obstacles to cause any undue delays.
3. **Realistic time estimate.** This is the time estimated to be the most probable for the completion of the various elements in the marketing program by considering that all normal problems or difficulties to be encountered will be routine in nature.

The detailed application of the PERT method requires that each marketing activity that has several components be sequenced in the order needed for the most efficient completion. This means that each activity must be segregated by indicating the predecessors for each part of the activity. To prepare a graphic representation of the network of activity components, each of them is assigned a number or a letter as an identification symbol. Time estimates are made for each activity segment in order to predict the total elapsed time to complete the program. The various activities are segmented in a network of predecessors and successors that provides a visual representation of the total coordination situation as well as specific completion requirements. Figures 15-4 and 15-5 represent a relatively uncomplicated bank marketing program, including the network and the computer printout using the PERT coordination program.

303

Figure 15-4. Sample PERT Program

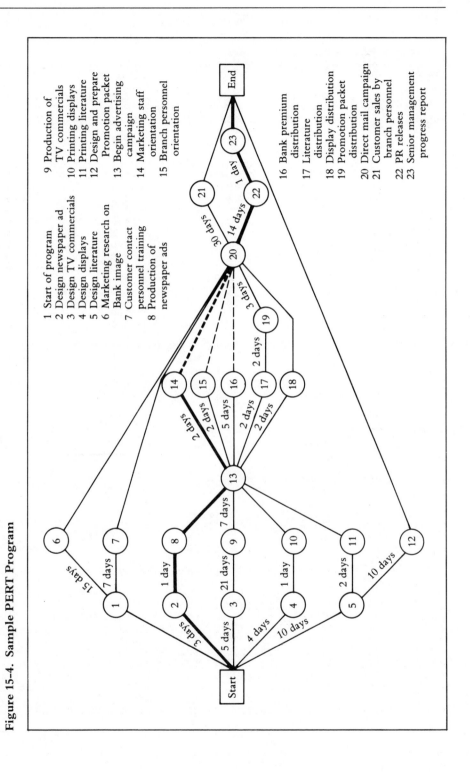

1 Start of program
2 Design newspaper ad
3 Design TV commercials
4 Design displays
5 Design literature
6 Marketing research on Bank image
7 Customer contact personnel training
8 Production of newspaper ads
9 Production of TV commercials
10 Printing displays
11 Printing literature
12 Design and prepare Promotion packet
13 Begin advertising campaign
14 Marketing staff orientation
15 Branch personnel orientation
16 Bank premium distribution
17 Literature distribution
18 Display distribution
19 Promotion packet distribution
20 Direct mail campaign
21 Customer sales by branch personnel
22 PR releases
23 Senior management progress report

Figure 15-5. PERT Program Computer Printout

Input

NUMBER	NAME OF JOB	NUMBER OF IMMEDIATE PREDECESSORS	NAMES OF IMMEDIATE PREDECESSORS	TIME TO COMPLETE JOB OPTIM	MOST PROBABLE	PESSIM
1	START	0	--	--	--	--
2	A	1	START	2.0	3.0	4.0
3	B	1	START	3.0	5.0	7.0
4	C	1	START	3.0	4.0	6.0
5	D	1	START	8.0	10.0	15.0
6	E	1	START	10.0	15.0	20.0
7	F	1	A	5.0	7.0	10.0
8	G	1	A	0.5	0.5	1.0
9	H	1	B	14.0	21.0	30.0
10	I	1	C	0.5	1.0	1.5
11	J	1	D	1.0	2.0	3.0
12	K	1	E	7.0	10.0	13.0
13	L	1	E	6.0	7.0	8.0
14	M	1	F	1.0	2.0	3.0
15	N	1	G	1.0	2.0	3.0
16	O	1	H	4.0	5.0	6.0
17	P	1	I	2.0	2.0	3.0
18	Q	1	J	2.0	2.0	3.0
19	R	1	K	2.0	2.0	3.0
20	S	1	L	2.0	3.0	4.0
21	T	4	O,P,Q,R	25.0	30.0	35.0
22	U	4	O,P,Q,R	12.0	14.0	16.0
23	V	4	O,P,Q,R	1.0	1.0	1.0

Output

JOB	EXPECTED TIME FOR JOB	START - TIMES EARLY	LATE	FINISH - TIMES EARLY	LATE	SLACK	CRITICAL JOB
A	3.00	0.00	49.17	3.00	52.17	49.17	
B	5.00	0.00	0.00	5.00	5.00	0	YES
C	4.17	0.00	24.00	4.17	28.17	24.00	
D	10.50	0.00	16.67	10.50	27.17	16.67	
E	15.00	0.00	4.17	15.00	19.17	4.17	
F	7.17	3.00	52.17	10.17	59.33	49.17	
G	0.58	3.00	58.75	3.58	59.33	55.75	
H	21.33	5.00	5.00	26.33	26.33	0	YES
I	1.00	4.17	28.17	5.17	29.17	24.00	
J	2.00	10.50	27.17	12.50	29.17	16.67	
K	10.00	15.00	19.17	25.00	29.17	4.17	
L	7.00	15.00	66.33	22.00	73.33	51.33	
M	2.00	10.17	59.33	12.17	61.33	49.17	
N	2.00	3.58	59.33	5.58	61.33	55.75	
O	5.00	26.33	26.33	31.33	31.33	0	YES
P	2.17	5.17	29.17	7.33	31.33	24.00	
Q	2.17	12.50	29.17	14.67	31.33	16.67	
R	2.17	25.00	29.17	27.17	31.33	4.17	
S	3.00	22.00	73.33	25.00	76.33	51.33	
T	30.00	31.33	31.33	61.33	61.33	0	YES
U	14.00	31.33	47.33	45.33	61.33	16.00	
V	1.00	31.33	60.33	32.33	61.33	29.00	

There are other less comprehensive methods for coordinating bank marketing programs. The time line method is a graphic visualization using a detailed bar chart. The time elements are sequenced horizontally with the marketing activities listed vertically; the length of the bar is used to indicate the starting and completion times for each of the activities. The disadvantage of this method of program coordination is that it does not indicate the way the activities are interrelated and their dependency on each other. Another less comprehensive method, which continues to be used by many bank marketing managers, is the chronological task method. This is merely a simplistic list of marketing activities entered according to the starting dates and placed in chronological order; a second list is required to indicate the desired completion dates. Since the starting times and the completion dates are on two separate lists, it is difficult to track each activity in terms of percentage completed. This method is only applicable for bank marketing programs that have an extremely limited number of activities to be coordinated.

Proper marketing and marketing support program coordination can also be accomplished by establishing coordination procedures that are continuous within certain functions involving several bank departments. These procedures become part of the standard method of operating within the bank and do not require special coordination techniques such as PERT because the activities are never-ending in a sense. These procedures are very desirable particularly when the coordination effort involves crucial functions and requires the participation of several staff or line units for the completion of the activity. The activities necessary for the marketing of a commercial loan is a case in point. There are several areas of activity that must be considered during the boarding of a commercial loan—the marketing effort, the loan processing, and the administration after the loan has been funded. An indication of the various functions that require close coordination is given by Figure 15-6. Note the many diverse functions that must be performed in each major activity area.

BANK MARKETING CONTROL. To initiate adequate control of the marketing effort, the bank marketing manager can rely on several methods to provide the necessary feedback of information on which control is dependent. Control has been characterized as the supreme management function. In marketing, it is used to make certain that the marketing programs have been or are being implemented according to plan. This requires information on total bank performance that can be obtained either inside or outside the bank. Some of the internal reports that can be useful to the bank marketing man-

Figure 15-6. Marketing Coordination with Commercial Lending

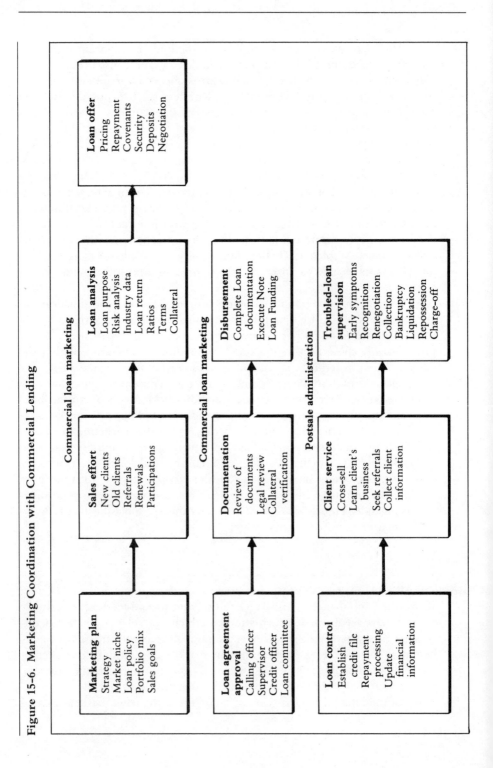

ager to indicate performance and compare it with the marketing objectives and goals are the following:

1. **Balance sheet.** The asset and liability accounts can be compared with previous periods to indicate the state of the bank.
2. **Income and expense statement.** The categories of income and expenses are detailed to show a comparison of current bank operating results with those of previous marketing efforts.
3. **Operating ratios.** The operating results can be compared in terms of ratios such as earnings per share, return on equity, capital to deposits, and loans to deposits. These are very significant ratios to indicate improvement in the marketing performance.
4. **Bank liquidity.** The form and maturity of bank assets as related to the demand for loans not only verify the forecasts made in the marketing plan but give an indication of changes in product or service emphasis that may be advisable.
5. **Loan reports.** The internal review of loans by categories such as the number and type of new loans, those renewed, large payouts, or problem loans provides a base for analysis of the competitive situation for asset-based products and services.
6. **Audit report.** The results of the internal audit program should be reviewed by the bank marketing manager, making particular note of any exceptions that might affect the marketing effort.
7. **Profit plan forecast.** Any variances from the annual bank plan as reflected in the approved budget should be analyzed and explained to senior management in terms of possible effects on the bank marketing objectives and goals.
8. **Call reports.** These reports on calling officer programs should indicate any significant business development activities regarding new or closed accounts, increases in existing relationships, or other changes that may require appropriate marketing staff response.

BUDGETING. The best known and used management control device is the annual budget. It provides the necessary quantitative values to the marketing plan, it helps identify the areas of marketing activity, and it allocates the bank resources needed to implement the plan to those responsible for its success. A marketing budget should be considered as part of the course of action that is planned for the commitment of bank resources. It also serves as an important control tool that monitors the marketing activities to measure deviations from the preplanned course that may indicate a need for corrective action. As a control tool, the budget has four dimensions—standards of anticipated performance, reports of actual performance, a system for comparative analysis, and a means for making necessary changes.

Every bank has its own approved technique or practices for the budgeting process. Regardless of the format, a chart of accounts is required for listing the individual income and expense items in sufficient detail to permit proper cost control and to apply accepted accounting procedures. In the marketing budget for staff support, only expenses are budgeted. In its preparation, the bank marketing manager often makes the mistake of grouping substantial expense items under a single heading without identifying the separate cost items. If bank marketing management does not have a detailed chart of accounts, it cannot separate cost items for close control and effective analysis. The chart of accounts in Table 15-2 is suggested for use in the budgeting process.

If the bank has a large staff marketing organization with specialized departments including product management, the procedures used in preparing the various parts of the marketing budget must also be coordinated. Senior bank management provides general or, perhaps, specific bank objectives in the form of revenue or income targets, cost reduction requirements, or earnings levels. These objectives and goals are cascaded to the organization through the various supervisory strata in a profit planning mode. The needs of the various marketing components may be defined in a budgetary form that is consistent with the senior-management constraints and guidelines. As the recommendations are forwarded through the various staff department and line unit approval stages, the marketing budget may be refined and the proposals tempered. In its final form, the marketing budget

Table 15-2. Bank Marketing Chart of Accounts

Personnel
Salaries
Benefits
Employee incentives

Facilities
Rent
Utilities
Equipment
Maintenance

Sales
Sales aids (presentations, films, charts)
Travel and entertainment
Sales training
Sales incentives
Meetings and conventions

Table 15-2 (continued)

Sales promotion _____
Literature _____
Contests and premiums _____
Signs and displays _____
Shows and exhibits _____
Advertising specialties _____

Advertising _____
Advertising media
  Newspapers _____
  Magazines _____
  Television _____
  Radio _____
  Business papers _____
  Outdoor/transportation _____
  Direct mail _____
  Catalogs/directories _____
Advertising production _____
Inquiry handling _____
Agency fees _____

Public relations _____
Public relations materials _____
Service publicity _____
Branch openings/special events _____
Customer relations _____
Financial relations _____
Government relations _____
Employee relations _____
Agency fees _____

Marketing research _____
Branch location _____
Industrial studies _____
Test marketing _____
Consumer attitudes _____
Performance measurement _____

Marketing administration _____
Travel and entertainment _____
Telephone and telegraph _____
Postage and supplies _____
Legal _____
Professional services _____
Temporary employees _____
Equipment rental _____
Dues and subscriptions _____
Contributions _____
Continuing education _____

Corporate administration _____
General overhead allocation _____
Corporate support services _____

Total marketing budget ==================

must be comprehensive since it is tangible evidence of the qualitative marketing course of action, expressed in quantitative terms. Since the marketing budget is part of an action plan, it is not intended to be an absolute expression or commitment to income and expenses, only a thoughtful, targeted estimate. Variations can be expected as part of the function of planning and control within an ever-changing marketing environment.

The final control element is the marketing audit. This is a control tool after the fact that attempts to measure the qualitative results beyond the quantitative data provided by the budget. It compares the objectives and goals of the marketing plan with the actual results obtained and tries to identify any reasons for the variances. Competitor performance is compared with the bank's performance during the same period. The findings of the audit should be distributed to bank marketing management as well as to senior management. It should be as objective as possible and include the identification or major deviations from the original plan. Recommendations for revisions of marketing objectives and goals, new strategies, and organizational changes should be included in the report. After a review of the marketing audit, both senior management and the bank marketing manager should determine corrective action and necessary revisions in the strategic or tactical plans.

VI

EPILOGUE

16

THE FUTURE AND BANK MARKETING

It is impossible for any futurist to make responsible projections without considering the impact of the computer. The world is in the age of information, and computers are the dominant force in any data seeking environment. The expanding applications in telecommunications have had a tremendous impact on marketing, whether involved with high-tech products, mass marketing or delivery of financial services. As the future evolves, telecommunication networks will abound and the telecomputer will become an instrument offering the ultimate in ubiquity. The current state of satellites, fiber optics, cellular radio, and point-to-point video is only a primitive forerunner of what bank marketing managers can expect to have at their command in the future.

The marketing environment of the future will be computer-friendly in every respect. Ours will be a home central society in which the human work function will change from production to information processing. Consumers will live and work in "electronic cottages," which will require a revolutionary change in shopping and traffic patterns. Coincident with this change, will be new merchandising techniques and customer service requirements for financial institutions. The marketing strategies will be oriented to the vast information networks provided by computer terminals in the home, in the banks, in retail stores, and in public places. Both consumer demographic and psychographic characteristics will be altered as the present baby boomer's concentration becomes a part of a more aging population. The trend in deregulation will also continue as regulated industries become less able to compete in the free markets. Banking, in particular, will benefit from deregulation because of the competitive environment provided by nonbank institutions in markets formerly the province of banks.

The impact of future change will affect marketing as an essential function of all business. Those in the manufacturing industries will become both machine- and capital-intensive as they seek improvements in processing methods. The role of automation in the distribution function will also gain in importance. Materials handling will become highly computerized with the use of scanners and robotic assemblers. Purchase orders will be processed by creating and transmitting invoices electronically. The complete logistical function will be shortened with robotic pick-up, packaging, and shipment. The tremendous capital requirements will provide increased marketing opportunities for financial services institutions. Of particular interest to asset-based lenders will be the changes in inventory control that will result in real-time information. Physical inventories will be taken by using hand-held scanning devices tied in with host computers. These will be programmed to calculate as well as project inventory levels based on the existing inventory, ongoing sales and receiving, as well as intercompany transfers of merchandise. The real-time information will also be transmitted directly to the bank for a review of lending formulas and funding requirements; less reliance will have to be placed on field audits.

DELIVERY SYSTEMS. Banking, as well as other financial institutions, will be forced to seek a more cost-effective delivery system. One approach that may become more widespread is shared delivery systems. Today, some commercial banks and thrift institutions have branch offices located in the stores of mass merchandisers even though they are not chartered by the retailer concerned. Others, such as Sears and Penneys, have bank charters and are part of the retail conglomerate. The alternative for many financial institutions will be joint ventures with shared delivery systems; insurance companies and securities firms will have sales offices on the platforms of bank branches. In contrast to joint ventures of separate financial institutions, the merger mania will continue unless Congress takes some legislative action. If the present antitrust climate remains, there will be a reduction in small firms as deregulation is completed. Many bankers predict that the number of banks by 1995 will decline by one-third. The *Wall Street Journal* reported that respondents in a survey of securities firms predicted that 80 percent of the market would eventually be captured by only twenty-five brokerage firms.

The financial services market will include all of the present types of banks, including commercial, mortgage, investment, and other specialists as well as all thrift institutions, credit unions, brokerage houses, and insurance companies. They will offer a selective line of financial products and services from mutual funds, to stock underwritings, to credit cards. The present banking regulations will ultimately be revised to permit a free national market but with a modicum of controls placed equally over all participants. As a true free market evolves, customer loyalty, the patronage habits, and preferences of the past will slowly diminish. Traditional product lines will become blurred, and many customers will seek financial supermarkets that offer one-stop financial shopping; others will opt for a specialty or boutique-type bank with customized, personal service while offering a limited product line

CONSUMERS. The consumer of the future will be affected most by the changes in market participants as well as by the concurrent information explosion. More detailed information will reduce consumer consensus as they avail themselves of information in depth from the expanded data base that will be readily accessible. This will result in diversity rather than conformity as consumers filter the information in their own self-interest. This will result in a greater variety of financial services provided to serve the many, highly polarized customer groups. Buying patterns will change with the home-maker no longer the dominant shopper. The male will assume greater importance as a retail shopper to be courted, and the heaviest purchasing power will be transferred to the older segment of the population. Retailing, including the selling role of the branch bank, will be conducted in several different ways. Products and services will be provided by direct sales through computer terminals in superstores as well as specialty shops; ATMs will be located in most retail establishments where store traffic warrants it. In the future retailing environment, home banking will become more practical with technological improvements. Some retailers will emphasize personal service and deliver it in an in-store environment that is psychologically suggestive for making purchases; this will require a greater use of sensual stimulants of lights, music, video, and appropriate furnishings. The low-cost, high-volume retail store will reduce service and be less convenient by offering a standardized selection in a relatively sterile, efficient environment. It is not likely that a large number of banking customers will accept this approach.

PRODUCTS AND SERVICES. Most retail banking installations will continue to provide easy access but with a more limited range of bank products and services. They will be offered through a greater variety of delivery vehicles from ATMs, to videotex, to financial supermarkets. The product promotion function will undergo a drastic change in both personal sales and sales promotion techniques. Telebuying will feature three-dimensional holographic merchandise displays that will also include rates and terms for financing. Loan applications will become part of the product display and the telebuying technology will permit the customer to fill out the loan application at the same time as the order is placed. Terminals at retail stores will also offer a three-dimensional mannequin which will permit rooms in a home to be displayed empty before they are furnished graphically and in color. Individuals can try on clothing through computer graphics in the same manner. This can be done to display how the merchandise will look once purchased. It is becoming more apparent that the technological advances will result in much of the financial marketing occurring at the point of purchase outside of the branch offices. Bank products and services will be delivered electronically through a variety of convenient networks, linked together for real time transactions similar to the present telephone systems.

The long promoted concept of relationship banking will receive greater emphasis, and, contrary to the views of some banking futurists, the branch will not become an endangered species. The branch office of the bank will serve as the nucleus for marketing nontraditional banking services such as insurance and securities sales. It will also function as the administrative base for off-premises sales and service to customers in offices and homes, similar to the present activities of direct sales agents. Routine banking transactions will become primarily self-service. Customers will interact with improved versions of automated teller machines that dispense exact cash in coin and bill mixtures. These will be located at the teller stations and replace live personnel. Stewards and stewardesses will be stationed in the lobby to assist customers in their automated transactions.

PRICING. Bank pricing policies will also change in the future as most of the free services are offered on a fee basis. Bank pricing will be structured according to the cost to the bank and the attractiveness of the consumer benefit, mindful of competition and the price-value relationship perceived by the customer. In keeping with every market environment, competition will determine the range of interest paid or charged; however, the pricing of fee-based services will vary greatly according to the nature of the service and its differentiation. Those banks providing less service will charge less; those offering exceptional personalized attention will be able to charge more. The traditional practice of retail merchandising to offer loss leaders in order to increase floor traffic and permit an opportunity for the switch selling of the consumer to an upgraded, more expensive product or service will be adapted to banking. There is some evidence of this at the present time as banks use the basic credit card as an introduction to a banking relationship by eliminating the annual fee normally charged or waiving the fee if other services are used. Other future pricing policy changes will provide for cash rebates for multiproduct usage; volume usage will also permit price adjustments for the customer.

In banking as in other retailing endeavors, the plastic card will become even more prevalent. Although the requirement for cash will never disappear, all of the present cash intensive retailers such as supermarkets and service stations will ultimately require plastic cards as part of an electronic checkout system. Such a system will be mandatory because it will also provide for inventory control and ordering for resupply. The GIRO system of payment will also facilitate check clearance. The complaints of consumers and the political issue recognized by legislators involving check clearance will be neutralized when the funds become available from the day of deposit through the GIRO system or its successors. Most company payrolls will be automated with the added feature of direct bank deposit. This will eliminate the delays for receiving paychecks when employees are ill or on vacation, a very worthwhile benefit that is already available. The use of float in the future will lessen gradually, but during the transition, there will be value dating techniques used to charge for or to issue credit for funds that are used by either the bank, the check writer, or the depositor during the float period.

DEREGULATION. There is a growing movement in Congress that is questioning the size of banking institutions. The recent liquidity and capital adequacy difficulties of some of the large banks because of energy-related situations as well as Third World credits, have caused some legislators to consider that there is some correlation between size and risk. They have been concerned with the possibility of large bank failures that might affect many of the other banks which use these failing institutions as intermediaries for reserve deposits and loan participations. The view of many bank futurists is that size in banking can offer desirable economies of scale as in any other industry and that risk is mitigated better when it is spread over a wide, diversified base of customers and markets. This movement to limit size and place other restrictions on operating will be blunted as nonbank institutions continue to enter the banking arena. This is particularly true since most of the nonbank entrants represent some of the largest corporations in the country. Wholesale financial markets require astronomical sums and will become increasingly integrated in the world markets of the future. Because of the sums involved, these markets will become the province of banks with sufficient size to operate in such a highly competitive financial environment involving the large foreign banks. Smaller regional banks in the United States will not have the resources to participate and will concentrate on domestic markets in their geographic areas of emphasis.

The dynamics of deregulation in other industries have been intensive. Changes in the airline, trucking, and securities industries came after a lengthy period of changing attitudes by the public and the regulators. Once deregulation begins, industries adjust rapidly and those who fail to plan adequately for change fall behind or are acquired by others. The differences in performance among firms widens after deregulation so that strong companies become stronger and the weak become weaker. As banking deregulation unfolds, these characteristics will also apply. There will be severe pressure on pricing and some of those products and services which were profitable before deregulation may turn out to be marginal at best. Bank products will become unbundled, and there will be trade-offs between bank products and the service provided. If prices are structured at the low end, customer service will be reduced; higher prices will result in better service. Initially, there will be a profit squeeze that will cause the banks to enter an era of rapid cost cutting. The banks will become more machine driven in an effort to reduce personnel costs. Thus, the capital requirements for banks will increase. The low-cost producers will market to those bank customers who are price-sensitive such as retirees seeking high deposit rates. As banks uncover new markets and adjust their ways of conducting business, the merger and acquisition activity will also increase.

STRATEGIC OPTIONS. As the banking industry adjusts to the free market in a deregulated environment, each bank will face the choice between three strategic options. The large money center banks such as Citibank, Chase, and Security Pacific that have ample resources will market nationally on a selective, interstate basis. These banks will be heavily capitalized for such expansion because of low debt-to-equity ratios. They will possess excellent management capability, particularly in marketing, and will emphasize cost reduction and control. These banks must increase their marketing awareness and allocate ample funds for promotion. They will probably make selective acquisitions along the way to add management expertise and broader market coverage. There will also be new financial institutions who will become the low-cost producers in the marketplace. These relatively new entrants will offer only a narrow product line and provide minimal banking service. The organizational emphasis will be on the line units instead of staff support departments. Prices will be discounted and the delivery system of the bank will be dependent upon ATM networks and mini-branches; communication messages will also emphasize price as the most important product benefit. The extensive training effort normally associated with banks will be replaced by a policy of hiring experienced people from competitive institutions.

The third strategy option is to become a specialty bank. This option will be selected by many of the existing local and regional banks. Their marketing strategy will be based on product or customer segmentation. These banks will offer an unbundled line of products that are not price-driven. Their target markets will be convenience-oriented rather than price-sensitive. For income purposes, these specialty banks will emphasize fee-based services in an attempt to dominate a well-defined market segment or niche. Any acquisitions of other banks will be made to deepen rather than to broaden their marketing capabilities. The communication message content will feature information instead of price or institutional image. In summary, the implications of the three possible strategies are that there will be relatively few interstate banks. Most of the existing banks will become specialty institutions with well-defined product lines being marketed to easily identified customer segments or niches. Some of the present banks that are relatively large may be unable to find the product or market niches to support their current overhead. These banks will face the choice of merger or a drastic reduction in operating expenses. The entrance of any new financial institutions will be by low-cost producers competing on the basis of price and minimal service. The banking structure as we know it today will be altered considerably in the future.

THE FUTURE IS NOW. Exciting events that are already occurring should whet the appetite of a bank marketing manager poised for the future. Many of the innovations in other industries, although not directly applicable, indicate some of the imaginative innovations that can occur in an era of change. For example, Elizabeth Arden is marketing a system that allows a woman to sit in front of a video camera and have her picture transferred to a computer screen. A cosmetologist can then try a variety of makeup on the screen image without touching the customer's face. The most acceptable combination of cosmetics can be viewed; a computer printout then indicates which products are the ones selected for purchase. A similar system has been developed for the eyeglass division of Cole National. Florsheim Shoe has a video system that displays styles, sizes, and colors that are not stocked in their conventional retail stores but can be seen by customers and are available on order from the factory. These advancements in the use of computer graphics can be applied in financial counseling and other banking activities for information on comparative investment options and outcomes using colorful performance charts, pies, and graphs.

Technological progress in banking has not been slow. The IBM automated teller station that not only accepts paper transactions but dispenses coins and bills in exact amounts is now on line in several banks. The Bank of Canada and Carleton University have designed a device that identifies, in English and in French, paper currency from one dollar to one hundred dollars. The customer places the bill into a small, checkbook-size reader, which deciphers the bar codes and activates a voice synthesizer that indicates the correct denomination; this device has an obvious application for the blind. The "Smart Card" is also beyond the test marketing stage. These integrated circuit cards have unique advantages over present cards serving as electronic money. They have an expanded memory for credit data storage, can be used for machine access, and have the advantage of providing a more secure identification. Even though it may be issued by a bank, the "Smart Card" can be programmed for use with pay telephones, for storage of medical records on person, and for allowing entry to restricted areas with an electronic authorization. The many uses of this card will justify a higher fee for the issuing bank.

The forces of change have indicated that the bank of today will not be the bank of tomorrow. The economic changes and the increasing financial sophistication of the various bank publics are responsible for the movement of banking as a secular industry into the mainstream of financial services. The growing competition from nonbank institutions and the pressure for greater profitability in an era of rising costs make changes in the way banks do business not only inevitable, but crucial. The deregulation process has added to this pressure, with interest rates now governed by the free market. Coincident with the interest rate situation are the increased capital requirements that have reduced the leverage of the banks and their potential earning power. Such a situation demands not only diversification and differentiation in products and markets but new, more innovative ways of doing business. Marketing, with the customer primarily in mind, provides the direction for the future.

Thus, the need for imaginative and highly effective bank marketing was never greater or more opportune, not only for commercial banks, but for our country as a whole. Foreign banks are enlarging their presence in the marketplace and are learning our lessons well through experience as well as acquisition. To meet this foreign competition as well as the onslaught from nonbank institutions, the surviving bank marketing managers must leave very little to chance. Professional marketing planning and meticulous execution can prevent costly mistakes and reduce the incidence of poor marketing performance. As the foremost proponents of the marketing concept, bank marketing managers have the power to begin the renaissance of commercial banking in an arena filled with nonbank institutions that not only are well capitalized and have well-recognized and accepted brand names, but have the depth of experience in marketing to make them immediate contenders for market share. In unmistakenly blunt terms, the U.S. Comptroller of the Currency made an observation of the current marketing environment for financial services, "the public wants financial services, but it could care less whether it gets them from banks." This, then, is the challenge for bank marketing managers now and in the future.

APPENDIX

SOURCES FOR ADDITIONAL READING

Books

Aaker, David A. *Strategic Market Management*. New York: John Wiley & Sons Inc., 1984.

Aaker, David A. and Day, George S. *Marketing Research*. New York: John Wiley & Sons Inc., 1983.

Austin, Douglas V., and Mandula, Mark S. *Bankers Handbook for Strategic Planning: How to Develop and Implement A Successful Strategy*. Boston: Bankers Publishing Company, 1985.

Berry, Leonard L., Futrell, Charles M., and Bowers, Michael R. *Bankers Who Sell: Improving Selling Effectiveness in Banking*. Homewood, Illinois: Dow Jones-Irwin, 1985.

Bovee, Courtland L., and Arens, William F. *Contemporary Advertising*. Homewood, Illinois: Richard D. Irwin Inc., 1982.

Burns, Thomas J. *Effective Communications and Advertising for Financial Institutions*. Englewood Cliffs, New Jersey: Prentice-Hall Inc., 1986.

Crawford, C. Merle *New Products Management*. Homewood, Illinois: Richard D. Irwin Inc., 1983.

Davis, Kenneth R. *Marketing Management, Fifth Edition*. New York: John Wiley & Sons Inc., 1985.

Day, George S. *Analysis for Strategic Market Decisions*. St. Paul: West Publishing Company, 1985.

Donnelly, James H. Jr., Berry, Leonard L., and Thompson, Thomas W. *Marketing Financial Services: A Strategic Vision*. Homewood, Illinois: Dow Jones-Irwin, 1985.

Engel, James F., et al. *Consumer Behavior*. Hinsdale, Illinois: The Dryden Press, 1986.

Engel, James F., et al. *Promotional Strategy*. Homewood, Illinois: Richard D. Irwin, Inc., 1983.

Govoni, Norman A., et al. *Promotional Management*. Englewood Cliffs, New Jersey: Prentice-Hall Inc., 1986.

Guiltinan, J.P., and Paul, G.W. *Marketing Management*. New York: McGraw Hill Book Company, 1982.

Hughes, C. David, and Singler, Charles H. *Strategic Sales Management*. Reading, Massachusetts: Addison-Wesley Publishing Company Inc., 1983.

Jain, Subhash C. *Marketing Planning and Strategy, Second Edition*. Cincinnati: South-Western Publishing Company, 1985.

Kinnear, Thomas C., and Bernhardt, Kenneth L. *Principles of Marketing*. Glenview, Illinois: Scott, Foresman & Company, 1986.

Kotler, Philip. *Marketing Management: Analysis, Planning and Control, Fifth Edition*. Englewood Cliffs, New Jersey: Prentice-Hall Inc., 1984.

Larreche, Jean–Claude, and Strong, Edward C. *Readings in Marketing Strategy.* Palo Alto: The Scientific Press, 1982.

Levitt, Theodore. *The Marketing Imagination.* New York: Free Press, 1983.

Porter, Michael E. *Competitive Advantage: Creating and Sustaining Superior Performance.* New York: Free Press, 1985.

Reidebach, Eric R., and Pitts Robert E. *Bank Marketing: A Guide to Strategic Planning.* Englewood Cliffs, New Jersey: Prentice-Hall Inc., 1986.

Richardson, Linda. *Bankers in the Selling Role: A Consultive Guide to Cross-Selling Financial Services.* New York: John Wiley & Sons Inc., 1981.

Seglin, Jeffrey, and Lauterbach, Jeffrey. *Personal Financial Planning in Banks: A Handbook for Decision Making.* Boston: Bankers Publishing Company, 1986.

Shaw, Roy, and Semenik, Richard J. *Marketing, Fifth Edition.* Cincinnati: South-Western Publishing Company, 1985.

Sinkey, Joseph, F. Jr. *Commercial Bank Financial Management, Second Edition.* New York: Macmillan Publishing Company Inc., 1986.

Periodicals

ABA Banking Journal. Published monthly by American Bankers Association, Subscription Department, P.O. Box 466,, Village Station, New York, New York 10014.

Advertising Age. Published weekly by Crain Communications, Inc., 740 Rush Street, Chicago, Illinois 60611.

American Banker. Published daily except Saturday, Sunday and holidays. Subscription Department, One State Street Plaza, New York, New York 10004.

Bank Directors Report. Published monthly by Warren, Gorham & Lamont, 210 South Street, Boston, Massachusetts 02111.

Bank Marketing Newsletter. Published monthly by American Bankers Association, 1120 Connecticut Avenue, N.W., Washington, D.C. 20036.

Bank Marketing Report. Published monthly by Warren, Gorham & Lamont, 210 South Street, Boston, Massachusetts 02111.

Bank Marketing. Published monthly by Bank Marketing Association, 309 West Washington Street, Chicago, Illinois 60606.

Credit Union Magazine. Published monthly by Credit Union National Association, 5710 Mineral Point Road, Madison, Wisconsin 53705.

Direct Marketing. Published monthly by Hoke Communications, Inc., 224 Seventh Street, Garden City, New York 11530.

Independent Banker. Published monthly by Independent Bankers Association, P.O. Box 267, Sauk Centre, Minnesota 56378.

Journal of Marketing. Published quarterly by American Marketing Association, 250 S. Wacker Drive, Chicago, Illinois 60606.

Journal of Retail Banking. Published quarterly by Lafferty Publications (USA), 3945 Holcomb Road, Suite 301, Norcross, Georgia 30092.

Magazine of Bank Administration. Published monthly by Bank Administration Institute, 60 Gould Center, Rolling Meadows, Illinois 60008.

Sales & Marketing Management. Published sixteen times a year by Bill Communications, Inc., 633 Third Avenue, New York, New York 10017.

Savings Institutions. Published monthly by the United States League of Savings Institutions, 111 E. Wacker Drive, Chicago, Illinois 60601.

United States Banker. Published monthly by Kalo Communications, Inc., One River Road, Cos Cob, Connecticut 06807.

Federal Reserve Bank Publications

Business Review, Federal Reserve Bank of Philadelphia. Published six times a year by Department of Research, Federal Reserve Bank of Philadelphia, Ten Independence Mall, Philadelphia, Pennsylvania 19106

Economic Perspectives, Federal Reserve Bank of Chicago. Published six times a year by Public Information Center, Federal Reserve Bank of Chicago, P.O. Box 834, Chicago, Illinois 60690.

Economic Review, Federal Reserve Bank of Atlanta. Published six times a year by The Information Center, Federal Reserve Bank of Atlanta, 104 Marietta Street, N.W., Atlanta, Georgia 30303.

Economic Review, Federal Reserve Bank of Cleveland. Published quarterly by Public Information Department, Federal Reserve Bank of Cleveland, P.O. Box 6387, Cleveland, Ohio 44101.

Economic Review, Federal Reserve Bank of Dallas. Published six times a year by Public Affairs Department, Federal Reserve Bank of Dallas, Station K, Dallas, Texas 75222.

Economic Review, Federal Reserve Bank of Kansas City. Published six times a year by Research Division, Federal Reserve Bank of Kansas City, 925 Grand Avenue, Kansas City, Missouri, 64198.

Economic Review, Federal Reserve Bank of Richmond. Published six times a year by Public Services, Federal Reserve Bank of Richmond, P.O. Box 27622, Richmond, Virginia 23261.

Economic Review, Federal Reserve Bank of San Francisco. Published quarterly by Public Information Department, Federal Reserve Bank of San Francisco, P.O. Box 7702, San Francisco, California 94120.

Federal Reserve Bulletin. Published monthly by Publication Services, Board of Governors of the Federal Reserve System, Washington, D.C. 20551.

New England Economic Review, Federal Reserve Bank of Boston. Published six times a year by Research Department, Publications Section, Federal Reserve Bank of Boston, Boston, Massachusetts 02106.

Quarterly Review, Federal Reserve Bank of Minneapolis. Published quarterly by Research Department, Federal Reserve Bank of Minneapolis, Minneapolis, Minnesota 55480.

Quarterly Review, Federal Reserve Bank of New York. Published quarterly by Public Information Department, Federal Reserve Bank of New York, 33 Liberty Street, New York, New York 10045.

Review, Federal Reserve Bank of St. Louis. Published six times a year by Research and Public Information, Federal Reserve Bank of St. Louis, P.O. Box 442, St. Louis, Missouri 63166.

Directories

American Savings Directory. Published by McFadden Business Publications, 6195 Crooked Creek Road, Norcross, Georgia 30092.

Callahan's Credit Union Directory. Published by Callahan & Associates, Inc., 1001 Connecticut Avenue, Suite 728, Washington, D.C. 20031.

Polk's World Bank Directory. Published semi-annually by R.L. Polk & Company, P.O. Box 1340, Nashville, Tennessee 37202.

INDEX

INDEX

Videotex, for bank advertising, 239
Visa, 8, 115
Volume, 143–144

Wall Street Journal, 168, 314
Waste circulation, 236
Wear out, 105

Weighted data, 105
Wells Fargo, Gold Account, 56
Western Savings, California, 231
Westinghouse Credit, 41
White-collar class, 90

Your Money, 207–208